# THROUGH SHAKESPEARE'S EYES

JOSEPH PEARCE

# THROUGH SHAKESPEARE'S EYES

## Seeing the Catholic Presence in the Plays

IGNATIUS PRESS    SAN FRANCISCO

Dustjacket art:
Top:
Portrait of William Shakespeare
© Antar Dayal / Illustration
Works / Corbis

Bottom:
The discovery of Yorick's skull by gravediggers
in a scene from the play *Hamlet*, by William Shakespeare.
Original Artwork: Engraved after a painting by Eugene Delacroix.
Photo by Hulton Archive / Getty Images

Dustjacket design by Roxanne Mei Lum

©2010 Ignatius Press, San Francisco
All rights reserved
ISBN 978-1-58617-413-2
Library of Congress Control Number 2009930112
Printed in the United States of America ∞

For
**Margaret Patricia Pearce**
1939–2009
*May flights of angels sing thee to thy rest*

# CONTENTS

Preface 9

Acknowledgments 11

Prologue: Through Shakespeare's Eyes 13

1. Of Jews and Jesuits 15

2. Venetian Blindness: Critical Mistakes and Dramatic Errors 20

3. "I have much ado to know myself" 25

4. Portia: Gate of Virtue 30

5. Shylock the Usurer 38

6. The Right to Choose 46

7. To Choose the Right 58

8. Lead, Kindly Light 66

9. The Vice of Vengeance 75

10. The Testing of Shylock 87

11. The Testing of Bassanio 97

12. Light and Lightheartedness 101

13. To Be or to Seem to Be: That Is the Question 112

14. Hamlet and the Ghost 118

15. Ophelia 125

16. Lies, Spies, and Fishmongers 132

17. True Mirrors and Deceitful Clouds 138

18. Inversion and Perversion 146

19. A *Memento Mori* 152

20. The Triumph of Sanity 157

21. "And flights of angels sing thee to thy rest" 165

22. Love's Silence 166

23. The Wisdom of Fools and the Sanity of Madmen 171

24. "When madmen lead the blind . . ."                           176

25. Reason in Madness                                            180

Epilogue: Why Protestants Should Not Be Scared of the
  Catholic Shakespeare                                           186

Appendix A: Shakespeare's Shocking Catholicism                  191

Appendix B: How to Read Shakespeare (or Anyone Else)            199

Subject Index                                                    209

Index of Fictional Characters                                    221

# PREFACE

This volume is intended as a companion to *The Quest for Shakespeare*,[1] in which the historical, biographical, and documentary evidence for Shakespeare's Catholicism is given. It is, however, not merely an appendix to *The Quest for Shakespeare* but is very much its equal. Whereas the earlier volume assembled the considerable body of evidence pointing to Shakespeare's Catholicism that can be found in the facts of his life, the present volume presents a sample of the even greater body of evidence of his Catholicism to be gleaned from his works.

It is only a sampling of the evidence because it would take numerous books to present such evidence systematically. One could easily envisage one separate book for each of the plays, and two more books to present the evidence for the Catholicism in the sonnets and the longer poems. Thus, in order to discover the superabundance of textual evidence for Shakespeare's Catholicism, one would have to write not merely a book but a library, or at any rate a whole shelf full of books, totaling more than three dozen volumes. This enormous undertaking, necessitating a close reading of the plays and poems in the light of Shakespeare's known Catholicism, is a challenge that I hope will be met by future generations of scholars. In this light, the present volume is little more than a gauntlet thrown down to initiate such a challenge.

The present volume examines only three of the Bard's works, *The Merchant of Venice*, *Hamlet*, and *King Lear*, and does so, as its title suggests, by endeavoring to see the plays through Shakespeare's own eyes, which is to see them through the eyes of a believing Catholic living in Elizabethan and Jacobean England. The endeavor may seem preposterously large or even preposterously presumptuous, but the alternative is not to see them in any meaningful sense at all. If we see them only through our own eyes, with no effort to see the text in its context, we will not see them as they are but only as we perceive them to be from the shuttered perspective of our own time and our own prejudices. We will not see them objectively but only subjectively. If we see them through

---

[1]Joseph Pearce, *The Quest for Shakespeare* (San Francisco: Ignatius Press, 2008).

the eyes of critics or "experts", we might receive greater insights into the plays' meaning than we would have if unaided by such guidance, but how do we know that such guides can be trusted? What criterion do we use to differentiate between genuine insight and mere sophistry? Who is the guide whom we can most trust?

Clearly the most reliable guide to a work is the author himself, who has the fullest grasp of all the contextual ingredients that inform and flavor the text. It is, therefore, necessary to understand as much about the author as possible, and as much as possible about the time and culture in which he lived. We need to know the author's most important beliefs, which are those beliefs that inform every aspect of his life. These are his theology and his philosophy. At this juncture we should remind ourselves that everyone works from theological and philosophical presumptions. Even atheism is theological, in the sense that the presumption that God does not exist informs the way that the atheist perceives everything else. The "Real Absence" of God is as crucial to the atheist as is his Real Presence to the believer. There is, therefore, no escaping God's primal importance, regardless of whether it springs from the primal assumption that he is or the primal assumption that he is not. It is one of the deepest paradoxes, and perhaps one of God's funniest jokes, that God is always present even when he is absent.

Returning to our quest for Shakespeare, it should now be obvious why it was necessary, in the first instance, to examine the facts of Shakespeare's life before proceeding to an examination of his work. We now know, from an examination of the biographical evidence, that Shakespeare was a Catholic at a time when Catholicism was illegal in England and at a time when Catholics were being persecuted and even put to death. In seeing the plays through Shakespeare's eyes, we will be seeing England through the eyes of one who had witnessed the persecution of family and friends and who may even have seen his friends executed by the state. In seeing the plays through Shakespeare's eyes, we will be seeing one of the darkest periods in history illuminated by one of its greatest geniuses. To reiterate the words of the preface to *The Quest for Shakespeare*, seeing the plays through Shakespeare's eyes is not merely enlightening but is an adventure in the presence of genius.

# ACKNOWLEDGMENTS

This volume differs significantly from its predecessor and companion, *The Quest for Shakespeare*, in the sense that the sources from which I have been working are the texts of the three plays *The Merchant of Venice*, *Hamlet*, and *King Lear*, along with some of the finer criticism of these plays. I did not have to trawl through dozens of biographies and other studies of Shakespeare in order to bring together all the different threads of his life into one volume. In this sense, the present volume might be said to have been easier to write than was its companion. It was, in any event, easier to research. I think, however, and in spite of such appearances to the contrary, that it was hardly easier to write. Grappling with a genius of Shakespeare's magnitude is never easy. It is as exhausting as it is exhilarating! Since, however, much of the book could be said to be a one-on-one encounter with the Bard, there are fewer obvious people to acknowledge for their help in the research and writing of the work. This is at least the case as long as I do not broaden the net of gratitude to include all those who have helped me to read, write, and think more clearly over the course of my life. Such a net deserves to be cast but would be too full to empty into the limited space traditionally allotted to acknowledgments. I shall, therefore, merely mention those names that most obviously and instantly come into my head and apologize for the inevitable oversights and sins of omission.

Those to whom I am indebted for either inspiring or encouraging my journey into the Bard-lands include Henry Russell; R. A. Benthall; Aaron Urbanczyk; Travis Curtright; Peter Milward, S.J.; and, last but not least, my father, Albert Pearce. I am grateful to Al Kresta for donating part of his library to the cause of bringing this book to life, and to those at Ave Maria University and Ignatius Press for making it possible for me to write and publish this and my other works.

My wife, Susannah, remains my greatest and dearest critic, reading every chapter as it was written, and our children, Leo and Evangeline, remain a source of inspiration, even though they are not able to read a single word!

# PROLOGUE: THROUGH SHAKESPEARE'S EYES

Every work of literature is the incarnation of the fruitful relationship between the artist and his Muse. From a Christian perspective, the Muse is the gift of grace; from an atheistic perspective, it is the author's subconscious. In both cases, the work of literature remains an expression of the personhood of the author. In the former case, the Christian believes that the gift of grace is freely given, like the talents in the Gospel parable,[1] and can be used or abused by the artist according to the predilections of his will (much as the gift of life is freely given and can be used or abused). In the latter case, the atheist believes that the subconscious "Muse" finds expression in the creative process. It can be seen, therefore, that Christians and atheists share the essential belief that the work is the creative incarnation of the personhood of the author. This being so, an author's theological and philosophical beliefs will be the most important influence upon the work, simply because they are the most important influence on the way in which the author perceives reality.

Since the evidence shows that Shakespeare was a believing Catholic,[2] it is clear that seeing his plays through his Catholic eyes is the best way, indeed the only way, of understanding the deepest meanings that they convey. This book endeavors, therefore, to see the plays through Shakespeare's eyes, giving us a "Bard's-eye" view of their true meaning.

---

[1] Cf. Matthew 25:14–30.

[2] For a summary of the key documentary and biographical evidence for Shakespeare's Catholicism, see appendix A, "Shakespeare's Shocking Catholicism". For a more extensive study of this historical evidence, see Joseph Pearce, *The Quest for Shakespeare: The Bard of Avon and the Church of Rome* (San Francisco: Ignatius Press, 2008).

# OF JEWS AND JESUITS

*The Merchant of Venice* was first registered[1] on July 22, 1598, but was probably written and first performed a few years earlier, perhaps as early as 1594 or 1595. It is likely that Shakespeare's initial inspiration for writing the play arose, in part, from the gruesome executions of two "traitors" on the orders of Queen Elizabeth. The first "traitor" was Roderigo López, the queen's personal physician, who was hanged, drawn, and quartered on June 7, 1594; the second was Robert Southwell, the Jesuit priest and poet, who was hanged, drawn, and quartered on February 20, 1595. Whereas the former may have served as the inspiration for Shylock, the latter can be seen as a ghostly presence flitting through the play as an allusion to the deeper meanings to be gleaned from the drama.

Roderigo López, a converted Portuguese Jew, had been appointed personal physician to the queen in 1586. Two years later he became official interpreter to Antonio Perez, pretender to the throne of Portugal, after Perez had sought sanctuary in England from the clutches of his enemy, King Philip of Spain. In 1590 López seems to have become embroiled in a Spanish plot to assassinate both Antonio Perez and Queen Elizabeth. Although he protested his innocence, he was found guilty and was sentenced to death. At his execution a large crowd bayed for his blood and bellowed anti-Semitic abuse.

In the wake of López's trial and execution, the Admiral's Men, an acting company, revived Christopher Marlowe's *Jew of Malta* as an entrepreneurial response to the tide of anti-Semitism that was sweeping through London. The play was a huge success, playing fifteen times to packed houses during 1594. It seems reasonable to assume, therefore, that Shakespeare wrote *The Merchant of Venice* in the same entrepreneurial spirit, seeking to cash in on the upsurge of anti-Semitism by writing his own

---

[1] All plays had to be registered with the Stationers' Company, an organization of printers and publishers that held a monopoly on the printing trade in Tudor England.

play about a villainous Jew. Such a supposition is supported by the fact that many critics have identified "the Venesyon Comodye", staged at the Rose Theatre in August 1594, with Shakespeare's play. From a purely business perspective, it makes sense that Shakespeare might write a play for his own company of players, the Lord Chamberlain's Men, to compete with the success of the revival of Marlowe's play by the Admiral's Men. Even if "the Venesyon Comodye" has nothing to do with Shakespeare's play but is merely a comedy set in Venice by an unknown playwright, it still seems likely that *The Merchant of Venice* was written as a response or reaction to López's conviction for treachery. Such a view is supported by a clue embedded within the text of the play that seems to connect López to Shylock. In act 4 of *The Merchant of Venice*, Gratiano describes Shylock as "a wolf . . . hang'd for human slaughter" (4.1.134),[2] which appears to be a pun on López's name, the Latin for "wolf" being *lupus*. López was indeed hanged for plotting human slaughter, and it is difficult to conclude anything but the obvious with regard to the connection between the real-life Jewish villain and Shakespeare's counterpart, especially considering that someone named Antonio is the intended victim in both cases.

Much more needs to be said about the alleged anti-Semitism of *The Merchant of Venice*, and we will return to the subject presently. First, however, let us look at the other real-life character who seems to have influenced the writing of the play.

There is an abundance of evidence to show that Shakespeare knew the Jesuit poet Robert Southwell prior to the latter's arrest in 1592, and it is possible that Shakespeare might have been among the large crowd that witnessed Southwell's brutal execution in 1595.[3] Furthermore, Shakespeare would have been writing *The Merchant of Venice* shortly after Southwell's execution or, if we accept the earliest possible dates for the play's composition, during the period in which the Jesuit was being tortured repeatedly by Richard Topcliffe, Elizabeth's sadistic chief interrogator. It should not surprise us, therefore, that we see Southwell's shadow, or shade, in Shakespeare's play. It is present most palpably in the haunting

---

[2] All quotations from *The Merchant of Venice* are from the edition published by Ignatius Press: *The Merchant of Venice*, ed. Joseph Pearce, Ignatius Critical Editions (San Francisco: Ignatius Press, 2009).

[3] For full details of the solid historical evidence for Shakespeare's friendship with Robert Southwell, see chapter 9 of Joseph Pearce, *The Quest for Shakespeare* (San Francisco: Ignatius Press, 2008), pp. 107–17.

echoes of Southwell's own poetry, which Shakespeare knew well and which he introduces into *The Merchant of Venice* on numerous occasions.[4] Take, for instance, Portia's words after the Prince of Arragon's failure in the test of the caskets: "Thus hath the candle sing'd the moth" (2.9.79). And compare it to lines from Southwell's "Lewd Love is Losse":

> So long the flie doth dallie with the flame,
> Untill his singed wings doe force his fall.[5]

Not only does the phraseology suggest Shakespeare's indebtedness to Southwell, but the very title of the poem from which the phrase is extracted suggests a connection to Shakespeare's theme that lewd love is loss. Arragon's love is lewdly self-interested, and his choice leads to the loss of his hopes to marry Portia. Shakespeare is not simply taking lines from Southwell; he is apparently taking his very theme from him.

In the final act, as Portia and Nerissa return to Belmont, they see a candle burning in the darkness. "When the moon shone, we did not see the candle", says Nerissa, to which the sagacious Portia responds: "So doth the greater glory dim the less" (5.1.92–93). Compare this to Southwell's "seeking the sunne it is ... booteles to borrowe the light of a candle."[6]

It is also intriguing that an expression ascribed by the *Oxford English Dictionary* to Shakespeare's coinage was actually coined originally by Southwell, to whom Shakespeare was presumably indebted. The phrase is Shylock's "a wilderness of monkeys" (subsequent to "a wilderness of Tygers" in *Titus Andronicus*), which owed its original source to Southwell's "a wilderness of serpents" in his *Epistle unto his Father*.[7]

If the foregoing should fail to convince the skeptical reader of Southwell's ghostly presence, the pivotal scene in which Bassanio triumphs in

---

[4] I am indebted in this discussion of Saint Robert Southwell's influence on *The Merchant of Venice* to the diligent research of John Klause. See John Klause, "Catholic and Protestant, Jesuit and Jew: Historical Religion in *The Merchant of Venice*", in *Shakespeare and the Culture of Christianity in Early Modern England*, ed. Dennis Taylor and David N. Beauregard (New York: Fordham University Press, 2003), pp. 180–221.

[5] James H. McDonald and Nancy Pollard Brown, eds., *The Poems of Robert Southwell, S.J.* (Oxford: Clarendon, 1967), quoted in Taylor and Beauregard, *Shakespeare and the Culture of Christianity*, p. 187.

[6] Robert Southwell, *Marie Magdalens Funeral Teares*, ed. Vincent B. Leitch (Delmar, N.Y.: Scholars' Facsimiles and Reprints, 1974), quoted in Taylor and Beauregard, *Shakespeare and the Culture of Christianity*, p. 187.

[7] Taylor and Beauregard, *Shakespeare and the Culture of Christianity*, p. 187. Southwell's *Epistle unto his Father* was written in 1588 or 1589, five years or so before Shakespeare used the similar phrase in *Titus Andronicus*.

the wisdom of his choice to "hazard all he hath", i.e., lay down his life
for his love, should prove sufficient to allay the most hardened skepticism. The Shakespeare scholar John Klause has shown how this scene
resonates as an echo of Southwell's *Marie Magdalens Funeral Teares*, in
which the saint is of a mind to "venture [her] life" for the love of her
Lord. Klause shows many suggestive parallels between Shakespeare's scene
and Southwell's earlier work, and yet nowhere is the allusion to Southwell more evident than in the exchange between Bassanio and Portia
before Bassanio makes his choice:

> *Bassanio.*                              Let me choose,
>     For as I am, I live upon the rack.
> *Portia.* Upon the rack, Bassanio! then confess
>     What treason there is mingled with your love.
> *Bassanio.* None but that ugly treason of mistrust,
>     Which makes me fear th' enjoying of my love;
>     There may as well be amity and life
>     'Tween snow and fire, as treason and my love.
> *Portia.* Ay, but I fear you speak upon the rack,
>     Where men enforced do speak any thing.
> *Bassanio.* Promise me life, and I'll confess the truth.
> *Portia.* Well then, confess and live.
> *Bassanio.*                              Confess and love
>     Had been the very sum of my confession.
>     O happy torment, when my torturer
>     Doth teach me answers for deliverance!
>     But let me to my fortune and the caskets.
> *Portia.* Away then! I am lock'd in one of them;
>     If you do love me, you will find me out. (3.1.24–41)

Since this exchange between the lover and the longed-for beloved
comes in the midst of an array of references to Southwell's poem, it is
difficult to avoid the conclusion that it represents a clear allusion to
Southwell's own recent experience "upon the rack" at the hands of a
torturer seeking to force him into a confession of the alleged crime of
"treason" with which he had been charged. Such a conclusion is
reinforced still further when juxtaposed with Southwell's own words in
his *Humble Supplication to her Maiestie*:

> What unsufferable Agonies we have bene put to upon the Rack....
> [One so tortured] is apt to utter anything to abridge the sharpnes and
> severity of paine. [Yet even an] unskillful Lay man ... [would] rather

venture his life by saying too much, then hazard his Conscience in not answering sufficient.[8]

What else is Bassanio doing, as he ponders the choices presented to him by the caskets, if not venturing his very life in the choice of death (lead) over worldly temptations (gold and silver)? He is willing to "hazard all he hath", as the casket demands, if it is the only way to gain his love. The parallels with Robert Southwell's willingness to die for his faith, hazarding all he has in his willingness to lay down his life for his friends, is obvious. And it is made even more so by the way in which Shakespeare artfully intersperses phrases from yet another Southwell poem, *Saint Peters Complaint*, into the words that Portia sings as Bassanio prepares to make his choice.[9]

It has been necessary to commence our exploration of *The Merchant of Venice* with the role that the Jew and the Jesuit played in its inspiration because, as we shall see, many of the mistakes made about the play have been the result of seeing the Jew and not the Jesuit. So much of the nonsense written about this most controversial of Shakespeare's plays arises from the opening of the wrong casket by worldly minded critics. The truth of the play, and the key to understanding it, is not to be found in the golden gaudiness of a materialistic perception of its meaning but from the lead-laden truth of the play's underlying Christian meaning. If we wish to understand where Shakespeare is leading us, we have to take up our cross and follow him. In doing so, we will be led by him to a region where hazarding all we have is the path to perception.

[8] Robert Southwell, *An Humble Supplication to her Maiestie*, ed. R. C. Bald (Cambridge: Cambridge University Press, 1953), pp. 34–35.

[9] For details of the similarities between Portia's song and *Saint Peters Complaint*, see Taylor and Beauregard, *Shakespeare and the Culture of Christianity*, p. 196.

# 2

# VENETIAN BLINDNESS:
## CRITICAL MISTAKES AND DRAMATIC ERRORS

Before we follow Shakespeare to where he seeks to take us, let us take a short detour in the company of the critics. We will begin by taking a look at the literary sources for *The Merchant of Venice* and will continue by examining the way in which the play has been perceived throughout the four centuries of its dramatic and critical history.

There is no single source for *The Merchant of Venice*, the plot of which seems to be a melding of three distinct stories: the story of the suitor and the usurer, the story of the caskets, and the story of the pound of flesh. It seems, however, that Shakespeare's principal source was *Il pecorone* (The dunce or The simpleton), a fourteenth-century story by Ser Giovanni Fiorentino. This is set in "Belmonte" and involves a quest by a suitor to win his mystical, otherworldly bride. As in Shakespeare's play, the suitor (Giannetto) receives money, in this case from his godfather, which has been borrowed from a Jewish usurer. Giannetto wins his bride with the assistance of the treachery of the lady's maid; the usurer demands payment, a lawyer intercedes, the lady appears in disguise, and the play ends with the business of the ring. It is, however, interesting that Shakespeare injects a specifically Christian morality into his recasting of the tale. Neither the hero nor the heroine is particularly devout in *Il pecorone*, and they choose to affront Christian morality by casually fornicating prior to their marriage. In comparison, the chastity of Portia and the chivalry of Bassanio stand in stark contrast to the moral obliquity of their literary prototypes, indicating Shakespeare's conscious decision to "baptize" his hero and heroine with Christian virtue.

Although the bare bones of much of the plot of *The Merchant of Venice* is to be found in *Il pecorone*, there is no trial of the suitors by means of the caskets in the earlier tale. This aspect of the drama might have been derived from any of several well-known versions of the casket story, such as John Gower's *Confessio amantis*, Boccacio's *Decameron*, or the anonymous *Gesta Romanorum*. In any event, as we have seen above, Shakespeare retold the casket story in his own inimitable fashion, injecting a Jesuitical metadramatic subtext into the tale.

The pound-of-flesh story was also widely known. Shakespeare might have read it in the anonymously authored "Ballad of the Crueltie of Geruntus" or in an "oration", recently translated from the French, entitled "Of a Jew, who would for his debt have a pound of flesh of a Christian". It was also included in the *Gesta Romanorum*, suggesting that this might have been the single source for both the casket and the pound-of-flesh stories. An earlier version appears in the tale of the fourth wise master in the "Seven Wise Masters of Rome" in *The Thousand and One Nights*, but since the *Nights* were not translated from the Arabic until the early eighteenth century, this version was presumably unknown to Shakespeare.

There is also the beguiling possibility that Shakespeare might have derived his own plot from an earlier play called simply *The Jew*, which was described by the English satirist Stephen Gosson in 1579 as "representing the greediness of worldly choosers and the bloody minds of usurers".[1] This description would suggest that the earlier play had a version of both the casket and the pound-of-flesh stories, but since the play is no longer extant, any further speculation is fruitless.

Finally, of course, there is the presence of Christopher Marlowe's *Jew of Malta*, which Shakespeare must have known very well. Although it seems likely that the successful revival of Marlowe's *Jew* in the wake of the López trial served as the motivation for Shakespeare's decision to write his own "Jewish" play, it would be a mistake to conflate the two plays. They have much in common, but it is in their differences, as distinct from their similarities, that we begin to perceive the injustice that has been done to Shakespeare's play by its critical misinterpretation over the centuries.

John Klause highlights "the moral vision of *The Merchant of Venice*, which is in some ways as idealistic as the ethos of Marlowe's play is cynical".[2] Whereas Marlowe made the antagonism between Christian and Jew the central element of his play, "cynically portraying Christian, Jew, and Turk as villains all",[3] the conflict between the two religions is

---

[1] Stephen Gosson, *The School of Abuse* (1579), quoted in Oscar James Campbell, ed., *The Reader's Encyclopedia of Shakespeare* (New York: MJF Books, 1966), p. 522.

[2] Dennis Taylor and David N. Beauregard, eds., *Shakespeare and the Culture of Christianity in Early Modern England* (New York: Fordham University Press, 2003), p. 185.

[3] Ibid., p. 183.

very much a secondary theme in Shakespeare's play, subsumed within the main episodes of the story line and subservient to the dominant moral theme. Take, for instance, the three main points of dramatic focus: the test of the caskets, the test of the trial, and the test of the rings. The conflict between Christian and Jew is entirely absent from the first and last of these dramatic nodal points, and it is present as a foil and not as the focus of the trial scene.

The moral focus during the drama of the trial revolves around notions of justice and mercy, or questions concerning the nature of law and ethics, and not about the hostilities between gentile and Jew. These hostilities are present, of course, and even prominent, but they are present as *accidents*, philosophically speaking,[4] and are not *essential* to the moral thrust of the plot. Considering the way in which the expression of these hostilities has distracted most critics from the essential morality of the play in pursuit of its accidental qualities, it could be argued convincingly that their inclusion was an "accident" in the more general sense of the word, i.e., a mistake on Shakespeare's part that led to the crashing of his play into the abyss of critical error.

If the gentile characters in the play, and by extension Shakespeare himself, can be accused of anti-Semitism or racism (a charge to which we shall return), it can be argued that the playwright has used immoral means to attain his moral ends, something beyond the pale from a Christian perspective. If so, the play, as a work of Christian literature, is an artistic failure. If the approach of the critics had followed this line of reasoning, one could scarcely fault their logic or their critical acumen. Unfortunately, however, their approach has all too often taken an entirely different and ultimately perverse course. Uncomfortable with the invective leveled against Shylock, the critics have leapt to his defense, enthroning him as the play's downtrodden hero and as its principal focus. This is absurd. Shylock is entirely uninvolved in two of the three pivotal turns in the plot and is only marginally and implicitly involved in the play's climactic denouement. To make Shylock the hero or the principal focus is to miss the whole point of the play. The play, we should remember, is called *The Merchant of Venice*, the merchant in question being Antonio and not Shylock, and is not called *The Jew of Venice* as an echo of Marlowe's *Jew of Malta*. Marlowe's play

---

[4] An accident, following the logic of Aristotle, is something that is irrelevant to the defining principle of a thing.

focuses on the Jew; Shakespeare's does not. In focusing too closely on Shylock, we lose the wider focus necessary to see the play as a whole.

This Shylockian heresy, to give it a name, is nothing less than a critical blindness. By way of analogy, let us look at two parallel characters in the works of Dickens that might be said to exhibit Shylockian attributes. The character of Ebenezer Scrooge in *A Christmas Carol* is so much at the center of the story line that stage and screen adaptations have adopted the title *Scrooge*. Though something of the artistic integrity of the work is lost in such a use of literary or dramatic license, one's critical sensibilities are not overly affronted by such an imposition. Scrooge is the principal focus of the work, and his becoming its eponymous hero seems understandable enough. If, on the other hand, screen adaptations of *Oliver Twist* had altered the focus of the story to such an extent that Fagin became the principal focus, we would immediately protest that an act of gross literary vandalism had been committed against the meaning and integrity of Dickens' novel. Since Fagin is not the principal character or focus but merely a powerful and integral part of the wider plot, we would be justifiably outraged at the grotesque parody of the original work inherent in such a shift of focus. And yet Shylock's role in *The Merchant of Venice* is much more akin to that of Fagin in *Oliver Twist* than it is to that of Scrooge in *A Christmas Carol*. It is, therefore, shocking that it has been the sad fate of *The Merchant of Venice* to suffer from the effects of the blindness of this Shylockian heresy on the part of those who have read it and staged it down the years.

From William Hazlitt's critical inversion of the play's deeper meaning in his defense of Shylock[5] to Henry Irving's celebrated stage portrayal of a Jew who is "conscious of his own superiority in all but circumstance to the oppressor",[6] it has been the play's fate to have its heroes demonized and its villain lionized. Perhaps this is the price that Shakespeare had to pay for his pandering to the anti-Semitic prejudices of his audience in the wake of the López trial. If so, after two hundred years of "substance abuse", in which the substantial meaning has been abused by the elevation of the accidental, it is surely time to

---

[5] William Hazlitt, *Characters of Shakespear's Plays* (London: George Bell and Sons, 1881), pp. 189–95. The work was first published by the London publisher Taylor and Hessey in 1817.

[6] From a review of Irving's performance of Shylock at London's Lyceum Theatre published in the *Saturday Review*, November 8, 1879.

insist that Shakespeare's debt has been paid. His words, having been made a pound of flesh, must now regain the spirit that gave life to the flesh in the first place. It is assuredly time to see *The Merchant of Venice* as Shakespeare saw it, as a work overflowing with Christian theological overtones.

## 3

## "I HAVE MUCH ADO TO KNOW MYSELF"

*Antonio.* In sooth, I know not why I am so sad;
It wearies me, you say it wearies you;
But how I caught it, found it, or came by it,
What stuff 'tis made of, whereof it is born,
I am to learn;
And such a want-wit sadness makes of me,
That I have much ado to know myself. (1.1.1–7)

With these melancholic lines Shakespeare opens his comedy and introduces us to its eponymous protagonist, Antonio, "the merchant of Venice". In doing so, he sets the scene for what follows by hinting at the dramatic dynamic that he is about to set in motion. Antonio, a wealthy merchant, would appear outwardly to have all that he needs and all that he desires. From a worldly perspective, he has made a success of his life. He has secured a great deal of wealth, a life of luxury, and all the financial security he could wish for. He has everything the world can offer. And yet he is not content; on the contrary, he is filled with "a want-wit sadness". But his opening words are not about the sadness but about the reasons for the sadness. Antonio is sad, but he does not know why he is sad. What wearies him is not the sadness but the unknown cause of the sadness. How did he catch it, or find it, or come by it? And what is it? What "stuff" is it made of? Is it something material, something that can be fixed by some worldly remedy; or is it spiritual, beyond the ability of the world to rectify? And what is its cause, whereof is it born? He does not know; he yet needs "to learn".

These are the questions that are preoccupying Antonio at the commencement of the drama, and they are, therefore, the questions that Shakespeare puts before us at the very outset of the play. Clearly, are they not meant to preoccupy us too? The very fact that the fifth line, "I am to learn", is left incomplete accentuates the importance of the questions being asked and, more important, the lack of answers to them. The words protrude in their metrical isolation, jarring with the flow of the pentameters and necessitating a pregnant pause after they are spoken. Antonio is "to learn", and Shakespeare clearly wants us to know that he is "to learn". And what exactly is he to learn? Not simply the reasons for his sadness or the "stuff" of which it is made, but the reasons for his very self and the "stuff" of which *he* is made:

> And such a want-wit sadness makes of me,
> That I have much ado to know myself.

And thus the play begins with one of the biggest questions facing all of us: Who are we? What is the "stuff" of which we are made? These are the questions that expose the shallowness of Polonius' "advice" in *Hamlet* that we must be true to ourselves above all else. How can we be true to ourselves unless we know who or what we truly are? This is the question with which Antonio agonizes at the beginning of *The Merchant of Venice*. His having "much ado" to know himself is not much ado about nothing but much ado about everything.

The question is teased out still further during Antonio's exchange with Salerio and Solanio as the scene unfolds. We discover that his sadness is not caused by any concern over the success of his business transactions or by any troubled romance:

> *Salerio.*                    I know Antonio
>    Is sad to think upon his merchandise.
> *Antonio.* Believe me, no. I thank my fortune for it,
>    My ventures are not in one bottom trusted,
>    Nor to one place; nor is my whole estate
>    Upon the fortune of this present year:
>    Therefore my merchandise makes me not sad.
> *Solanio.* Why then you are in love.
> *Antonio.*                              Fie, fie!
> *Solanio.* Not in love neither? (1.1.39–47)

Once again the question is begged. If Antonio's sadness is not caused by the love of gold or the love of woman, what exactly *is* the cause? Gratiano is the next to broach the question:

> *Gratiano.* You look not well, Signior Antonio,
>    You have too much respect upon the world.
>    They lose it that do buy it with much care.

Believe me you are marvellously chang'd.
*Antonio.* I hold the world but as the world, Gratiano,
A stage, where every man must play a part,
And mine a sad one. (1.1.73–79)

Since Antonio's sadness has no worldly cause, it is implicit that the cause or source of his sorrow is otherworldly; it is to be discovered beyond the world and its cares. Its source is spiritual.

As always, Shakespeare takes us beyond the myopia of materialism to show us the spiritual realm in which reality is played out. The world is but a stage on which men play the parts allotted to them. Each has a different part to play, and each can play his part well or badly, receiving the applause or condemnation that his performance merits after the final curtain falls. These oft-quoted lines do not imply, as some (post)-modern critics would have us believe, that nothing is real, that everything and everyone is but a mask, or a series of masks, that can be changed at will or at whim to make them something or someone else. On the contrary, the world is a stage because it has been built to serve the purpose of staging the play, and a play necessitates a Playwright. The world is a stage because the Deity is a Dramatist. The profound Christian aesthetic and philosophy of creativity rooted in this metaphor of Antonio's would be toyed with implicitly by Shakespeare in his final play, *The Tempest.*[1]

Having been introduced to "the merchant of Venice", Antonio, as one who is overcome with an unfathomable sadness, and having been told that the world, or life, is but the stage upon which we are called to play the parts allotted us (until the curtain of death falls), we are then introduced to Bassanio, Antonio's "noble kinsman" (1.1.57).[2] He is introduced to us as a sort of prodigal son confessing his sins to Antonio, who consequently emerges as a father figure. Like his biblical archetype, Bassanio laments the wasteful ways in which he has lived his life thus far:

---

[1] The same metaphor would also be explored more explicitly in terms of its philosophical and artistic ramifications by G. K. Chesterton in his play *Magic.*

[2] One of the many sins committed by critics against Antonio and Bassanio is the suggestion that their relationship is in some sense homosexual. Such a reading of their relationship is utterly unsustainable from any objective reading of the text and can be dismissed as the product of narcissistic and subjective misreadings of the play and its moral meaning. For a full discussion of the errors of "queer theory" in relation to Shakespeare and his work, see Joseph Pearce, *The Quest for Shakespeare* (San Francisco: Ignatius Press, 2008), chapter 11, "Red Herrings and Codpieces", pp. 129–34.

> 'Tis not unknown to you, Antonio,
> How much I have disabled mine estate,
> By something showing a more swelling port
> Than my faint means would grant continuance.
> Nor do I now make moan to be abridg'd
> From such a noble rate, but my chief care
> Is to come fairly off from the great debts
> Wherein my time something too prodigal
> Hath left me gag'd. To you, Antonio,
> I owe the most in money and in love,
> And from your love I have a warranty
> To unburthen all my plots and purposes
> How to get clear of all the debts I owe. (1.1.122–34)

Having met the benevolent father and the prodigal son, the stage is now set for the arrival of the play's blessed virgin. This is Portia, the Lady of Belmont, fairer than fair and "[o]f wondrous virtues" (1.1.162). Her being introduced to us with such grandiloquence serves the purpose of establishing our heroine's bona fides, a purpose that is fulfilled regardless of the fact that the words are uttered by the besotted Bassanio, who sees her through the eyes of a love that is not blind but sees truly, as is subsequently confirmed by his choice of the "true" casket.

Bassanio needs to borrow money if he is to be successful in his quest to woo the Lady of Belmont, and Antonio, generous as ever and convinced by Bassanio of the worthiness of the lady, agrees to lend his friend the necessary funds:

> Thou know'st that all my fortunes are at sea,
> Neither have I money nor commodity
> To raise a present sum; therefore go forth,
> Try what my credit can in Venice do.
> That shall be rack'd, even to the uttermost,
> To furnish thee to Belmont, to fair Portia.
> Go presently inquire, and so will I,
> Where money is, and I no question make
> To have it of my trust, or for my sake. (1.1.177–85)

Antonio's willingness to "be rack'd, even to the uttermost" to furnish the means by which Bassanio can win his "fair Portia" is destined to be put to the uttermost test as the drama unfolds. The word "rack'd", or "racked", is a portentous pun on "recked", in the sense of a reckoning, an account that must be paid, or a day of reckoning on which something must be atoned for or avenged, thereby linking the word with the Day of Atonement, the most solemn fast of the Jewish year, and by extension with the Christian Day of Atonement, Good Friday, on which the reconciliation of God and man is achieved through Christ's Crucifixion. The pun is indeed brilliant but should not detract from the literal meaning of the word "racked", i.e., tortured on the rack, which connects the text with the fate of the subtextually omnipresent Robert Southwell. In this way the words "racked" and "recked" become interchangeable. The merchant and the Jesuit on the rack are mystically united with Christ on the Cross.[3] The racking is the reckoning, the atonement for sin. For Antonio, it is not his wealth, or the money that he owes, that will be reckoned and racked. It will be his love for Bassanio, symbolized by the pound of flesh nearest his heart.

[3] And the same is true of Shakespeare's use of the imagery of the "rack" as Bassanio prepares for the trial of the caskets. In this case it is Bassanio and Southwell who are mystically united with the crucified Christ as they choose to "hazard all" for their love.

# 4

## PORTIA: GATE OF VIRTUE

> In Belmont is a lady richly left,
> And she is fair and, fairer than that word,
> Of wondrous virtues. Sometimes from her eyes
> I did receive fair speechless messages.
> Her name is Portia.... (1.1.161–65)

If Antonio is the eponymous hero of *The Merchant of Venice*, it is generally agreed that he is upstaged by the play's heroine, the fairer-than-fair Portia.

Among Portia's numerous admirers is Fanny Kemble, the celebrated Shakespearean actress and sometime critic who waxed lyrical, elevating Portia's "wondrous virtues" until she seems a veritable icon of idealized femininity:

> I chose Portia [as] my ideal of a perfect woman ... the wise, witty woman, loving with all her soul, and submitting with all her heart to a man whom everybody but herself (who was the best judge) would have judged her inferior; the laughter-loving, light-hearted, true-hearted, deep-hearted woman, full of keen perception, of active efficiency, of wisdom prompted by love, of tenderest unselfishness, of generous magnanimity; noble, simple, humble, pure; true, dutiful, religious, and full of fun; delightful above all others, the woman of women.[1]

William Hazlitt, on the other hand, true to his perverted inversion of the play's meaning, misreads Portia as he misreads Shylock:

> Portia is not a very great favorite with us; neither are we in love with her maid, Nerissa. Portia has a certain degree of affection and pedantry about her, which is very unusual in Shakespear's women.... The speech about Mercy is very well; but there are a thousand finer ones in Shakespear. We

---

[1] *Atlantic Monthly*, June 1876.

do not admire the scene of the caskets: and object entirely to the Black Prince, Morocchius.[2]

The best way of responding to Hazlitt's character assassination of Portia is to present the evidence that disproves his position.

Her virtue is established most convincingly by her own actions, and these we shall study presently at greater length, but it is also confirmed by the judgment of others. We have seen already the effusiveness with which Bassanio introduces her virtue to Antonio, and to us, and he reiterates his respect for her moral rectitude in his words to Gratiano in act 2. After Gratiano's insistence that he be allowed to accompany Bassanio on his journey to Belmont (Portia's home), Bassanio is at great pains to warn Gratiano that he must be on his best behavior in Portia's presence:

> But hear thee, Gratiano:
> Thou art too wild, too rude, and bold of voice—
> Parts that become thee happily enough,
> And in such eyes as ours appear not faults,
> But where thou art not known, why, there they show
> Something too liberal. Pray thee take pain
> To allay with some cold drops of modesty
> Thy skipping spirit, lest through thy wild behavior
> I be misconst'red in the place I go to,
> And lose my hopes. (2.2.180–89)

It is true that Bassanio has an ulterior motive for desiring that his friend conduct himself with modesty in Portia's presence, but this does not detract from the fact that modesty is becoming in her presence. Belmont is not Venice, and decorum dictates a degree of modesty and temperance in the one that may be lacking in the other.

Perhaps the greatest witness to Portia's virtue, apart from her own actions, is given by Jessica. On being asked by Lorenzo her opinion of Portia, her reply raises the Lady of Belmont's "wondrous virtues" to the very heavens:

> *Lorenzo.* And now, good sweet, say thy opinion,
> How dost thou like the Lord Bassanio's wife?

---

[2] William Hazlitt, *Characters of Shakespear's Plays* (London: George Bell and Sons, 1881), pp. 189–95.

*Jessica.* Past all expressing. It is very meet
  The Lord Bassanio live an upright life,
  For having such a blessing in his lady,
  He finds the joys of heaven here on earth,
  And if on earth he do not [merit] it,
  In reason he should never come to heaven!
  Why, if two gods should play some heavenly match,
  And on the wager lay two earthly women,
  And Portia one, there must be something else
  Pawn'd with the other, for the poor rude world
  Hath not her fellow. (3.5.71–83)

Although Bassanio is not present to hear Jessica's praise, we see in her words an echo of Bassanio's own advice to Gratiano. Bassanio, like his friend, must be on his best behavior in Portia's presence. There is, however, a crucial difference. Since Bassanio has succeeded in his quest to win the lady's hand in marriage, he must now be on his best behavior for the rest of his life!

Jessica's words are also awash with Christian typological significance. In describing Portia as the most blessed of all "earthly women", who has no equal in virtue anywhere in this "poor rude world", Shakespeare is clearly casting Portia as a Marian figure, a figure of the Blessed Virgin. Such a typological reading of her character is reinforced by her very name, Portia, which derives from the Latin word for gate (*porta*), an allusion to one of the Blessed Virgin's titles in the Litany of Loreto, where she is described as the "gate of heaven".[3] It is reinforced still further by the name assigned to Portia's home.[4] The atmosphere of Belmont is so different from the worldly dross that preoccupies the residents of Venice that the name's literal meaning, "mountain of beauty", seems singularly appropriate. The perspective of life that we attain from

---

[3] The Virgin's title in the litany is *janua caeli*, which means the same as *porta caeli*.

[4] Although "Belmonte" is the setting for *Il pecorone*, the source play for *The Merchant of Venice*, it is significant that Shakespeare chooses to retain the name, signaling his desire that the allegorical allusions with which it is pregnant are given birth within his own play. For those seeking biographical connections with Shakespeare's Catholicism, it is noteworthy that Belmont was also the Hampshire home of Thomas Pounde (1539–1615), a cousin of Shakespeare's benefactor, the Earl of Southampton, who had been an actor as a young man but was imprisoned for his active Catholicism and became a Jesuit lay brother in prison. He was still a prisoner at the time that Shakespeare was writing *The Merchant of Venice*, and it is entirely feasible, given what we know of Shakespeare's own Catholicism, that this was a further reason for his retaining Belmont as the home of his heroine.

the beautiful heights of Belmont, in the company of the "heavenly" Portia, is so different from the venality and vendettas of Venice. If Venice wallows in the gutters of life, Belmont seems to point to the stars, and to the heaven beyond the stars, and ultimately, suggests Shakespeare scholar Fernando de Mello Moser, to the Love that moves the heaven and the stars:

> It is surely significant that Shakespeare kept the place-name of Bel-mont, implying Beauty and the Heights! Poetically and symbolically, Belmont stands for a state of overpowering Joy, a joy that grows with Love and through Love, and—as elsewhere in Shakespeare—is revealed and communicated primarily through the heroine. Because Shakespeare, different as he is from Dante in so many ways, is like the great Florentine in [several] essential and interrelated points: both seem to have experienced what may be described as the "Beatrician vision" ... and Shakespeare, again and again, wrote about Love in terms that imply something more than merely human love, rather, beyond it, something like "l'amor che move il sole e l'altre stele".[5]

Fernando de Mello Moser's appraisal of the moral dimension of the play is as fresh and refreshing as it is rare and unusual. The problem that afflicts so much other Shakespearean criticism, of which William Hazlitt's criticism is typical, is that the so-called post-Christian age has lost the ability to see as Shakespeare sees, from the beautiful heights of Belmont. Lacking perspective, these critics are left with nothing but the perplexity that leads to apoplexy. They do not see Venice, as Portia sees it, from the heights of Belmont; they see Belmont only from the gutters of Venice. And from the gutters of Venice, you cannot really see Belmont at all. You have to hike to the heights to get Portia's perspective, and the true perspective of Portia's character, which Hazlitt clearly lacks. The *bella vista* can be seen only from the summit, and the summit can be reached only through an understanding of Christianity and an appreciation and apprehension of the Christian imagination that Shakespeare shared with his audience.

Two perceptive observations by Oscar Wilde come to mind at this juncture. The first are the words of Lord Darlington in *Lady Windermere's Fan*:

---

[5] Fernando de Mello Moser, *Dilecta Britannia: Estudos de cultura inglesa* (Lisbon, Portugal: Fundação Calouste Gulbenkian, 2004), p. 294. "L'amor che move il sole e l'altre stele" (The Love that moves the sun and the other stars) is the final line and climax of Dante's *Divine Comedy*.

"We are all in the gutter but some of us are looking at the stars." [6] And the other is from Wilde's preface to *The Picture of Dorian Gray*:

> Those who find ugly meanings in beautiful things are corrupt without being charming. This is a fault.
>
> Those who find beautiful meanings in beautiful things are the cultivated. For these there is hope.

If we are in the gutter and can see nothing but the gutter, we have made ourselves blind. If we are materialists or cynics and believe that there is nothing to see but the gutter, we will have been blinded by our own philosophy. It is not that we have to *be* Christians in order to see Christian art as it should be seen, but we have to *see* what Christians see in the way in which they see it. Even if sympathy is impossible, empathy is necessary. To see only through Venetian eyes is to suffer from Venetian blindness; to see only through Shylock's eyes, as does Hazlitt, is to suffer from Shylock's blindness; on the other hand, to see through Portia's eyes is to gain the clarity of vision necessary to see clearly, and to read *The Merchant of Venice* properly. This being so, let us get to know Portia better so that we can see as she sees.

Her very first words echo the very first words of Antonio, thereby connecting the first lines of the play's second scene with the first lines of its opening scene. "By my troth, Nerissa, my little body is a-weary of this great world" (1.2.1–2). So says Portia. "In sooth, I know not why I am so sad; it wearies me, you say it wearies you" (1.1.1–2). So says Antonio. Shakespeare, with his usual mastery of dramatic symmetry, connects his hero and his heroine in our minds; and the thing that they have in common, the thing that connects them, is their world-weariness. They are weary of the world and what it has to offer. They are otherworldly. They desire those things that the world cannot provide. They look beyond it and its limitations for the fulfillment of their desires. Note, however, that there is no suggestion that Portia does not know the reason for her world-weariness. She does not need to ask the fundamental questions about the meaning of life and the meaning of the self that preoccupy Antonio. By her "troth" (her faith), she already sees more clearly than he does. Note also that her lady-in-waiting, Nerissa, sees more clearly than do Antonio's friends, Salerio and Solanio. Whereas Antonio's friends suggested

---

[6] Act 3.

worldly causes for his world-weariness, Nerissa understands clearly that such weariness has nothing to do with worldly considerations:

> [F]or aught I see, they are as sick that surfeit with too much as they that starve with nothing. It is no mean happiness therefore to be seated in the mean: superfluity comes sooner by white hairs, but competency lives longer. (1.2.5–9)

Nerissa perceives that true happiness does not come with worldly riches and that, on the contrary, too much wealth can bring its own problems and anxieties. "Good sentences, and well pronounc'd", responds Portia, concurring with her lady-in-waiting's words of wisdom. It is evident that those in Belmont do not see as the world sees.

Implicit in the words enunciated by Nerissa is the teaching of Christ that "where your treasure is, there will your heart be also."[7] Portia's heart is not where her worldly treasure is—though she is very rich— nor is Antonio's. Portia's heart is set on the beautiful heights that can be seen more clearly from Belmont, the sphere of the spirit, than from Venice, the sphere of the world. Antonio's heart is also pining for the beautiful heights of this spiritual sphere, but because he does not see as those in Belmont see, he does not yet know what it is that his heart desires. He is in the dark but longing for the light. He is in the gutter but longing for the stars that he cannot yet see.

Compare Antonio's Venetian blindness with the Belmontian perspicacity of Portia and Nerissa:

> *Portia.* If to do were as easy as to know what were good to do, chapels had been churches, and poor men's cottages princes' palaces. It is a good divine that follows his own instructions; I can easier teach twenty what were good to be done, than to be one of the twenty to follow mine own teaching. The brain may devise laws for the blood, but a hot temper leaps o'er a cold decree—such a hare is madness the youth, to skip o'er the meshes of good counsel the cripple. But this reasoning is not in the fashion to choose me a husband. O me, the word choose! I may neither choose who I would, nor refuse who I dislike; so is the will of a living daughter curb'd by the will of a dead father. Is it not hard, Nerissa, that I cannot choose one, nor refuse none?
>
> *Nerissa.* Your father was ever virtuous, and holy men at their death have good inspirations; therefore the lott'ry that he hath devis'd in these three

---

[7] Matthew 6:21. All biblical quotations are from the King James Version.

chests of gold, silver, and lead, whereof who chooses his meaning chooses
you, will no doubt never be chosen by any rightly but one who you
shall rightly love. (1.2.12–33)

Portia understands the value and necessity of prudence and temperance, and the dangers of failing to act in accordance with these virtuous precepts. She also knows that it is easier to know virtue than to live
virtuously. If prudence is preached but not practiced, or if a "hot temper" is not tempered by temperance, "madness the youth" will go its
wicked way, ignoring the "good counsel" of wisdom in its pursuit of
selfish passion. And yet she bemoans the fact that "this reasoning is not
in the fashion to choose me a husband." Portia, it seems, is not free to
exercise prudence and temperance in her choice of a husband because
her right to choose has been refused by her recently deceased father.
"Is it not hard, Nerissa, that I cannot choose one, nor refuse none?"
    Although it is tempting to sympathize with Portia's plight, it is clear
that we are meant to resist such a temptation. Shakespeare is not an
emotion-driven romantic but a sober-minded Christian realist, and all
such sympathy for Portia is thrown into question by Nerissa's reply:
"Your father was ever virtuous, and holy men at their death have good
inspirations." Portia's father is not some control freak intent on ruining
his daughter's happiness; he is a holy man, "ever virtuous", who devised
the test of the caskets as a "good inspiration" at the moment of his
death. The test is, therefore, sanctioned by the sanctity and wisdom of
the father and is designed in such a way that the correct casket "will no
doubt never be chosen by any rightly but one who you shall rightly
love." In other words, the one who passes the test by choosing rightly
will have proven himself in wisdom and virtue to such a sublime degree
that Portia will herself be choosing rightly in accepting his hand in
marriage.
    And this brings us to the whole question of "choice". It seems from
this exchange between Portia and Nerissa that there are only two choices
facing Portia. She can choose rightly or she can choose wrongly. She
can make her choices based upon what she knows is right, or she can
choose on the basis of passion. She can choose *objectively* by subjecting
her passions to virtue, or she can choose *subjectively* by allowing her
passions to override her objective knowledge of the good. And this, of
course, is exactly Portia's point in contrasting the reasoning power of
the brain with the "hot temper" of the blood, or in contrasting "good

counsel" with the "madness" of youth. And one surmises that Portia is merely putting into words the thoughts of her "ever virtuous" father as he pondered the choices facing his daughter following his death. He knew that Portia knew right from wrong, but he knew, as Portia knows, that it is easier to teach others the good to be done than to do the good oneself. Preaching is easier than practicing what we preach. Portia is young; she is passionate. There is a danger that her knowledge of virtue might be overpowered by her youthful "madness". Mindful of this danger, Portia's holy father had the "good inspiration" to devise a plan whereby his daughter would be protected from the consequence of a bad choice through her acceptance of the consequence of a good choice. In making the right choice, the suitor *becomes* the right choice!

From a worldly perspective, and particularly from a (post)modern worldly perspective, the whole business of the caskets is nothing less than a denial of Portia's freedom to make her own choices. And from a feminist perspective, it is a patriarchal denial of a woman's right to choose. And yet this is not the way that Portia sees it. In an act of outrageous "political incorrectness", she *freely chooses* to do the will of her father: "I will die as chaste as Diana, unless I be obtain'd by the manner of my father's will" (1.2.106–8). In *freely choosing* this limitation on her freedom, Portia is not succumbing to a patriarchal imposition but is merely conforming her will to correct reason. Portia knows that to *choose* evil is not only wrong but irrational. And to be irrational is to be a slave to the "madness" of one's passions. Liberty and the libertine are at war with each other. This is one of the ironies and paradoxes at the heart of the whole drama and is the very gist of Portia's discourse on the importance of prudence and temperance in the face of unruly passion. It can be seen, therefore, that Portia truly lives up to her name. She is a gate of virtue. And if the gate is narrower than the world likes, it is because the world does not know her, nor does it wish to choose the casket of virtue that she offers it. The world chooses as it has ever chosen, following its unruly passions and binding itself with chains of gold and silver. Enslaving itself to its selfishness, it remains bereft of the joy it has not chosen.

# 5

# SHYLOCK THE USURER

If Portia is misunderstood by worldly critics, in their failure to perceive the unity of virtue and wisdom at the heart of her character, Shylock is equally misunderstood by the same critics, in their failure to perceive the vice and wickedness in his pride-hardened heart. A true appraisal of Shylock is, therefore, as necessary to a true understanding of the play as is a true knowledge of Portia.

One of the earliest Shakespearean critics, Nicholas Rowe, argued that Shylock should be seen as a truly tragic figure who transcends the merely comic aspects of his character. After comparing Shylock with comic characters such as Malvolio in *Twelfth Night* and Petruchio in *The Taming of the Shrew*, Rowe insists that *The Merchant of Venice* "was designed tragically by the author":

> There appears in it such a deadly spirit of revenge, such a savage fierceness and fellness, and such a bloody designation of cruelty and mischief, as cannot agree either with the style or characters of comedy.[1]

It needs to be noted that all the aspects of the play that turn it into a tragedy in Rowe's judgment are fatal flaws in one character. It is Shylock that carries within him "a deadly spirit of revenge"; it is Shylock whose every action is animated by "a savage fierceness and fellness"; it is Shylock who gives to the play its "bloody designation of cruelty and mischief". Is it any wonder that the very name of Shylock is generally believed to be derived from the Hebrew word *shalach*, meaning "cormorant", a creature that is synonymous with gluttonous excess? Similarly, is it any wonder that Shylock is often likened to Satan? Take, for instance, the words of Solanio at the beginning of act 3:

[1] Nicholas Rowe, *The Works of Mr. William Shakespear* (1709), quoted in Kenneth Myrick, ed., *The Merchant of Venice* (New York: Signet Classic, 1998), p. 109.

Let me say amen betimes, lest the devil cross my prayer, for here he comes in the likeness of a Jew. (3.1.19–21)

A few lines later, after Shylock states that his daughter is "damn'd" for her elopement with Lorenzo, Solanio responds that her damnation is "certain, if the devil may be her judge" (3.1.32–33). The riposte hits the mark. It is no sin to be "damn'd" by the Devil.

It is possible to sympathize with Shylock, in the sense that we can truly pity a person who is imprisoned by his own self-destructive pride, but it is wrong that we should sympathize with him in the sense of justifying his pride and his anger through a shifting of the blame onto others. The former approach represents true critical discernment, the latter a warped distortion of the play's integral meaning. The former approach displays a sympathy for the sinner, the latter a sympathy for the Devil.

Shakespeare leaves us in no doubt of Shylock's villainy and his hatred of Christianity in the way in which he introduces him to us. On being invited by Bassanio to dine with Antonio, Shylock responds with venomous invective:

Yes, to smell pork, to eat of the habitation which your prophet the Nazarite conjur'd the devil into. I will buy with you, sell with you, talk with you, walk with you, and so following; but I will not eat with you, drink with you, nor pray with you. (1.3.33–38)

The invective continues in the aside that Shylock utters to himself as he first sets eyes on Antonio:

How like a fawning publican he looks!
I hate him for he is a Christian;
But more, for that in low simplicity
He lends out money gratis, and brings down
The rate of usance here with us in Venice.
If I can catch him once upon the hip,
I will feed fat the ancient grudge I bear him.
He hates our sacred nation, and he rails
Even there where merchants most do congregate
On me, my bargains, and my well-won thrift,
Which he calls interest. Cursed be my tribe
If I forgive him! (1.3.41–52)

In the wake of the anti-Semitic (and anti-Christian) debauchery of the Third Reich, it is difficult to hear these words without shifting uncomfortably in our seats. Yet Shakespeare knew nothing of the Third Reich or of the pathological hatred of Hitler, and it is wrong to see such lines out of their true Elizabethan context. There is no way that Shakespeare's Christian imagination could conceive the post-Christian and anti-Christian hatred of the Nazis, and as such, it is wrong to accuse him of views that he could not even have contemplated or comprehended. Yet it is true that Shakespeare depicts a great enmity, an "ancient grudge", between Christian and Jew, an enmity that we will need to understand if we are to comprehend this particular aspect of the play, mindful nonetheless, and as we have already noted, that it represents a relatively minor aspect of the play compared to the moral dynamic inherent in the difference between Belmont and Venice.

Let it be understood from the outset that the enmity between Christian and Jew is not rooted in racism but in theology. This is clear from the fact that a Jew can become a Christian, whereas it is not possible for a Jew in Nazi Germany to become an Aryan or for a black man to become a member of the Ku Klux Klan. Shakespeare, as a Christian, believed that Christ was the Way, the Truth, and the Life and that none could come to the Father except through the Son. It was, therefore, good for Jews, Muslims, and pagans to convert to Christianity; their eternal souls were saved thereby. This might make the modern reader uneasy. We live in an age of pluralism and ecumenism, in which religious differences are not the topic of polite conversation, but Shakespeare did not live in such an age. He lived in an age in which people believed that Christ was the only way to salvation. We do not have to agree with Shakespeare, or the age in which he lived, but we do need to understand this stark reality—and we need to see that it is starkly different from the thoroughly modern disease of racism. Jessica, Shylock's daughter, is accepted with an open heart by all the Christian characters as soon as she expresses a desire to convert to Christianity. Her equality with them is not in question; she is not seen as racially inferior but as theologically flawed. As soon as she sees the error of her beliefs, and changes her mind and heart, she is united with her Christian brothers and sisters. This is seen most tellingly in Salerio's response to Shylock's insistence that Jessica "is my flesh and my blood":

There is more difference between thy flesh and hers than between jet
and ivory, more between your bloods than there is between red wine
and Rhenish. (3.1.39–42)


There is, therefore, no doubt that Shakespeare perceived the difference
between Christian and Jew as having nothing to do with race or "blood"
but as being rooted in issues of theology.

So much for the nonsensical conflation of the "ancient grudge"
between Christian and Jew with the new disease of racism. But what of
the apparent hatred between Shylock and his enemies? Hatred is certainly a sin even if it is not racial hatred, and it needs to be named as
such. Let us look a little closer, therefore, at the enmity between Shylock and Antonio.

Shylock hates Antonio because "he is a Christian", but this is mentioned almost in passing. The deeper reason is given immediately afterward, and at considerable length. He hates him because Antonio "lends
out money gratis", a practice that "brings down the rate of usance",
and although he attacks Antonio because he "hates [the Jews'] sacred
nation", it is once again the issue of usury that is the real immediate
cause of their enmity:


> He rails
> Even there where merchants most do congregate
> On me, my bargains, and my well-won thrift,
> Which he calls interest. (1.3.48–51)


It can be seen, therefore, that the real enmity between Antonio and
Shylock is rooted in their business practices. Shylock lends money at
interest, whereas Antonio, believing such practice to be immoral, lends
money interest free and berates Shylock in public for his "usury". The
fact that usury is the principal cause of division is emphasized throughout the remainder of the scene, in which the subject of usury is dominant. Shylock is, therefore, introduced to us primarily as a usurer. This
is his defining characteristic.

In the discussion of the morality or immorality of lending money at
interest, Shylock quotes from the book of Genesis to justify his actions,
thereby rooting the whole issue in the realm of theology. Antonio,
unimpressed with Shylock's argument from Scripture, responds in a way

that appears to be an implicit attack on the Protestant new theology of *sola scriptura*:[2]

> Mark you this, Bassanio,
> The devil can cite Scripture for his purpose.
> An evil soul producing holy witness
> Is like a villain with a smiling cheek,
> A goodly apple rotten at the heart.
> O, what a goodly outside falsehood hath! (1.3.97–102)

This apparent allusion to the contemporary theological divisions between Catholics and Protestants has led several scholars, including Clare Asquith, John Klause, Peter Milward, and Velma Richmond, to suggest a metadramatic allegorical dimension whereby Shylock is a thinly veiled personification of a Puritan and Antonio an equally thinly veiled personification of a Jesuit.[3] Evidence for such an allegorical reading is rooted in the thriftiness of the Puritans, who were called "Christian Jews" because of their work ethic, their refusal to associate with others (as Shylock refuses to associate with Christians), and their practice of usury in defiance of Christian convention. By extension, Antonio, as a victim of "Puritan" persecution, is seen as a long-suffering Jesuit who lays down his life for his friends. Here is Peter Milward on the subject:

> Though he is a Jew of Venice ... he might just as well have been, as he was no doubt in the dramatist's mind, one of the Puritan merchants of London. In fact, each of [Shylock's] characteristics is ascribed to the Puritans by celebrated Anglican authors of the time—by John Whitgift, later Archbishop of Canterbury, writing against the Puritan leader Thomas Cartwright; by Richard Bancroft, later Bishop of London and subsequently Archbishop of Canterbury, against the anonymous Puritan authors

---

[2] *Sola scriptura* (Latin for "by Scripture alone") was one of the foundational doctrinal principles of the Protestant Reformation as promulgated by Martin Luther. The implicit condemnation of the doctrine by the virtuous Antonio serves as textual evidence of Shakespeare's own disdain for this Protestant precept.

[3] See, for instance, Clare Asquith, *Shadowplay: The Hidden Beliefs and Coded Politics of William Shakespeare* (New York: Public Affairs, 2005), p. 114; John Klause, "Catholic and Protestant, Jesuit and Jew: Historical Religion in *The Merchant of Venice*", in *Shakespeare and the Culture of Christianity in Early Modern England*, ed. Dennis Taylor and David N. Beauregard (New York: Fordham University Press, 2003), pp. 208–10; Peter Milward, *The Catholicism of Shakespeare's Plays* (Southampton, Hampshire: Saint Austin, 1997), pp. 13–21; Peter Milward, *Shakespeare the Papist* (Naples, Fla.: Sapientia, 2005), pp. 93–102; and Velma Bourgeois Richmond, *Shakespeare, Catholicism and Romance* (New York: Continuum, 2000), pp. 122–23.

of the Marprelate tracts; and by Matthew Sutcliffe, Dean of Exeter, when returning to the attack on Cartwright and openly accusing him of engaging in detested usury. Moreover, this superimposition by Shakespeare of a Puritan character on a Jewish villain—which seems so paradoxical to traditionally minded Shakespeare scholars—is the more understandable when we reflect how little he would have had to do with Jews in his dramatic career, and how much with Puritans.[4]

Such speculation aside, there is little doubt that the division between the two protagonists is theological in nature, though whether purely on the literal level between Christian and Jew, or on the allegorical level between Catholic and Protestant, is open to conjecture.

In any event, the theological root of the argument between Antonio and Shylock is evident even in those speeches of Shylock in which it is usually overlooked. Take, for instance, Shylock's complaint that Antonio had spit on him in public, an act that is often taken to be indicative of blind bigotry on Antonio's part:

> Signior Antonio, many a time and oft
> In the Rialto you have rated me
> About my moneys and my usances.
> Still have I borne it with a patient shrug
> (For suff'rance is the badge of all our tribe).
> You call me misbeliever, cut-throat dog,
> And spet upon my Jewish gaberdine,
> And all for use of that which is mine own. (1.3.106–13)

It is scarcely surprising that the graphic visual image of Antonio spitting on Shylock should obscure or eclipse the actual meaning of Shylock's words, yet those words indicate that Antonio's act of disrespect had nothing to do with Shylock as a Jew and everything to do with Shylock as a usurer. Apart from Antonio calling him a "misbeliever", i.e., a non-Christian, the remainder of Shylock's complaint makes it abundantly clear that Antonio had attacked him for his immoral business practices, not for his Judaism. He was berated about his "moneys" and his "usances" and was called a "cut-throat dog", presumably for his

---

[4] Milward, *Shakespeare the Papist*, p. 98. There were virtually no Jews in England in Shakespeare's time, their having been expelled by Edward I in 1290, i.e., three hundred years earlier. Puritans, on the other hand, were rising in political and economic power and were highly critical of the stage, which they saw as evil and "papist".

lack of business ethics in his dealings with others. And why, exactly, was he spit upon? According to Shylock, it was "all for use of that which is mine own". In other words, Antonio was attacking Shylock not because he was a Jew but because he was angered by his usury.

Why such a fuss over the issue of usury? Why is it so important? Why does it cause such division between Shylock and Antonio? Is it, as many critics have seemingly believed, much ado about nothing; or did Shakespeare and his contemporaries feel as strongly about usury as does Antonio? Perhaps, in order to understand *The Merchant of Venice* in the way in which Shakespeare understood it, we need to see the issue of usury through Shakespeare's eyes. In doing so, we will see immediately that usury was seen in Elizabethan England as a grievous sin. Such a belief was rooted in the teaching of the Catholic Church and in the arguments of the greatest of ancient philosophers.

Plato, Aristotle, and Aristophanes all considered the charging of interest to be fundamentally unnatural, and Cato, Seneca, and Plutarch went so far as to condemn usury in terms that compared it to homicide. It is noteworthy in this regard that Antonio condemns usury in terms that resonate with the Aristotelian and Thomistic doctrine that the "breeding" of inanimate objects, such as money, through usury, was an offense against nature ("for when did friendship take / A breed for barren metal of his friend?" [1.3.133–34]). Similarly, when Antonio asks Shylock whether he considers his gold and silver to be ewes and rams, Shylock replies that he makes his gold and silver "breed as fast" (1.3.95–96).

The early Church also condemned usury, specifically at the First Council of Carthage in 345, and the condemnation continued throughout the Middle Ages, at the Council of Aix in 789 and at several councils thereafter. This was still the official teaching of the Catholic Church at the time that Shakespeare was writing *The Merchant of Venice*. By contrast, Calvin had permitted usury, and his disciple Salmasius had codified the rules by which interest-bearing loans were permissible. Thomas Cartwright, a contemporary of Shakespeare and one of the leading Calvinists in England, followed the teaching of Calvin and Salmasius and was consequently condemned for his defense of usury. It is also noteworthy that it was Henry VIII who altered the law forbidding usury, allowing for loans charging up to 10 percent interest. Edward VI abolished that allowance, prohibiting all interest, a prohibition that remained in force during the reign of the Catholic queen Mary Tudor. Queen Elizabeth reinstated Henry VIII's law, setting the legal limit of 10 percent. "While interest was legally allowed in Elizabethan England," writes the economist James E. Hartley, "there was little change in the perceived morality of usury. It was, in this respect, much like modern laws on adultery; while it is not a crime, there are few who think the act is morally acceptable." [5]

Clearly this was a hot topic in Shakespeare's day, and one that divided people along religious lines. It is interesting, therefore, that Shakespeare takes the Catholic side in the argument, as opposed to the Puritan position, a fact that surely heightens the possibility that Shylock is really a Puritan wearing a Jewish mask. Although such a possibility is all too often lost on modern readers of the play, it would clearly have been much more obvious and much more topical to the audience for which the play was written. For Antonio, and for Shakespeare, and for the vast majority of the audience in Elizabethan England, usury was not simply a crime but a sin, an evil practice that it was the duty of the virtuous to condemn.

[5] James E. Hartley, "Breeding Barren Metal: Usury and *The Merchant of Venice*", in *The Merchant of Venice*, ed. Joseph Pearce, Ignatius Critical Editions (San Francisco: Ignatius Press, 2009), pp. 210.

# 6

## THE RIGHT TO CHOOSE

> In terms of choice I am not soly led
> By nice direction of a maiden's eyes;
> Besides, the lott'ry of my destiny
> Bars me the right of voluntary choosing. (2.1.13–16)

We have already seen that issues of freedom and choice form the moral backbone of the drama in *The Merchant of Venice*, and nowhere is this more obvious than in the test of the caskets. In act 1 we are introduced to a number of would-be suitors who prove themselves unfit to choose through their unwillingness to risk the consequences of their choices. In act 2 the suitors are made of sterner stuff. The first, Morocco, is an infidel, a non-Christian who melds the paganism of classical antiquity with the Islam of the exotic East:

> Therefore I pray you lead me to the caskets
> To try my fortune. By this scimitar
> That slew the Sophy and a Persian prince
> That won three fields of Sultan Solyman,
> I would o'erstare the sternest eyes that look,
> Outbrave the heart most daring on the earth,
> Pluck the young sucking cubs from the she-bear,
> Yea, mock the lion when 'a roars for prey,
> To win [thee], lady. But alas the while!
> If Hercules and Lichas play at dice
> Which is the better man, the greater throw
> May turn by fortune from the weaker hand:
> So is Alcides beaten by his [page],
> And so may I, blind fortune leading me,
> Miss that which one unworthier may attain,
> And die with grieving. (2.1.22–38)

In this depiction of the presumably Muslim Morocco, Shakespeare emerges as a true inheritor of the literary tradition of medieval Christendom. In medieval works, such as *The Song of Roland*, the Muslim is a "paynim" (pagan), pure and simple. There is no suggestion that Muslims, Christians, and Jews are "people of the Book", united in their biblical roots;[1] on the contrary, Islam is the old enemy, intent on conquering the nations of Christendom and forcing all Christians to convert to the creed of "Mahound" (Muhammad). This conflation of ancient paganism and modern Muhammadanism emerges as surely in Shakespeare's characterization of the Prince of Morocco, the "tawny Moor", as it does in *The Song of Roland*. Morocco's conception of virtue is clearly non-Christian and is rooted in a classical eulogizing of prideful courage and in an apparent belief that "might is right." Such sentiments are intensified and Islamicized by the references to the scimitar and to "Sultan Solyman", presumably a reference to Süleyman the Magnificent, the sultan of Turkey whose armies invaded large parts of Christian Europe, including Belgrade and Budapest, in the same century in which Shakespeare was writing. And thus does Morocco meld the might of Hercules with the might of the Muslim hordes terrorizing Europe.

Morocco also exhibits an exotic understanding of the nature of freedom and choice. Since, in his understanding, fate or kismet is as unpredictable and as unalterable as playing at dice, freedom of choice is at the mercy of the follies of fortune. And since he is being led by "blind fortune", it is possible that the unworthy will prevail. This runs counter to the whole philosophy of Portia's father, who has devised the test of the caskets in the belief that choosing freely and virtuously will *prove* the worthiness of the suitor and will *win* him the reward of his heart's desire. Portia's father is akin to the Christian crusaders in Chesterton's "Lepanto":

> It is he that saith not "Kismet"; it is he that knows not Fate;
> It is Richard, it is Raymond, it is Godfrey in the gate![2]

Once again, Shakespeare is showing his masterful grasp of Catholic theology. On the one side, we have the "blind" determinism of the

---

[1] Take, for instance, Launcelot's affectionate description of Shylock's daughter, Jessica, as a "[m]ost beautiful pagan, most sweet Jew" (2.4.10–11).

[2] G. K. Chesterton, *Collected Works*, vol. 10, *Collected Poetry*, pt. 1 (San Francisco: Ignatius Press, 1994), p. 64–65.

pagan or the Muslim (and the "blind" predestination of the Calvinist Puritan); on the other side, we have the Catholic insistence on the freedom of the will and its necessity, under grace, for salvation. In this way, Shakespeare turns the test of the caskets into a touchstone of truth, making it serve as a powerful metaphor for a Catholic understanding of the role of free will in God's salvific plan, as opposed to the new theology of Calvinism with its insistence on predestination. And so, perhaps, Shakespeare uses the Muslim as well as the Jew as a thinly veiled mask for the Puritan.

Act 2, scene 7, in which Morocco agonizes over which of the caskets he should choose, abounds with the verbal dexterity for which the Bard of Avon is rightly celebrated. We are led from casket to casket, agonizing with the proud Prince over the meaning of the inscriptions and the symbolic significance of the gold, silver, and lead of which the caskets are made.

Although there are three caskets, it should be noted that Morocco and the other suitors have only two choices, not three. They have three things from which to choose—gold, silver, or lead—but they can ultimately choose only correctly or incorrectly. To choose gold or silver is to make the wrong choice, i.e., a choice lacking in virtue, whereas to choose lead is to choose virtuously. This is the wisdom of Belmont, a wisdom that in the eyes of Venice and the world is but foolishness. Thus the proudhearted and worldly Prince ponders the meaning of the inscription on the leaden casket ("Who chooseth me must give and hazard all he hath") and concludes instantly that to hazard all for "worthless" lead is utter foolishness:

> Must give—for what? for lead, hazard for lead?
> This casket threatens. Men that hazard all
> Do it in hope of fair advantages;
> A golden mind stoops not to shows of dross.
> I'll then nor give nor hazard aught for lead. (2.7.17–21)

From a worldly perspective, whether Venetian or Moroccan, the Prince's reasoning is perfectly valid. Those who think and choose selfishly can hardly be expected to make great sacrifices for "dross", especially when the lure of gold and silver is present as an alternative. For the self-centered, sacrifices are made only in the "hope of fair advantages". What other reason can there be for inconveniencing ourselves than the expectation of material gain? This is the reasoning of the world and the foundation of modern economics. Morocco has simply made the obvious choice that anyone in Venice would have made in the same circumstances. The problem for such worldly choosers is that the ways of Belmont are not the ways of the world. Portia's father, in his Belmontian (Christian) wisdom, knew that the worldly would choose according to their own lights and, in so doing, would choose incorrectly. Since all men are made in the image of God and therefore are made mystically equal, the worldly suitors have the *right* to choose the good (i.e., Portia, as an allegorical representation of virtue), but they lack the wisdom to choose *rightly*. Portia's father understood the ways of the world and knew that the test of the caskets would protect his daughter from such unwelcome advances.

Portia is also endowed with her father's wisdom, wishing Morocco a "gentle riddance" after he has made his hasty and crestfallen departure and adding her desire that "all of his complexion choose me so" (2.7.78–79). Her reference to "his complexion" is often taken as a racist gibe by Portia against the dark color of the Prince's skin, an assumption that seems justified at first perusal considering that Morocco had introduced himself to her with a request that his skin color should not prejudice her against him:

> Mislike me not for my complexion,
> The shadowed livery of the burnish'd sun,
> To whom I am a neighbor and near bred. (2.1.1–3)

It would seem reasonable to assume that Portia's reference to "his complexion" must allude to his skin color, indicating that she does indeed "mislike" him for it. Yet such an assumption is a little premature for a number of reasons. First, and most obvious, the word "complexion" means "temperament", "character", "personality", or "the *complexity* of qualities that constitute the nature of a person or thing", as well as "skin color". Considering Shakespeare's penchant for puns, it is probable that Portia uses the word as a deliberate double entendre alluding to Morocco's initial use of the word but employs it with the alternative meaning in mind. She does indeed "mislike" him, but it is for the overall complexion of his character rather than for the superficial coloring of his skin. Such a view is reinforced by Portia's actual response to Morocco's initial request that she not "mislike" him for his skin color:

In terms of choice I am not soly led
By nice direction of a maiden's eyes;
Besides, the lott'ry of my destiny
Bars me the right of voluntary choosing.
But if my father had not scanted me,
And hedg'd me by his wit to yield myself
His wife who wins me by that means I told you,
Yourself, renowned Prince, then stood as fair
As any comer I have look'd on yet
For my affection. (2.1.13–22)

She begins by assuring him that her "choice" or personal preference is
not "soly led" or dictated by "nice direction of a maiden's eyes". The modern colloquial use of the word "nice" as referring to something agreeable
or attractive would lead us to conclude that Morocco's dark complexion
is not "nice" and that if Portia were concerned with such niceties his complexion would tell against him. Even if we were to accept this definition
of "nice", which is unlikely to have been a definition with which Shakespeare would have been familiar, it is clear that Portia is insisting that she
is *not* concerned with such niceties, i.e., that they are not important to
her. Yet the older meaning of "nice" as "fastidious", "scrupulous", "dis-
criminative", or even "punctiliously petty" suggests that Portia is using
the word in a pejorative sense, as referring to something that is not nice
at all! She would not dream of allowing such prejudice to cloud her judgment, if indeed she were free to judge. And we can take this etymolog-
ical defense of Portia still further. The Middle English meaning of the word
"nice" was "stupid" or "wanton", having entered the English language,
via Old French, from the Latin word *nescius*, which actually means "ignorant", from whence we have the modern-day word "nescience". If this
older meaning of the word was intended by Shakespeare, we can see that
Portia is actually saying that judging Morocco on the basis of his complexion would be ignorant, stupid, and wanton, none of which charac-
teristics can be ascribed to Shakespeare's wondrously virtuous heroine.

As if the foregoing would not be sufficient to acquit Portia of the
heinous charge of racism, she makes it patently clear in the passage just
quoted that the "renowned Prince . . . stood as fair / As any comer [she
has] look'd on yet / For [her] affection." To put the matter plainly, he is
as fair to her as the suitors from England, France, Scotland, Germany,
and Italy, all of whom were impeccably white! Clearly she does not

judge or prejudge on the basis of skin color. It is true, of course, that her comments are barbed, in the sense that she "mislikes" all the other suitors for their unworthiness, but she "mislikes" them for their lack of virtue, not for their outward appearance.

Seen in this light, it is abundantly clear that Portia's desire that "all of his complexion choose me so" refers to the complexion of his moral character, not to the complexion of his skin (apart from the word's employment as a pun). This being so, Portia clearly "mislikes" Morocco for the complexion of his "golden mind" that "stoops not to shows of dross". Ironically, it is his pride, his arrogance, and his superciliousness, the classic traits of the racist, that cause Portia's disdain for him. The "golden-minded" snob will no more condescend to the level of "dross" than will the "golden-haired" racist to the level of those who wear the "shadowed livery of the burnish'd sun".

With his customary sense of dramatic symmetry, Shakespeare shifts the focus from the golden-minded arrogance of Morocco to the golden-minded avarice of Shylock. As one scene closes with the curtains being drawn on the courtly ambitions of one who chose a fool's gold over the pearl of great price,[3] the next scene opens with the discussion of another fool who chooses gold over his own daughter. Act 2, scene 8, opens with Salerio and Solanio discussing Shylock's reaction to the discovery that his daughter, Jessica, has eloped with Lorenzo, taking some of Shylock's money and jewelry as her dowry. Solanio's reporting of Shylock's avaricious rage is comic but, at the same time, and as Nicholas Rowe surmised, truly tragic:

> I never heard a passion so confus'd,
> So strange, outrageous, and so variable
> As the dog Jew did utter in the streets.
> "My daughter! O my ducats! O my daughter!
> Fled with a Christian! O my Christian ducats!
> Justice! the law! my ducats, and my daughter!
> A sealed bag, two sealed bags of ducats,
> Of double ducats, stol'n from me by my daughter!
> And jewels, two stones, two rich and precious stones,
> Stol'n by my daughter! Justice! find the girl,
> She hath the stones upon her, and the ducats." (2.8.12–22)

---

[3] Matthew 13:46.

Here we see a transformation, a metamorphosis reminiscent of Dr. Jekyll's transmutation into Mr. Hyde. Shylock begins, apparently, with a genuine concern for his daughter and ends with a fulminating tirade against her, demanding her arrest. It is as though his natural parental affections are at war with his unnatural lust for his material possessions. At first, his thoughts for his daughter seem to predominate: "My daughter! O my ducats! O my daughter!" Soon, however, his desire for his ducats rivals his thoughts for his daughter: "Justice! the law! my ducats, and my daughter!" And finally, like Morocco in the previous scene, he chooses the fool's gold over the love of the girl:

> Stol'n by my daughter! Justice! find the girl,
> She hath the stones upon her, and the ducats.

It is as though we have just witnessed a perverse alchemy in which the true gold of a father's love for his daughter is transmuted into the baseness of a miser's lust for his possessions. And it gets worse. In the following act, he not only wishes the weight of justice and the law to fall upon his daughter, but he actually wishes her dead:

> Two thousand ducats in that, and other precious, precious jewels. I would
> my daughter were dead at my foot, and the jewels in her ear! Would she
> were hears'd at my foot, and the ducats in her coffin! (3.1.86–90)

And the tragicomedy continues. When Tubal informs Shylock that Jessica had spent "fourscore ducats" in a single night, Shylock's suffering is intense: "Thou stick'st a dagger in me. I shall never see my gold again. Fourscore ducats at a sitting, fourscore ducats!" (3.1.110–12). He is not concerned that he may never see his daughter again, merely that he will not see his gold. His whole moral outlook is perverse. As a usurer, he boasts of the fertility of his finances. He makes his gold and silver "breed as fast" as ewes and rams, yet he wishes his daughter dead.

Those who wish to exonerate Shylock from any culpability for his actions point to Jessica's original sin in eloping with Lorenzo, without her father's permission, and, as though to add insult to injury, her stealing money and jewels from him into the bargain. It is evident that Shylock can be seen as justified in feeling infuriated by his daughter's conduct, but is he justified in wishing her dead, and is he justified in valuing his ducats more than his daughter? It is as though the whole relationship is a paradoxical inversion of the parable of the prodigal son. Jessica might be seen as a prodigal daughter, but Shylock is the very antithesis of the forgiving father. Such an allusion serves to accentuate the Christian relationship between Antonio and Bassanio, which we have already identified as being akin to that between the forgiving father and the prodigal son, the healthiness of the one relationship heightening our awareness of the pathological nature of the other.

In Jessica's defense, we can see that she does not enjoy a father's love and that she seems to have been treated as merely one of his possessions—and evidently not a particularly valued one:

> Alack, what heinous sin is it in me
> To be ashamed to be my father's child!
> But though I am a daughter to his blood,
> I am not to his manners. O Lorenzo,
> If thou keep promise, I shall end this strife,
> Become a Christian and thy loving wife. (2.3.16–21)

We know also that Jessica was horrified by her father's vengeful plans to "have Antonio's flesh" (3.2.286), and she knew that her father would never permit her to marry Lorenzo, a Christian. Even her taking of Shylock's money would not have been considered as grievous a crime as theft from an honest man. We need to remember that usury was seen as a sin and that a usurer's profit was considered almost as theft in itself.[4] Seen in this light, Jessica's helping herself to a dowry that her father would otherwise have unjustly denied, especially as it was taken from his ill-gotten gains, might have been condoned or even applauded by Shakespeare's audience. It is almost as though Jessica is cast in the romantic role of a Robin Hood who steals from the rich thief to give to the poor bride and groom. Nor can it be purely coincidental that the gold that she takes from her father is kept in a casket. "Here, catch this casket," she exclaims to Lorenzo, "it is worth the pains" (2.6.33).

There is no escaping the connection between the two caskets of gold, and clearly we are meant to see a dramatic parallel between them. On one level, it could be said that Shakespeare is leveling a criticism at Jessica for choosing to take the casket, a possibility that is supported by her own words as she elopes with Lorenzo and the gold:

---

[4] There is a hint of the immoral nature of usury in Solanio's reporting of Shylock's reaction to the theft of his money: "A sealed bag, two sealed bags of ducats, / Of double ducats. . . ." It is almost as though Shylock cannot even talk about money without making it "breed"!

I am glad 'tis night, you do not look on me,
For I am much asham'd of my exchange.
But love is blind, and lovers cannot see
The pretty follies that themselves commit,
For if they could, Cupid himself would blush
To see me thus transformed to a boy. (2.6.34–39)

On the literal level, Jessica is clearly embarrassed by the fact that she is forced to don the disguise of a boy. The "exchange" of which she is "asham'd" is her change of clothes. Yet it is difficult to avoid the suggestion that she, or at least we, should be somewhat ashamed of the elopement and the theft of the ducats, even if, for the reasons enumerated above, our sympathies are with the lovers and not with the father of the bride-to-be. Their love is "blind", and the lovers cannot see the "pretty follies" that they commit. Theirs is the type of love that Portia condemns when first we meet her in the play's second scene. Jessica's and Lorenzo's "hot temper" eludes the demands of temperance, and their youthful "madness" skips with the wantonness of a March hare from "the meshes of good counsel". Theirs is the sort of love that would make even Cupid blush!

And yet, on a deeper level, Jessica's choosing wrongly in taking the casket pales into relative insignificance beside the wrong choice of her father in choosing the casket and its gold over the love of the girl, his daughter. It is Shylock's choice that most closely parallels Morocco's choice, and it is Shylock who is ultimately destined, like Morocco, to leave empty-handed, without either the girl or the gold. And there is an even deeper parallel between Shylock's casket and Portia's. In the test of the caskets devised by Portia's father, the correct choice is lead, signifying death, necessitating that we hazard all we have for the beloved and that we lay down our lives for our friends. Shylock does the complete opposite, inverting the choice infernally. He does not choose to die himself for those he loves; he chooses the death of others to feed his frenzy for revenge. And such is the depth of his hatred that he wishes death not merely on his enemies, such as Antonio, but on his very family. And the parallel between the caskets serves to point to the parallel between the fathers. Portia's father loves her from beyond the grave, making sagacious provision for her welfare after his death; Jessica's father wishes his very daughter in the grave so that he can gloat over her body and reclaim his precious gold. The difference between the two father figures could not be starker or more horrific.

As act 2 draws to a close, the Prince of Arragon claims his right to choose the casket that, he hopes, will win him Portia's hand in marriage. Dismissing the baseness of the lead casket without so much as a second look, he proceeds to the gold:

> What says the golden chest? Ha, let me see:
> "Who chooseth me shall gain what many men desire."
> What many men desire! That many may be meant
> By the fool multitude that choose by show,
> Not learning more than the fond eye doth teach,
> Which pries not to th' interior, but like the martlet
> Builds in the weather on the outward wall,
> Even in the force and road of casualty.
> I will not choose what many men desire,
> Because I will not jump with common spirits,
> And rank me with the barbarous multitudes. (2.9.23–33)

The irony inherent in Arragon's reasoning is evident in his contempt for those who "choose by show" when he has himself, moments before, dismissed the lead casket contemptuously with the remark that "base lead" would need to "look fairer ere I give or hazard" (2.9.20, 22). He has already chosen by show and has, in so doing, condemned himself to a wrong choice. Having dismissed the "base lead" as unworthy of his attention, he is doomed to failure no matter how much he considers the relative merits of gold and silver. Nonetheless, and blissfully ignorant of his failure, he exhibits a supercilious arrogance, not dissimilar to that which had characterized Morocco, in his insistence that he "will not choose what many men desire", feeling himself superior to the "common spirits" of the "barbarous multitudes". Proceeding to the silver casket, he has his pride preened by the inscription he reads: "Who chooseth me shall get as much as he deserves." This is much more to his liking:

> And well said too; for who shall go about
> To cozen fortune, and be honorable
> Without the stamp of merit? (2.9.37–39)

Having seen his presumed merit reflected back to him in narcissistic self-centeredness, he needs look no further for the choice he presumes to be correct:

> Well, but to my choice:
> "Who chooseth me shall get as much as he deserves."
> I will assume desert.[5] Give me a key for this,
> And instantly unlock my fortunes here. (2.9.49–52)

Opening the silver casket, he discovers to his horror that he has indeed received "as much as he deserves": "What's here? the portrait of a blinking idiot" (2.9.54). Having interpreted the inscription narcissistically, he sees a reflection of himself in the mirror of truth that the casket represents. He is indeed "a blinking idiot":

> Did I deserve no more than a fool's head?
> Is that my prize? Are my deserts no better? (2.9.59–60)

Portia answers the fool's questions with her customary brilliance:

> To offend and judge are distinct offices,
> And of opposed natures. (2.9.61–62)

Literally she is simply saying that the offender is not the judge of his own crimes, but she is also making a clear allusion to the words of Christ: "Judge not, that ye be not judged. For with what judgment ye judge, ye shall be judged: and with what measure ye mete, it shall be measured to you again. And why beholdest thou the mote that is in thy brother's eye, but considerest not the beam that is in thine own eye?"[6] The Prince of Arragon has been judged in the manner in which he judged. Having dismissed the "barbarous multitudes" for the motes in their eyes that prevented them from seeing clearly, he had been blinded by the beam of pride in his own eyes. He received the judgment that his own judgment deserved.

After Arragon's departure, Portia bids farewell to the last of the unworthy suitors with words that encapsulate the reason for their unworthiness:

---

[5] Those looking for coded references to the contemporary theological controversies of the Reformation, which were still new and raging at the time that Shakespeare was writing, may discern in Arragon's assumption of desert a connection with the Protestant belief in *sola fide*, the doctrine of justification by faith alone, and also the Calvinist belief in predestination. If so, it can be seen that Shakespeare is taking the Catholic position that such a belief constitutes the sin of presumption. To "assume desert", or presume that we are "saved", displays a supercilious arrogance that is clearly being condemned in the prideful nature of Arragon's deliberations and the consequences of his presumption.

[6] Matthew 7:1–3.

Thus hath the candle sing'd the moth.
O, these deliberate fools, when they do choose,
They have the wisdom by their wit to lose. (2.9.79–81)

We have already discussed the likelihood that Portia's reference to the candle singing the moth was taken from Robert Southwell's poem "Lewd Love is Losse":

So long the flie doth dallie with the flame,
Untill his singed wings doe force his fall.

The connection between Portia's words and Southwell's poem are further strengthened by Nerissa's words immediately after Portia's allusive words are uttered:

The ancient saying is no heresy,
Hanging and wiving goes with destiny. (2.9.82–83)

From a Catholic perspective, Robert Southwell was hanged as a priest, and, as a priest, *in persona Christi*, he had chosen the Church as his Bride (hence the vow of celibacy taken by the Catholic clergy). In choosing the Church as his "wife", he had accepted "hanging" as his destiny. Southwell, like all the Jesuit missionaries to Elizabethan England, expected to be brutally put to death if caught by the authorities. Nerissa's words, coming immediately after Portia's allusion to Southwell's poem, can be seen as a coded tribute to the recently martyred or soon-to-be-martyred priest, a fact that is highlighted still further by Nerissa's declaration that the "ancient" is "no heresy", i.e., that the old faith was not heretical.

Southwell's theme, "Lewd Love is Losse", is also Shakespeare's. The lewdness of Arragon's love and his dallying with the flames of his own prideful passion have led to the loss of his heart's desire. Portia also perceives, with her usual unerring moral perspective, that the deliberations of Morocco and Arragon were ultimately foolish because their fallacious philosophies, fueled with pride, have "outwitted" wisdom. Or, to put the matter the other way around, the wisdom of Portia's father had outwitted the "wit" of the worldly-wise. Portia's father knew, as does Portia, that the right to choose is not enough to merit the reward. To win our heart's desire, we must use the right to choose to choose the right.

# 7

## TO CHOOSE THE RIGHT

As Arragon makes his hasty departure, Portia asks Nerissa to "draw the curtain" (2.9.84) over the caskets, and thereby draws the final curtain on the unworthy suitors. The stage is now set for the curtain to open on the worthy suitor, and, right on cue, he is announced:

> Madam, there is alighted at your gate
> A young Venetian, one that comes before
> To signify th' approaching of his lord,
> From whom he bringeth sensible regrets:
> To wit (besides commends and courteous breath),
> Gifts of rich value. Yet I have not seen
> So likely an embassador of love.
> A day in April never came so sweet,
> To show how costly summer was at hand,
> As this fore-spurrer comes before his lord. (2.9.86–95)

The messenger's announcement of Bassanio's impending arrival is so ripe and replete with the burgeoning promise of impending fruitfulness that we cannot fail to see his effusiveness as anything but a prophecy of the arrival of the worthy one who will eclipse the very memory of his unworthy predecessors. It is, therefore, hardly surprising that Nerissa ends the scene by putting into words the thoughts and hopes of her mistress: "Bassanio, Lord Love, if thy will it be!" (2.9.101).[1]

Following a short digressive scene in which Shylock is likened to the Devil and in which he pleads the "justice" of his planned vengeance on

---

[1] Although "Lord Love" is usually glossed as "Cupid", which is appropriate enough considering that Cupid is mentioned by name in the preceding line, it also conveys to Shakespeare's Christian audience the "Lord of Love" himself, a fact that is accentuated by the resonance between the words that follow, "if thy will it be", and the words of the Lord's Prayer: "Thy will be done". In this, as in numerous other instances throughout the length and breadth of the play, there is no escaping the Christian providential dimension in the plot's unfolding.

Antonio, we arrive, at last, at the pivotal scene in which Bassanio passes the test of the caskets and wins Portia's hand in marriage.

In order to understand Shakespeare's deepest meaning, we need to learn, with Bassanio, the importance of his choosing the right casket and the logical and theological reasoning by which he does so. We must begin, as Shakespeare does, by reminding ourselves once again of the allusive connection between Bassanio and Robert Southwell. Having heralded Bassanio's arrival, at the end of act 2, with an allusion to the Jesuit's poem, followed by the equally poignant ecclesiological metaphor of the Bride and the Bridegroom, and with the suggestive connection between "hanging and wiving", Bassanio's casket scene continues this allusive theme with Jesuitical dexterity. Portia complains that "these naughty times / Put bars between the owners and their rights", a phrase that suggests a connection between the wicked times in which Shakespeare and his audience found themselves and the imprisonment of those who sought the right to practice their faith without harassment or persecution. For Shakespeare and his Catholic contemporaries, there was no right in law to choose the right. The state's anti-Catholic laws put bars between the Catholic laity and the practice of their faith, and, in the case of priests such as Southwell, put prison bars between the ordained and the faithful they sought to serve. Taken by itself, in isolation from what comes before and after it, the allusion might be considered somewhat tenuous, but taken together with the allusions that precede it and the exchange between Bassanio and Portia about living "upon the rack" that immediately succeeds it,[2] the convergence of so many similar allusive images becomes convincing. Let us assume, therefore, as we look at the unfolding drama of this crucial part of the play, that Shakespeare always has one eye on the ghostly presence of Robert Southwell as he puts his weighty and weighted words into the mouths of his protagonists.

Having perceived the Bard's deeper meaning, we are not surprised to discover that Portia's words, as Bassanio prepares to make his choice, are pregnant with theological symbolism:

> He may win;
> And what is music then? Then music is
> Even as the flourish when true subjects bow

[2] See pages 16–19 above for a reminder of the allusions to Robert Southwell in this exchange.

To a new-crowned monarch; such it is
As are those dulcet sounds in break of day
That creep into the dreaming bridegroom's ear,
And summon him to marriage. Now he goes,
With no less presence, but with much more love,
Than young Alcides, when he did redeem
The virgin tribute paid by howling Troy
To the sea-monster. I stand for sacrifice;
The rest aloof are the Dardanian wives,
With bleared visages, come forth to view
The issue of th' exploit. Go, Hercules,
Live thou, I live; with much, much more dismay
I view the fight than thou that mak'st the fray. (3.2.47–62)

If we desire to unlock the rich theological symbolism in these beautiful lines, we need to remember the ecclesiological metaphor of the
Bride and the Bridegroom that Shakespeare employs so often in his
plays. Portia, as the desired bride, is a metaphor for the Church, the
gate (*porta* in Latin) to heaven; Bassanio, as the bridegroom, is a metaphor for Christ and, by extension, a metaphor for Robert Southwell,
who, as a priest, is *in persona Christi* not merely during the Mass but in
the very essence of his priesthood. Such symbolism is largely unknown
to the modern reader or the postmodern critic, but it was most certainly not unknown to Shakespeare and his largely Catholic audience.

The metaphor is strengthened still further by its connection to the
nature of the choice facing Bassanio. We know already, through the
failure of the unworthy suitors to choose correctly, that he must spurn
the follies of pride and the gaudiness of the world and that he must
embrace the death that awaits him in the lead-lined coffin in which is
to be found his heart's desire and his true reward. He must choose
death over life in order to attain the love of his life. This, of course, is
the crux of the choice facing all Christians at all times, and the crux of
the choice facing the persecuted Catholics of Elizabeth's England: "He
that findeth his life shall lose it: and he that loseth his life for my sake
shall find it." [3] The choice of death, or choosing to die to oneself, is
the only way to obtain the fullness of life, the love of the Other beyond
the self, the Beloved that every rational heart desires.

---

[3] Matthew 10:39. The whole of this chapter from Matthew's Gospel resonates powerfully
with the moral drama of *The Merchant of Venice*.

Although the foregoing is deducible through the employment of the marriage metaphor at the heart of Catholic ecclesiology, it is made more obviously manifest through Portia's likening of Bassanio to Alcides, or Hercules. In making the analogy between Bassanio and Hercules, Portia is also making both of these heroes a metaphor for Christ himself. Like Dante and Chaucer before him, Shakespeare makes liberal use of the living heritage of the Greek classics as illustrations, or metaphorical foreshadowings, of the truth of the Gospel. In the story to which Portia alludes, Hercules saves Priam's sister, Hesione, from being devoured by the sea monster, to which she was being sacrificed. In the Christian metaphor, Hercules metamorphoses into Christ by saving the virgin, Hesione (humanity), from the sea monster or dragon (Satan). This metaphorical metamorphosis is made more manifest by the language that Portia employs. Bassanio goes "with no less presence, but with much more love" than Hercules because, as a Christian hero, Bassanio is motivated by love, not by pagan pride. He does not kill the monster through the power of his warcraft, and the pride that is its master, but through the power of his love, and the humility that is its handmaid. In the baptizing of the metaphor, it is not pride's physique but love's physic that saves the virgin from the dragon. Portia makes this christening of the metaphor even more evident through the use of the word "redeem" to signify her salvation from the clutches of the Beast.

Compare this Christian employment of the metaphor with its earlier pagan employment by the unworthy suitor Morocco:

> By this scimitar
> . . . . . . . . . . . . . . . . . .
> I would o'erstare the sternest eyes that look,
> Outbrave the heart most daring on the earth,
> Pluck the young sucking cubs from the she-bear,
> Yea, mock the lion when 'a roars for prey,
> To win [thee], lady. But alas the while!
> If Hercules and Lichas play at dice
> Which is the better man, the greater throw
> May turn by fortune from the weaker hand:
> So is Alcides beaten by his [page],
> And so may I, blind fortune leading me,
> Miss that which one unworthier may attain,
> And die with grieving. (2.1.24, 27–38)

The blind pagan, led by blind fate, is felled by the folly of his own pride and fails to win the lady. Bassanio, on the other hand, spurning the might of sword or scimitar, proceeds to the choice that faces him armed only with love and the wisdom of humility. Pagan fate is no match for Christian faith, and the slavery of pagan fatalism no match for the freedom of Christian choice.

The right or the freedom to choose is, however, not enough to win the desired reward. "I stand for sacrifice", says Portia, and this is the key to understanding how to make the right choices. Literally, of course, Portia is simply putting herself into Hesione's shoes. Portia is "the virgin tribute" who will be sacrificed to the Beast unless she is "redeemed" by Bassanio's love. Yet her words are charged with deliberate ambiguity, enabling us to see that she "stands for sacrifice" in the deeper sense that she represents the need for sacrifice as the only means to win the Belmontian, i.e., heavenly, reward that our hearts desire. It is only through self-sacrifice, and not by might or power, that the heavenly Portia can be won.

Portia's perspicacity appears to know no bounds, with Shakespeare pouring all the wisdom that he possesses into the words she enunciates. Having waxed lyrical on the self-sacrificial character of true love, she exposes the superficiality of false loves in a song that represents the death knell of vanity:

> Tell me where is fancy bred,
> Or in the heart or in the head?
> How begot, how nourished?
> . . . . . . . . . . . . .
> It is engend'red in the [eyes],
> With gazing fed, and fancy dies
> In the cradle where it lies.
> Let us all ring fancy's knell.
> I'll begin it. Ding, dong, bell. (3.2.63–71)

Portia answers her own rhetorical questions, showing that fancy, or false love, is not bred in either the heart or the head. It is not the stuff of either faith or reason but is begotten and fed by the vanity of the eyes. As the product of pride, it has no life-sustaining power and dies in the falsehood in which it had lived, a fact that is emphasized by the pun on the word "lies".

All of the foregoing seems obvious enough. Yet there are none so blind as postmodern critics, and there are few things more maliciously misleading than modern stagings of the play and postmodern misreadings of it. Such stagings and misreadings have even transformed the high philosophy of Portia's sublimely succinct ringing of "fancy's knell" into nothing but a cynical attempt by the unprincipled heroine to defy her father's will. In these postmodern misreadings, Portia brazenly cheats by emphasizing those words in her song that rhyme with "lead", i.e., "bred", "head", and "nourished" (pronounced "nourishèd", as three syllables), in order to provide Bassanio with heavy-handed hints that he should choose the lead casket. In choosing to cheat, Portia descends from the heights of Belmont into the gutters of Venice, and in so doing, she removes the whole Christian heart of the drama, plunging the plot into cynical depths in which the play becomes a ploy for heartless sophistry on all sides. Such productions sacrifice truth on the altar of zeitgeist-conforming "originality" and constitute an original sin against the work. This is postmodernism as vandalism. It is the philandering of the philistine.[4]

These misreadings do violence to the entirety and integrity of the work, flying in the face of the holistic harmony with which the work has been constructed and contradicting the known Catholicism of the play's author. As such, they barely merit any serious attention. Nonetheless, and as an object lesson in the follies and perils of subjective reading, we will expose the self-evident falsity of these efforts to pervert Portia's purity.

It is, for instance, intriguing that a better textual argument could be made for Portia's cheating in order to help the earlier suitors choose correctly than can be made for her cheating in favor of Bassanio. Portia says to Morocco, "First, forward to the temple; after dinner / Your *hazard* shall be made" (2.1.44–45, emphasis added); and to Arragon she says, "To these injunctions every one doth swear / That comes to *hazard* for my worthless self" (2.9.17–18, emphasis added). It will be remembered that the inscription on the lead casket reads, "Who chooseth me must give and *hazard* all he hath" (2.7.9, emphasis added). It is clear, therefore, that Portia's "clues" to the unworthy and unwanted suitors were far more likely to lead them to the lead casket than the words of

---

[4] A similar postmodern perversion of the play's meaning was witnessed by the present writer during a production at the Theatre Royal in the English city of Norwich in which Bassanio and Antonio were characterized as skinheads who punctuated their dialogues with Shylock by punching and kicking him and spitting in his face.

her song. It is equally clear, of course, that she did not intend her unwitting use of the hazardous word to lead them to hazard the correct answer. It is surely even clearer that the rhyme of her song was not intended to offer any clues, not least because Shakespeare provides no stage direction that the rhymes should be emphasized, whereas the stage directions that are given indicate that Bassanio was probably not even listening to the words of the song when Portia was singing them. On the other hand, Portia's use of the "h-word" was given in direct speech to Morocco and Arragon, indicating that, unlike Bassanio, they had actually heard the so-called "clue" when it was given them. As the critic Daniel Lowenstein observes: "If either of these had been the lucky suitor, critics would have had a stronger case for Portia cheating than they have with respect to Bassanio." [5] Lowenstein also offers additional evidence to refute the suggestion that Portia was dishonest in the way she administered the casket test to Bassanio:

> There are many textual indications that she does not cheat, including, most persuasively, the usually poised and self-assured Portia's manifest nervousness in her long speech to Bassanio immediately before he chooses (3.1.1–24). Why should she be so nervous if she is planning to cheat?[6]

Lowenstein's arguments are more than sufficient to expose the absurdity of this postmodern libeling of Portia, but for good measure, we will offer further evidence of her obvious and transparent honesty. It is clear, for instance, that Portia sends Bassanio out of earshot as soon as he asks to be led to the caskets and that she asks everyone else to "stand aloof", i.e., separate, while he is pondering his choice. It is to these people, safely distant from the deliberating Bassanio, that she addresses her words:

> *Bassanio.* But let me to my fortune and the caskets.
> *Portia.* Away then! I am lock'd in one of them;
> If you do love me, you will find me out.
> Nerissa and the rest, stand all aloof.
> Let music sound while he doth make his choice;
> Then if he lose he makes a swan-like end,
> Fading in music. (3.2.39–45)

[5] Daniel H. Lowenstein, "Law and Mercy in *The Merchant of Venice*", in *The Merchant of Venice*, ed. Joseph Pearce, Ignatius Critical Editions (San Francisco: Ignatius Press, 2009), p. 222.
[6] Ibid., p. 221.

Apart from the fact that Portia sends Bassanio "away", out of ear-shot, and that she is addressing her words to those who have joined her in standing "aloof" from the deliberating suitor, her words are also masked from Bassanio's ears by the music that she orders to be played while he makes his choice. Furthermore, the stage direction makes it clear that Portia's song is sung "whilst Bassanio comments on the caskets to himself"; i.e., he is deep in his own thoughts about the meaning of the riddles and is not listening to the song.

Any honest and objective reading of the play cannot avoid the obvious conclusion that Bassanio was not listening to Portia's words, or the equally obvious conclusion that Portia's words were not intended for his unhearing ears. Couple this patently obvious and unavoidable conclusion with Portia's earlier insistence that she would willingly comply with her father's will, and there is no escaping the transparent honesty of both Bassanio and Portia. Indeed, Portia insists quite openly that she will not cheat in order to allow Bassanio to choose correctly:

> I could teach you
> How to choose right, but then I am forsworn.
> So will I never be.... (3.2.10–12)

Let us remind ourselves that to be "forsworn" is to be a "renouncer of an oath", or one who "swears falsely" or who "perjures oneself".[7] This is someone who Portia will "never be".

It is, in fact, the postmodernists who are "forsworn"; it is they who cheat and swear falsely, perjuring themselves in order to defame the honesty and integrity of Shakespeare's heroes and heroines. Unable to accept virtue when they see it, the postmodern critic denies it and defames it by turning every virtuous word and action into a cynical lie on the hero's or heroine's part. This is nothing less than a sinful perversion of the truth through a cynical inversion of it.

Let us leave the postmodernists wallowing in the gutter of their own Venetian self-deception and rejoin the virtuous Portia and Bassanio in the heavenly heights of Belmont.

---

[7] *Concise Oxford Dictionary*, 5th ed.

8

# LEAD, KINDLY LIGHT

As Portia waxes lyrical about the necessity of sacrifice and the folly of vanity, Bassanio ponders the meaning of the three caskets ranged before him. Oblivious to Portia's words, he is led by the kindly light of the lead itself to the truth it symbolizes:

> So may the outward shows be least themselves—
> The world is still deceiv'd with ornament.
> In law, what plea so tainted and corrupt
> But, being season'd with a gracious voice,
> Obscures the show of evil? In religion,
> What damned error but some sober brow
> Will bless it, and approve it with a text,
> Hiding the grossness with fair ornament?
> There is no [vice] so simple but assumes
> Some mark of virtue on his outward parts.
> How many cowards, whose hearts are all as false
> As stairs of sand, wear yet upon their chins
> The beards of Hercules and frowning Mars,
> Who inward search'd, have livers white as milk,
> And these assume but valor's excrement
> To render them redoubted! Look on beauty,
> And you shall see 'tis purchased by the weight,
> Which therein works a miracle in nature,
> Making them lightest that wear most of it.
> So are those crisped snaky golden locks,
> Which [make] such wanton gambols with the wind
> Upon supposed fairness, often known
> To be the dowry of a second head,
> The skull that bred them in the sepulchre.
> Thus ornament is but the guiled shore

To a most dangerous sea; the beauteous scarf
Veiling an Indian beauty; in a word,
The seeming truth which cunning times put on
To entrap the wisest. Therefore then, thou gaudy gold,
Hard food for Midas, I will none of thee;
Nor none of thee, thou pale and common drudge
'Tween man and man; but thou, thou meagre lead,
Which rather threaten'st than doth promise aught,
Thy paleness moves me more than eloquence,
And here choose I. Joy be the consequence! (3.2.73–107)

Bassanio's speech has been quoted *in extenso* because it conveys so much of vital importance. Its preoccupation with the distinction between that which truly *is* and that which only *seems* to be is a recurring feature in Shakespeare's work, a theme that, in *Hamlet*, would become the very core and essence of the drama. Why is such a distinction so important to Shakespeare? Why is it the very key to Bassanio's success in the test of the caskets?

First and foremost, Shakespeare is using Bassanio's approach to the conundrum of the caskets as a launching pad into those fundamental issues of metaphysics that had been dividing philosophers since the advent of the nominalism of William of Ockham almost three hundred years earlier. The fact that Shakespeare invariably comes down on the side of the *realism* of Plato, Aristotle, and Thomas Aquinas and against the *nominalism* of Ockham and the protorelativism that it represents is further convincing evidence of the Bard's Catholicism. According to the realists, the *essence* or *being* of a thing[1] is immutable and is contrasted with those attributes of a thing that are changeable or *accidental*, or, to employ Bassanio's phrase, merely *ornamental*. To the postphilosophical culture in which we find ourselves, such distinctions might themselves seem irrelevant or merely ornamental, but to Shakespeare and the culture of sixteenth-century Europe, such issues were at the center of the cauldron of controversy and conflict that had been bubbling since the Renaissance and had been boiling over since the Reformation.[2] For Shakespeare and his contemporaries, the battle between

---

[1] *Esse* is "to be" in Latin.

[2] Nominalism would soon find powerful champions in the philosophical writings of Francis Bacon (1561–1626), Thomas Hobbes (1588–1679), and René Descartes (1596–1650). Shakespeare's own position is clearly inimical to that professed by these pioneers of modern philosophy.

realism and nominalism was a very hot topic, and Shakespeare clearly takes a position in defense of the former against the latter.

By Shakespeare's time, the war between the two positions had evolved into a more complex conflict between an increasingly secularized humanism and an entrenched but defiant scholasticism.[3] The humanists adopted an anthropocentric view of the world and reality, believing that the best way of studying man was through man, thereby marginalizing God; the scholastics, on the other hand, insisted on a theocentric view of the world and reality, stressing that man was best understood in the light of his Creator. In *The Merchant of Venice*, the world of secular humanism and its intrinsic materialism is to be found in Venice, whereas the otherworld of scholasticism and its intrinsic Catholic spirituality is to be found on the lofty heights of Belmont. One is tempted indeed to see a parallel with Augustine's distinction between the City of Man and the City of God, and one wonders whether Shakespeare had Augustine in mind as he highlighted the difference between worldly Venice and otherworldly Belmont.

Having discussed the philosophical backdrop to Bassanio's famous casket speech, let us return to the speech itself, studying it in greater detail. His opening words distinguish that a thing's "outward shows", i.e., its *accidental* or *nominal* qualities, may "be least themselves". In other words, the *essence* of a thing, its *reality*, is not defined by, or dependent upon, its accidental or ornamental qualities. Yet the world, i.e., Venice and its humanism and nominalism, "is still deceiv'd with ornament". It sees only the nominal truth of reality and not its spiritual essence. Once one undermines the *essential reality*, i.e., the immutable objectivity, of a thing, its very being becomes nominal, i.e., subject to change and dependent on how it is perceived relative to other things. This philosophical nominalism has wide-ranging ramifications. If all things are relative, our concepts of right and wrong must be merely relative also. In such circumstances, the moral objectivity of Christianity is replaced with the moral relativism of the Machiavel:

---

[3] Secular humanism had been a rising force in the sphere of political philosophy since the publication of Machiavelli's *Il principe* (*The Prince*) in 1532, and much of Shakespeare's work can be seen as a dialectical clash between this new spirit of cynical secularism and the time-honored understanding of virtue espoused by orthodox Christianity. Shakespeare's positioning of himself on the side of the Church against the humanists is evident from the fact that his villains are Machiavellians and his heroes and heroines are traditionally virtuous.

In law, what plea so tainted and corrupt
But, being season'd with a gracious voice,
Obscures the show of evil?

Again, we must remember that Bassanio's speech comes at a point in the play in which the ghost of Robert Southwell is present in the background, his appearance being brought to our attention repeatedly by the power of allusion. For Shakespeare, as a Catholic who probably knew Southwell well, Bassanio's words would encapsulate the travesty of justice that saw the saintly priest put to death.[4] The Jesuit, as a priest of the Catholic Church, was a representative of objective truth whose saintly virtue was obscured in his trial by the "tainted and corrupt" pleas of serpent-tongued lawyers who, with "gracious voice", obscure "the show of evil" with the appearance of justice. For Shakespeare, the show trial was itself a "show of evil".

Following Bassanio's implicit attack on the Machiavellian use of the law to perpetrate injustice in the name of "justice", he proceeds to an attack on the use of Scripture to justify "damned error":

In religion,
What damned error but some sober brow
Will bless it, and approve it with a text,
Hiding the grossness with fair ornament?

We must remember that Shakespeare lived in the cauldron of change following the Reformation, a time in which Scripture was used by all sides to justify their respective positions and to condemn the "damned errors" of their opponents. It was a time in which, to employ Chesterton's words,[5] "Christian killeth Christian in a narrow dusty room" as theological scholars, "full of tangled things and texts and aching eyes", condemned each other as heretics.[6] This being so, it is tempting to see these words of Bassanio as a condemnation of all theological disputes, a denunciation in which he, and by implication Shakespeare also, is seen

---

[4] These lines might represent evidence that *The Merchant of Venice* was written after Southwell's trial and execution in 1595. Yet even if the lines were written before his trial, they were certainly written while Southwell was in prison awaiting trial, and Shakespeare had plenty of experience of previous show trials of priests and other "papists", including his own relatives, who were subsequently executed for their Catholic faith.

[5] In "Lepanto"; see G. K. Chesterton, *Collected Works*, vol. 10, *Collected Poetry*, pt. 1 (San Francisco: Ignatius Press, 1994), p. 550, line 82.

[6] Ibid., line 84.

to criticize both the Catholics and the Protestants for the theological frenzy initiated by the Reformation, saying, with Mercutio in *Romeo and Juliet*, "a plague o' both your houses".[7]

Yet Bassanio's words must be seen within the context of the times in which Shakespeare was writing, and they must be read in the light of the philosophical backdrop of nominalism and realism that colors the whole of his speech. If this is done, it is clear that Bassanio is condemning the implicit nominalism and de facto relativism of the Protestant doctrine of *sola scriptura*. The inevitable consequence of this doctrine, which was championed by Martin Luther and is a cornerstone of the Reformation, was that Protestant Christians began to read the Bible subjectively, which is to say that they interpreted its meaning in light of their own presuppositions and prejudices, without the requirement of subjecting such subjectivity to the touchstone of objectivity inherent in the teaching authority of the Church. Under the doctrine of *sola scriptura*, the Bible becomes a text disembodied from its context and from the authority inherent in its Author. From a Catholic perspective, the Church, as the Mystical Body of Christ, had stamped her authority on the Bible, editing the Scriptures in the light of the Holy Spirit and deciding which of the ancient texts should be incorporated into the divinely sanctioned Book and which were to be omitted. This being so, the truth of Scripture, i.e., its objective and authentic meaning, was to be found in the teaching of the Church, in her unique position as the divinely appointed authority sanctioned by the Book's Author. By contrast, the Protestant doctrine of *sola scriptura* can be seen as the root and archetype of all forms of subjective reading, even if this was not the intention of its original advocates.

Before we return to Bassanio's words, it might prove helpful to examine the way that G. K. Chesterton compared Shakespeare's objectivity in matters of faith with the subjectivity of the Bard's great Protestant literary counterpart, John Milton:

> Nearly all Englishmen are either Shakespearians or Miltonians. I do not mean that they admire one more than the other; because everyone in his senses must admire both of them infinitely. I mean that each represents something in the make-up of England; and that the two things are so antagonistic that it is really impossible not to be secretly on one side or the other. . . .

---

[7] *Romeo and Juliet*, The Riverside Shakespeare, 2nd edition (Boston/New York: Houghton Mifflin, 1997), p. 82, 3.1.91.

Shakespeare represents the Catholic, Milton the Protestant. . . . Whenever Milton speaks of religion, it is Milton's religion: the religion that Milton has made. Whenever Shakespeare speaks of religion . . . it is of a religion that has made him.[8]

Not surprisingly perhaps, Chesterton was asked to clarify the rationale behind his assertion of Shakespeare's Catholicism:

A correspondent has written to me asking me what I meant by saying that Shakespeare was a Catholic and Milton a Protestant. That Milton was a Protestant, I suppose, he will not dispute. . . . But the point about the religion of Shakespeare is certainly less obvious, though I think not less true. . . . These impressions are hard to explain. . . . But here, at least, is one way of putting the difference between the religions of Shakespeare and Milton. Milton is possessed with what is, I suppose, the first and finest idea of Protestantism—the idea of the individual soul actually testing and tasting all the truth there is, and calling that truth which it has not tested or tasted truth of a less valuable and vivid kind. But Shakespeare is possessed through and through with the feeling which is the first and finest idea of Catholicism that truth exists whether we like it or not, and that it is for us to accommodate ourselves to it. . . . But I really do not know how this indescribable matter can be better described than by simply saying this; that Milton's religion was Milton's religion, and that Shakespeare's religion was not Shakespeare's.[9]

Chesterton's comparison of Shakespeare with Milton sheds some intriguing light on our present discussion of *sola scriptura*, indicating that, in Chesterton's judgment, the former conformed to the objective teaching of the Catholic Church whereas the latter had embraced *sola*

---

[8] G. K. Chesterton, *Illustrated London News*, May 18, 1907.

[9] Ibid., June 8, 1907. Intriguingly, and astonishingly, a letter to the *Tablet*, published May 23, 1908, less than a year after Chesterton wrote these words, provides documentary evidence of the unthinkable fact that Milton may also have died a Catholic. As unbelievable as this may seem, the evidence is provided by the respected historian W. H. Grattan Flood from a reputable source. While searching in the seventh report of the Historical Manuscripts Commission, Grattan Flood came across the following statement from the autobiography of Sir John Percival, in volume 2 of the Egmont papers: "Milton, the poet, died a Papist. Dr Charlotte, Master of University College, Oxford, told me lately at Bath that he remembers to have heard from Dr Binks that he was at an entertainment in King James' reign, when Sir Christopher Milton, one of the Judges, and elder brother to the famous Mr Milton, the poet, was present; that the Judge did then say publicly his brother was a Papist some years before he died, and that he died so. I am still more persuaded of it from what Dr English told me that he often heard Mr Prior, the poet, say that the late Earl of Dorset told him the same thing."

*scriptura*, employing it with implicit relativism to construct a custom-built or personalized faith. Whereas there is nothing in Shakespeare's work that indicates nonconformity with the teachings of Catholicism, Milton, in *Paradise Lost*, renounces the Trinity and relegates Christ to the role of a mere creature created by the Father after the creation of Satan.

It is, therefore, in the context of the heated debate over the consequences of *sola scriptura* that Bassanio's words should be judged. From a Catholic perspective, his complaint that "damned error" was being approved "with a text" encapsulated the very nub of the Church's objection to the plethora of subjective interpretations of Scripture that had followed in the wake of the Reformation.

The remainder of Bassanio's speech twists and coils around the central difference between that which truly *is* and that which only *seems* to be. Everywhere the "grossness", i.e., objective evil, is hidden "with fair ornament". Vice is concealed by the "mark of virtue on his outward parts"; cowards conceal their milk-livered and falsehearted cowardice by donning the mask of Hercules or Mars; ugliness is concealed behind a mask of cosmetics; and physical beauty, poisoned with a narcissistic pride in itself, conceals the true deadliness of its vanity:

> So are those crisped snaky golden locks,
> Which [make] such wanton gambols with the wind
> Upon supposed fairness, often known
> To be the dowry of a second head,
> The skull that bred them in the sepulchre.

The connection between sin and death is made repeatedly by Bassanio as he endeavors to make sense of the riddle of the caskets, and his words represent one of the numerous examples of Shakespeare's employment of the *memento mori*. This literary device or motif was particularly popular in medieval art and represented a sobering reminder of the Four Last Things to be remembered by all Christians: death, judgment, heaven, and hell. The reminder of *death* in the image of the skull and the sepulcher is united with the *hell* to which it leads for those self-condemned in the *judgment* of their sin. Shakespeare's repeated use of the *memento mori* throughout his work is itself a further potent indication of his orthodox Christianity.

The juxtaposition of "snaky" and "golden" in the depiction of the beautiful "locks" of hair serves to show that "supposed fairness" is no substitute for the real beauty of virtue. "Snaky" signifies the serpentine, i.e., satanic, connection between outward beauty and inner corruption, and its use in conjunction with "golden" signifies a clue that Bassanio needs to shun the show of seeming beauty or seeming virtue and seek instead the real virtue that is not "deceiv'd with ornament":

> Thus ornament is but the guiled shore
> To a most dangerous sea....
>
> . . . . . . . . . . . . . .
>
> The seeming truth which cunning times put on
> To entrap the wisest. Therefore then, thou gaudy gold,
> Hard food for Midas, I will none of thee;
> Nor none of thee, thou pale and common drudge
> 'Tween man and man;but thou, thou meagre lead,
> Which rather threaten'st than dost promise aught,
> Thy paleness moves me more than eloquence,
> And here choose I. Joy be the consequence!

And so, in one of the most powerful passages in the entire Shakespearean canon, Bassanio chooses the true casket over its seductive rivals, opting for the authentically *real*, the very *essence* of virtue, over the superficial "ornament" of false virtue that still deceives the world.

Portia is so overwhelmed with utter elation when she sees that her beloved is making the right choice that she fears that the surfeit of ecstasy will prove too much for her:

> O love, be moderate, allay thy ecstasy,
> In measure rain thy joy, scant this excess! (3.2.111–12)

This is hardly the reaction of one who has cynically cheated by practically telling her lover the answer to the riddle!

Seeing Portia's painted image, Bassanio is overcome with the beauty of it and marvels at the majesty of the artistic powers that had made such a likeness. Yet he realizes that even the most beautiful art is no match for the real Portia, who stands in his presence:

> Yet look how far
> The substance of my praise doth wrong this shadow
> In underprizing it, so far this shadow
> Doth limp behind the substance. (3.2.126–29)

Once again, Shakespeare is placing the drama on a firm philosophical footing. The painting, though beautiful, is but a pale reflection or a mere shadow
of the *real* or *essential* Portia, her *substance*. Bassanio's love and desire will
not be satisfied with a mere image of Portia, a thing that merely *seems* to
be her; he seeks complete communion and unity with her real presence
and will settle for nothing less. Bassanio's language alludes perhaps to the
allegory of the cave in Plato's *Republic*, with its distinction between the
shadows of reality and reality itself, or perhaps to Aristotle's discussion of
primary and secondary substances. Either way, Bassanio's philosophy is in
complete conformity with the philosophical realism espoused by the Catholic Church in the Christian Platonism of Augustine or the Christian Aristotelianism of Thomas Aquinas and is in dialectical opposition to the
nominalism that had been condemned by the Church. As with his theology, Shakespeare's philosophy is entirely orthodox.

Taken within the philosophical context of the lines that immediately
precede it, Bassanio's tribute to Portia as a "thrice-fair lady" (3.2.146)
presents itself as a metaphysical riddle in need of unraveling. It is hard
for a Christian reader to avoid a suggestion of the Trinity in such phraseology, but the phrase is more likely to be an allusion to Plato's "trinity"
of the good, the true, and the beautiful in his *Dialogues* than a direct
reference to the Father, Son, and Holy Spirit. Yet Christian metaphysics is rooted in the assumption that God *is* the Good, the True, and the
Beautiful. And since God is One, though containing three distinct yet
unified Persons, the Good, the True, and the Beautiful are also One:
the Good is True, the Truth is Beautiful, and Beauty is Good. Plato's
trinity is, therefore, subsumed within and consumed by the Trinity, which
is its source and inspiration. Bassanio's "thrice-fair lady" reflects the
goodness, truth, and beauty of God himself. And this, of course, is the
*real* goodness, truth, and beauty for which Bassanio, Portia, and Antonio are searching, as distinct from the travesty of falsehood masquerad-
ing as the good, the true, and the beautiful that is manifest in the play's
less virtuous characters. In the eyes of the latter, who are blinded by
their ability to see only what seems to be, Bassanio's choice of voluntary poverty over the gaudy pomp of temporal riches is but foolish. Yet
it is the worldly choosers, and not Bassanio, who leave empty-handed,
bereft of the pearl of great price that is beyond the reach of gold or
silver; and it is Bassanio, and not the worldly choosers, who achieves
the joy of his heart's desire. Led by the light of his own humility, he
sees beneath the superficial surface to the very heart of reality.

# 9

## THE VICE OF VENGEANCE

It is now time to turn our attention from the real world of Belmont to the fake world of Venice, passing from the heavenly test of the caskets in Belmont to the testing of Antonio and Shylock at the Venetian courts of justice.

Against all odds, none of Antonio's merchandise reaches its destination, thereby preventing him from being able to repay the loan within the allotted time and putting him at the mercy of Shylock:

> Hath all his ventures fail'd? What, not one hit?
> From Tripolis, from Mexico, and England,
> From Lisbon, Barbary, and India,
> And not one vessel scape the dreadful touch
> Of merchant-marring rocks? (3.2.267–71)

The shipwreck of all of Antonio's ships in such disparate parts of the world beggars belief. Such a catastrophic coincidence defies all laws of probability and leaves the reader feeling that Shakespeare has stooped to a cheap dramatic ploy in building his plot upon such a highly improbable foundation. And yet Shakespeare does not make a habit of erecting his edifying edifices upon fallacious foundations, nor does he stoop to such incredible dramatic devices unless he intends to conquer thereby. If this is so, we should look beyond the mundane assumption of ineptitude on the author's part and seek instead the real reason for Shakespeare's employment of such an unlikely coincidence. Assuming that it is not a clumsy flaw in his dramaturgy, it must be designed to serve the dramatic symmetry of the plot in some allegorically significant way. If the event beggars belief on the level of worldly coincidence, we are left with no alternative but to accept that the incredible turn of events illuminates the hand of providence in the catastrophe, a deus ex machina that is as decorous in the supernaturally supercharged plots of Shakespeare as it is indecorous in the godless machinery of much of today's secular drama. What, then, is the allegorical significance of, and the dramatic symmetry in, the incredible catastrophe?

Considering its pivotal importance to the subsequent denouement, it is surely evident that the multiple shipwrecks serve as the touchstone by which we are to judge Antonio and Shylock; or, to put the matter more correctly and objectively, they serve as the touchstone by which Antonio and Shylock will be judged, not by us but by the Judge of all men. Such a purpose is made manifest by Shakespeare's stooping to the same literary ploy in his later play *The Tempest*, in which it is stated explicitly that the wreck was providentially designed to serve the purpose of restoring harmony among the characters. Modern readers might also be reminded of God's paradoxically providential hand in Gerard Manley Hopkins' "Wreck of the Deutschland", in which a natural disaster that claims the lives of many people, drowned in the tempest, serves as an instrument of God's grace:

> [I]s the shipwreck then a harvest,
> Does tempest carry the grain for thee? (lines 247–48)

In Shakespeare's play, as in Hopkins' poem, the shipwreck is a harvest; and Shakespeare's tempest, like Hopkins', carries the grain of truth that will come to fruition as the plot unfolds. The harvest will prove bitter to those who thought it most sweet, and sweet to those who thought it most bitter. Shylock, who had rejoiced at the news of the wrecked ships, will see himself wrecked by his response to it; Antonio, who had thought himself ruined, will discover unexpected riches in the wrecks' wake. In both cases, the wrecks are a reckoning.

Antonio, like the unworthy suitors in the casket test, has placed his trust in gold and silver. Yet, unlike the unworthy suitors, he had not seen his gold or silver as the means of achieving his heart's desire, a fact about his character that is made clear in the play's opening scene (see chapter 3). He might have trusted too much in material wealth, as is evident from the dashing of his material hopes on the "merchant-marring rocks", but, when tested, he had opted, like his friend Bassanio, to "hazard all he hath" for his love of another. In freely choosing the burden of sacrifice, the lead of love, the Cross of Christ, he was showing the greatest love of all in laying down his life for his friends. Antonio, like Bassanio, had shown himself worthy by making the right choice and passing the test of virtue.

It is, however, not the testing of Antonio but the testing of Shylock that forms the centerpiece of the drama in the court of justice, a drama made possible by the loss of Antonio's wealth on the high seas. Will Shylock pass the test of virtue by showing mercy to his debtor? Will he pass the even tougher test of forgiving—or even loving—his enemy? Or will he fail miserably in the ignominy of his own hatred, gripping his victim in the vice of vengeance and demanding his bond at all costs?

From the outset, Shylock seems intent on vengeance. When Antonio seeks to reason with him, Shylock's heart is hardened to his enemy's pleas:

> Antonio.            Hear me yet, good Shylock.
> Shylock. I'll have my bond! Speak not against my bond!
>     I have sworn an oath that I will have my bond.
> . . . . . . . . . . . . . . . . . . .
> Antonio. I pray thee hear me speak.
> Shylock. I'll have my bond; I will not hear thee speak.
>     I'll have my bond, and therefore speak no more.
>     I'll not be made a soft and dull-ey'd fool
>     To shake the head, relent, and sigh, and yield
>     To Christian intercessors. Follow not,
>     I'll have no speaking, I will have my bond. (3.3.3–5, 11–17)

Shylock exits the stage, intent on "justice" and deaf to Antonio's adjurations; and lest we should forget the real cause of Shylock's hatred, we are reminded once again by Antonio that their enmity is rooted in the problem of usury:

>                         Let him alone,
>     I'll follow him no more with bootless prayers.
>     He seeks my life; his reason well I know:
>     I oft deliver'd from his forfeitures
>     Many that have at times made moan to me;
>     Therefore he hates me. (3.3.19–24)

Shakespeare is clearly intent on showing us, at every opportunity, that the question at issue is that of usury, not one of racial hatred or even religious differences, though the latter, unlike the former, is certainly present, albeit to a subordinate degree. Antonio's "crime", in the eyes of Shylock, and the reason that he is hated, is that he paid off the penalties due to Shylock from those who had forfeited their bonds through late payment. In freeing Shylock's debtors from their bondage to him, Antonio was acting charitably, according to Christian teaching, in alleviating the evil consequences of an immoral act, i.e., a usurious loan. As such, Shylock's villainy, as a usurer, is exacerbated by his hatred of Antonio's virtue.

The stage is now set for the court case, the second of the three tests that Shakespeare presents to us in the unfolding of the drama.

In the first test, in Belmont, we were shown the inseparability of love and sacrifice. "I stand for sacrifice", says Portia. She is sacrificed by the love of her father and can be won only by the self-sacrificial love of the worthy suitor. She sacrifices herself freely to the one who will sacrifice himself freely for her. True love is about spurning the world and all it has to offer in order to gain the pearl of great price that lies beyond the world's reach. True love, and true life, is about dying to ourselves so that we may enjoy a richer, deeper life and love that is unattainable without such sacrifice. Portia stands for sacrifice because true love *is* sacrifice. This is the lesson that is learned in the test of the caskets, and it is, of course, a lesson that is at the very heart of Christianity.

In the second test, in the court case in Venice, we are shown the inseparability of justice and mercy. "I stand for judgment", says Shylock, and later: "I stand here for law" (4.1.103, 142). There is no doubt that Shylock has the letter of the law on his side, but he lacks the mercy necessary to transform the law from a heartless pharisaical legalism into anything genuinely just. This is made clear from the very outset of the trial in the introductory words of the Duke to Antonio:

> I am sorry for thee. Thou art come to answer
> A stony adversary, an inhuman wretch,
> Uncapable of pity, void and empty
> From any dram of mercy. (4.1.3–6)

At this juncture it is important to remind ourselves of the metadramatic role of Robert Southwell throughout the drama. We have seen how the Jesuit's allusive presence is evident in many parts of the play, most particularly during the test of the caskets in which Bassanio's hazarding all he has is connected to Southwell's willingness to lay down his life for his love of Christ and his Church. As we move to the courtroom scene, Southwell's ghostly presence passes from Bassanio to Antonio, as the latter finds himself at the mercy of a merciless persecutor. We have also seen how several scholars have suggested a metadramatic connection between Shylock, as a thinly veiled personification of a Puritan, and Antonio, as an equally thinly veiled personification of a Jesuit.[1] Such a connection adds a crucial allegorical dimension to the whole courtroom scene, in which Shakespeare effectively recreates the trial of his friend Robert Southwell so that it is presented from the true vantage point of Belmont (Catholicism) and not from the gutter perspective of Venice (Elizabethan state propaganda). Once such a connection is made, the very "justice" demanded by Shylock becomes uncannily and uncomfortably close to the "justice" meted out by Elizabeth's court to Southwell. Shylock demands that he has a right to cut a pound of flesh nearest to the heart of Antonio. It is the law, written in the bond, and he demands that the law be obeyed. In Robert Southwell's case, the law demanded that Jesuit "traitors" should be hanged, drawn, and quartered. This involved the convicted "traitor" being hanged by his neck but cut down before he lost consciousness. He would then be cut open, while still alive, and his heart and other internal organs removed. In Southwell's case, the prosecutors did not only demand a pound of their victim's flesh, nearest his heart, but they actually obtained it.

There is, however, another allegorical dimension to this scene that should not be overlooked. The whole trial can be seen as an allegory of salvation history in which the old law of the Jews is fulfilled by the new law of Christianity. Shylock stands for the old "law" and the old "judgment"—the judgment of the old law of the pagans no less than the judgment of the old law of the Jews, the judgment of Aeschylus' *Oresteia* no less than the judgment of Moses' Exodus. In short and in sum, Shylock stands for the law and the judgment that demands an eye for an eye. This is the situation, the impasse, in which we find ourselves at the beginning of the trial.

The first hint of the healing balm of the new law comes in an angry exchange between the unrelenting Shylock and the unforgiving Gratiano:

*Bassanio*. Why dost thou whet thy knife so earnestly?
*Shylock*. To cut the forfeiture from that bankrout there.
*Gratiano*. Not on thy sole, but on thy soul, harsh Jew,
  Thou mak'st thy knife keen; but no metal can,
  No, not the hangman's axe, bear half the keenness
  Of thy sharp envy. Can no prayers pierce thee?

---

[1] See pages 42–43 above for a fuller discussion of this metadramatic connection and the scholarly work that underpins the discussion.

*Shylock.* No, none that thou hast wit enough to make.
*Gratiano.* O, be thou damn'd, inexecrable dog!
    And for thy life let justice be accus'd. (4.1.121–29)

Although this vindictive and vituperative exchange seems a long way from the Gospel, it is nonetheless suggestive of Christ's teaching that we judge not, lest we be judged. In sharpening his knife of envy on the sole of his shoe to take the life of his enemy, Shylock is sharpening the knife of judgment that will take the life of his own soul. In judging, he will be judged. Shakespeare's thematic linking of Exodus 21:23–27 (an eye for an eye) with Matthew 7:1–5 (judge not, lest ye be judged) illustrates his profound understanding of the typology that underpins biblical theology. Whereas in Exodus, the man who took the eye of another in a fight is instructed to pluck out his own eye and offer it in just compensation, the passage in Matthew responds to such a notion of justice by pointing at the plank in our own eye that should prevent us judging the mote in the eyes of others.

> Judge not, that ye be not judged. For with what judgment ye judge, ye shall be judged: and with what measure ye mete, it shall be measured to you again. And why beholdest thou the mote that is in thy brother's eye, but considerest not the beam that is in thine own eye? Or how wilt thou say to thy brother, Let me pull out the mote out of thine eye; and, behold, a beam is in thine own eye? Thou hypocrite, first cast out the beam out of thine own eye; and then shalt thou see clearly to cast out the mote out of thy brother's eye.[2]

Here we see how the new law of Christ perfects the old law of Moses. Shylock should look at the sins of his own heart before seeking to pluck out the heart of another. If not, he will be judged with the same hardness of heart with which he has judged. And yet his heart is so hardened in hatred against Antonio that there are no prayers that can pierce the hardness of it. Or perhaps, and delving even deeper into the mystery, Shylock's hardened heart cannot be pierced by the prayers of those who are as hardhearted as he is. "Can no prayers pierce thee?" asks Gratiano. "No, none that *thou* hast wit enough to make", responds the usurer (emphasis added). Gratiano's venomously judgmental response to his opponent's riposte exposes Gratiano's own hardhearted hypocrisy, a hypocrisy that can serve only to harden his enemy's heart still further:

[2] Matthew 7:1–5.

> O, be thou damn'd, inexecrable dog!
> And for thy life let justice be accus'd.

Having warned Shylock that he will be judged in the manner in which he is passing judgment, Gratiano condemns both Shylock and even justice itself to hell. In so doing, Gratiano, the so-called Christian, condemns himself to the hellish justice that he wishes on another. "For with what judgment ye judge, ye shall be judged . . ." It is perhaps no wonder that Gratiano's very next words illustrate the fickleness of his faith:

> Thou almost mak'st me waver in my faith
> To hold opinion with Pythagoras,
> That souls of animals infuse themselves
> Into the trunks of men. (4.1.130–33)

Gratiano's lack of Christian virtue and his hypocritical inability to practice what he preaches leaves him susceptible to a relapse into paganism. Where the new law has not taken root, the old law will prevail. It is almost as though Shakespeare is saying that the Christian hypocrite is no better than the infidel. The former confuses, and the latter refuses, the teaching of Christ. And perhaps it is in this light that we should view Gratiano's decidedly un-Christian gloating over Shylock's downfall later in the scene. It is also perhaps in this light that we should view Shylock's most famous speech in which he complains of the hardheartedness of his Christian enemies:

*Salerio.* But tell us, do you hear whether Antonio have had any loss at sea or no?

*Shylock.* There I have another bad match. A bankrout, a prodigal, who dare scarce show his head on the Rialto; a beggar, that was us'd to come so smug upon the mart: let him look to his bond. He was wont to call me usurer, let him look to his bond. He was wont to lend money for a Christian cur'sy, let him look to his bond.

*Salerio.* Why, I am sure if he forfeit thou wilt not take his flesh. What's that good for?

*Shylock.* To bait fish withal—if it will feed nothing else, it will feed my revenge. He hath disgrac'd me, and hind'red me half a million, laugh'd at my losses, mock'd at my gains, scorn'd my nation, thwarted my bargains, cool'd my friends, heated mine enemies; and what's his reason? I am a

Jew. Hath not a Jew eyes? Hath not a Jew hands, organs, dimensions, senses, affections, passions; fed with the same food, hurt with the same weapons, subject to the same diseases, heal'd by the same means, warm'd and cool'd by the same winter and summer, as a Christian is? If you prick us, do we not bleed? If you tickle us, do we not laugh? If you poison us, do we not die? And if you wrong us, shall we not revenge? If we are like you in the rest, we will resemble you in that. If a Jew wrong a Christian, what is his humility? Revenge. If a Christian wrong a Jew, what should his sufferance be by Christian example? Why, revenge. The villainy you teach me, I will execute, and it shall go hard but I will better the instruction. (3.1.44–73)

There is no doubt that Shylock's plaintive invective serves as a rebuke to those hardhearted Christians, such as Gratiano, who fail in their duty to love their neighbor—and their enemy. In pointing an accusing finger at Christian hypocrites, Shakespeare is following in the inestimable footsteps of Dante and Chaucer, his great Catholic forebears. It would, however, be a gross misreading of the playwright and his play to see Shylock's words as being indicative of Shakespeare's disdain for Christianity itself. As with Dante and Chaucer, Shakespeare was motivated in his attacks on hypocrisy by his love for the Church, not by his disdain for it. Hypocritical Christians cause scandal and turn souls away from Christ and, as such, are a fitting and necessary target for the Christian poet. And in any case, Shylock's attack on his hypocritical Christian neighbors is unconvincing as an attack on Christianity because it is nothing but an *argumentum ad hominem*.[3] The authority of Christ is not diminished by the doubting of Thomas, the cowardice of Peter, or the treachery of Judas; nor is the authority of the Church diminished by the actions of the sinners whom she calls to repentance.

In recent years, in the wake of Nazi anti-Semitism, the *argumentum ad hominem* has been joined by the *argumentum ad captandum*,[4] the rhetorical

---

[3] An *argumentum ad hominem*, an "argument against the man", is a rhetorical tactic appealing to feelings and passions rather than reason and intellect. One who argues *ad hominem* avoids any engagement with the subject under discussion by deflecting the discussion to an attack on an opponent's character. Arguments *ad hominem* are considered to be logically inadmissible because they fail to prove a point by failing to address it. Such arguments are, however, the very "stuff" of opportunist politicians and postmodern critics.

[4] An *argumentum ad captandum*, like an *argumentum ad hominem*, appeals to feelings rather than reason. It is an argument designed to arouse the passions and prejudices of the masses. As with arguments *ad hominem*, arguments *ad captandum* are logically fallacious because they fail to prove a point by failing to address it.

weapon of the demagogue who seeks to replace rational discussion with the passions of prejudice. Whereas Shylock employs arguments *ad hominem* to justify his actions, postmodern critics employ arguments *ad captandum* to foment the passions associated with the Nazi holocaust in their discussion of Shylock's role in the play. Thus Shylock becomes a personified abstraction, signifying the holocaust and the horrors of Auschwitz, and by extension, his opponents become personified abstractions of Nazism and the horrors of racism. As if by magic, by a literary sleight of hand, Shylock is metamorphosed into the role of victim, and therefore into the role of tragic hero, and Portia, Bassanio, Antonio, et al. are metamorphosed into the role of persecutors or racists, and therefore into the role of villains. This is nothing less than the inversion of meaning through the perversion of perception. It is the sacrificing of Shakespeare on the altar of the ethnomasochistic angst that is the bane of postmodernism. It is the crucifixion of the Bard by the Pharisees and the Philistines.

And it is, of course, ironic that the crime against Shakespeare's humanity perpetrated by these postmodern critics is very similar in tone to the crimes against humanity perpetrated by the Nazis themselves. The Nazis were masters of the argument *ad captandum* in their war against the Jews, and the postmodernists are equally adept at arguing *ad captandum* in their war against Christian culture. The Nazis had an irrational hatred of the Jews, and the postmodernists have an irrational contempt for anything dead, white, European, or male. And although it would be an exaggeration to accuse the postmodernists of being quite as rabid as the Nazis, it is nonetheless true that they vent their spleen with venomous invective against anything tainted with the mark of the West, almost as if it were the mark of the Beast.

It is, however, time to move beyond the argument *ad hominem* of Shylock or the argument *ad captandum* of the postmodernists to the much surer footing of the *argumentum ab auctoritate*, the argument based on genuine authority. If we seek to understand the text by seeing it as the author saw it, as far as possible, and by seeing its parts as being integrated with the literary integrity of the text as a whole, we will see instantly how Shakespeare's perception of Shylock differs fundamentally from the misperceptions of his modern and postmodern critics.

The selective reading, out of context, of Shylock's most famous speech exposes the blindness of the critics to the bigger picture that Shakespeare presents. The speech is normally referred to by the line "Hath not a Jew eyes?" thereby stressing Shylock's role as victim, whereas, in fact, the speech is far more about vengeance than victimhood. Shylock begins his speech with the rhetorical statement that he will use the pound of Antonio's flesh as mere fish bait, adding that if the flesh "will feed nothing else, it will feed my revenge". It ends with the word "revenge" emphatically spoken twice, followed by a promise by Shylock that he will prove better at the "villainy" of vengeance than his Christian enemies. It is this emphasis on the vice of vengeance that dominates the speech, with the oft-quoted "victim" lines serving merely as a means by which Shylock seeks to justify his vice. The whole speech is, in fact, an iteration by Shakespeare of the concept of "an eye for an eye", or merciless justice, which is the dominant theme of the third act. Shylock feels wronged, and he will wrong those who have wronged him. This is Shakespeare's theme, and Shakespeare's point, and it is wrong to manipulate his words to imply an alternative meaning.

It is also interesting that modern and postmodern critics deviate from the conventional practice of referring to the speech by its opening line. Portia's "quality of mercy" speech is referred to as such because this is the opening line and the subject of her discourse. Hamlet's soliloquy, "To be, or not to be", is referred to by its opening line because it *is* the opening line and because it summarizes the nub of the question that the soliloquy addresses. According to this convention, Shylock's vengeful invective should be referred to as the "To bait fish withal" speech, a line that encapsulates the spitefulness of the speech succinctly. To refer to it by the words "Hath not a Jew eyes?", plucked out of context from the heart of the speech, is to pluck the very heart from the speech itself, thereby killing its meaning through subjective distortion. And this serves as a useful metaphor for the way that modern and postmodern critics have murdered the text. They have removed the pound of flesh nearest the Christian heart of the play and have killed it thereby.

If we look at Shylock's speech within the context of the lines that immediately precede it, we will see even more clearly that Shakespeare's purpose has been studiously ignored by proponents of Shylock's tragic heroism:

*Solanio.* Let me say amen betimes, lest the devil cross my prayer, for here he comes in the likeness of a Jew.

*Enter Shylock.*

How now, Shylock, what news among the merchants?

*Shylock.* You knew, none so well, none so well as you, of my daughter's flight.

*Salerio.* That's certain. I for my part knew the tailor that made the wings she flew withal.

*Solanio.* And Shylock for his own part knew the bird was flidge, and then it is the complexion of them all to leave the dam.

*Shylock.* She is damn'd for it.

*Salerio.* That's certain, if the devil may be her judge.

*Shylock.* My own flesh and blood to rebel!

*Solanio.* Out upon it, old carrion, rebels it at these years?

*Shylock.* I say, my daughter is my flesh and my blood.

*Salerio.* There is more difference between thy flesh and hers than between jet and ivory, more between your bloods than there is between red wine and Rhenish. (3.1.19–42)

The imagery that proliferates in these lines suggests something satanic in Shylock's evil intentions. He is heralded upon his arrival as being the very Devil himself, and when he announces that his own daughter is "damn'd", the response is that she will indeed be damned "if the devil [Shylock] may be her judge". The play on the word "rebel" reinforces the satanic connotations, considering that Satan is the primal and archetypal rebel, and even the word "carrion" carries with it the odor, the ordure, of hell. Shylock is "old carrion" in the sense that his flesh is death itself, stinking and rotting,[5] and also perhaps in the sense that he is a carrion crow, who feeds on dead flesh. In the former sense, Shylock's dead and stinking flesh could not be more different from the living, virtuous flesh of his daughter. In the latter sense, his words a few lines later that Antonio's flesh will feed his revenge gain added infernal power.

It should be noted that there is no reference to Shylock's being hated because he is Jewish. On the contrary, he is despised solely because of his evil character. He is not a devil *because* he is a Jew; he is a devil who

[5] Here, of course, "flesh" is being employed as a metaphor for "soul".

comes in the *likeness* of a Jew. His flesh and blood is not despised because it is Jewish but because it is carrion; it is dead and rotten, and reeks of decay. Jessica's flesh and blood is as Jewish as her father's, yet it is fresh and virtuous, and is as different from her father's as jet and ivory or red and white wine. In short, Shylock is not despised because of his race or his religion but because of the vice of vengeance that defines his character. It should also be noted that Shylock's merciless justice is likened to the way in which Satan passes judgment on the whole of humanity. If the Devil may be our judge, it is certain that we shall all be damned. And this is, of course, an implicit foreshadowing of Portia's words to Shylock:

> Therefore, Jew,
> Though justice be thy plea, consider this,
> That in the course of justice, none of us
> Should see salvation. (4.1.197–200)

The exchange between Shylock, Solanio, and Salerio, in which Shylock's evil character is likened to the Devil, is followed by Shylock's malicious attack on Antonio, in which Antonio is attacked not for his alleged anti-Semitism but for his opposition to Shylock's usury:

> He was wont to call me usurer, let him look to his bond. He was wont to lend money for a Christian cur'sy, let him look to his bond.

Shylock's hatred of Antonio is rooted in the latter's moral opposition to the practice of usury and also in Antonio's practice of lending money interest free as a Christian courtesy. And this harmonizes with, and confirms, Antonio's insistence that it is the issue of usury that has caused the enmity between them.

These, therefore, are the lines that immediately precede Shylock's most famous and most misinterpreted speech. They show beyond any reasonable doubt that Shylock is a thoroughgoing rogue in the tradition of other Shakespearean villains, such as Iago in *Othello* or Edmund in *King Lear*, and though we may sympathize with the suffering of a Jew living in a Christian culture, as we may sympathize with Edmund's plight as an illegitimate son, it does not justify the evil that they perpetrate. Vengeance is a vice, and evil, by any other name, still smells as foul.

# 10

# THE TESTING OF SHYLOCK

As Gratiano and Shylock take it in turns to strike the other's cheek, the stage is set for the arrival of the Savior who will show them a new law of mercy, and it is surely no coincidence that Portia's arrival is announced immediately after the angry exchange between the heardhearted Jew and the equally hardhearted Christian. And surely it is no coincidence that she is introduced as "a young doctor of Rome", suggesting a connection between the Eternal City and the eternal verities that she is about to espouse. If Belmont signifies the City of God and Venice the City of Man, Rome signifies the place where the former is made manifest to the latter. Portia descends from the heavenly heights of Belmont to the venal depths of Venice robed with the majesty and authority of Rome. She is set to show the people of Venice, both Jew and gentile alike, the new law that will set them free from the bondage of merciless justice. She is *Portia*, the *gate* of heaven, the means by which people can be raised from the venal gutters to the virtuous heights. She is the conduit of wisdom and grace. In short, she is a symbol of the Church herself!

While we are exploring the play's metadramatic dimension, it might be worth conjecturing an allegorical significance to the name that Portia chooses for her alter ego. In deciding to call herself Balthazar in her guise as the mysterious lawyer from Rome, she is connecting herself to the equally mysterious Magus in the Gospel narrative. The suggestive symmetry between the three caskets of gold, silver, and lead and the three caskets of gold, frankincense, and myrrh strengthens the likelihood of an allegorical significance to Portia's choice of name. The Magi, or Wise Men, are an integral part of the Epiphany, the showing of Christ to the gentiles, the moment at which God reveals himself to the whole world and not merely to the Chosen People. As such, the arrival of the Magi at the manger represents the first manifestation of the new law, signified by the birth of Christ, which will reconcile Jew and gentile, the old and the new, in the revelation of the New Covenant of sacrificial *love* and merciful *justice*. In the test of the caskets, the correct choice was lead, signifying death or self-sacrifice, as the necessary prerequisite of true *love*; in the test of the court scene, the correct choice is mercy, i.e., to judge others in the manner in which we hope God will judge us, as the necessary prerequisite of true *justice*. This profoundly Catholic understanding of the theological foundations of justice is made manifest in the way in which Portia approaches the problem presented to her by Shylock's merciless legalism:

> *Portia.*          Do you confess the bond?
> *Antonio.* I do.
> *Portia.*      Then must the Jew be merciful.
> *Shylock.* On what compulsion must I? tell me that.
> *Portia.* The quality of mercy is not strain'd,
>     It droppeth as the gentle rain from heaven
>     Upon the place beneath. It is twice blest:
>     It blesseth him that gives and him that takes.
>     'Tis mightiest in the mightiest, it becomes
>     The throned monarch better than his crown.
>     His sceptre shows the force of temporal power,
>     The attribute to awe and majesty,
>     Wherein doth sit the dread and fear of kings;
>     But mercy is above this sceptred sway,
>     It is enthroned in the hearts of kings,
>     It is an attribute to God himself;
>     And earthly power doth then show likest God's
>     When mercy seasons justice. Therefore, Jew,
>     Though justice be thy plea, consider this,
>     That in the course of justice, none of us
>     Should see salvation. We do pray for mercy,
>     And that same prayer doth teach us all to render
>     The deeds of mercy. I have spoke thus much
>     To mitigate the justice of thy plea,
>     Which if thou follow, this strict court of Venice
>     Must needs give sentence 'gainst the merchant there. (4.1.181–205)

Mercy, Portia tells us, is a gift of grace, "an attribute to God himself", that "droppeth as the gentle rain from heaven". It is "twice blest" in that it profits both parties in the transaction, the one who gives and the one who receives. Where mercy is present, there are no losers. Everyone is better off. On the other hand, the absence of mercy impoverishes both parties, the one who refuses to give it as much as the one to whom it is refused. Whereas the latter will suffer temporal impoverishment from the lack of mercy, the former will be cursed eternally, being refused the mercy from God that he had refused his neighbor. Therefore, if justice be our plea, we should consider the justice we render unto others and the mercy of which we are ourselves in need:

> We do pray for mercy,
> And that same prayer doth teach us all to render
> The deeds of mercy.

In the light of Portia's words, we should not overlook the way in which Shakespeare is punning on the words "mercy" and "merchant", both of which are derived from the Latin word *mercedem*, meaning "reward". Etymologically and ethically, a true merchant must be united with true mercy and should be grateful for the reward that such unity brings. Mercy and gratitude are indivisible, as is signified by their linguistic unity in modern French, in which *merci* means "mercy" but also "thank you". This is true economics, the knowledge of the economy of grace that governs the commerce and communion of all men. This is the true law of supply and demand that supplies all our needs and desires but demands our grateful compliance with our side of the bargain. This is the true sign of the Hidden Hand that governs all human transactions. This is the economics of Love, the economics of Belmont, the economics of the Catholic Church as manifested in her social teaching down the centuries. It is the antithesis of the economics of self-interest, the economics of Venice, the economics of the Enlightenment as manifested in the implicit materialism of modern economic thought. Once again, Shakespeare shows himself a Catholic in his treatment of the controversies and struggles between Catholic tradition and Enlightenment innovation.

Considering the theological heights to which we have seen that Shakespeare ascends, we might also wish to ponder the significance of the phrase "twice blest" in relation to the quality of mercy. If "thrice-fair" as a description of Portia reminds us insistently of the Trinity, "twice blest" as a description of mercy reminds us equally insistently of the Incarnation, the real sign of God's mercy to mankind. The Trinity is "thrice-fair" as three Persons in one Being; Christ is "twice blest" as two natures in one Person, the divine and the human. Thus Portia is showing us that the mercy of God, incarnated in the Person of Jesus, is the model and type of the mercy we must show to each other. The words of "Balthazar" are a true epiphany!

It is, however, surely significant that much of Portia's speech is concerned with the necessity of kings and monarchs to show mercy:

> 'Tis mightiest in the mightiest, it becomes
> The throned monarch better than his crown.
> His sceptre shows the force of temporal power,
> The attribute to awe and majesty,
> Wherein doth sit the dread and fear of kings;
> But mercy is above this sceptred sway,
> It is enthroned in the hearts of kings,
> It is an attribute to God himself;
> And earthly power doth then show likest God's
> When mercy seasons justice.

Considering the omnipresence of Robert Southwell's ghostly presence throughout this play, it is hard to see these lines as anything but a plea to Queen Elizabeth that she should show mercy to the Jesuits whom her courts were regularly putting to bloody death. Perhaps these lines indicate that the play was written prior to Southwell's execution, though they could serve equally as a plaintive criticism, after the execution, of the absence of mercy that had been shown to the martyred priest.

The Christological dimension of Portia's words is confirmed by Shylock's response to them:

> My deeds upon my head! I crave the law,
> The penalty and forfeit of my bond. (4.1.206–7)

To Shakespeare's Christian audience, which was far better versed in Scripture than are the Bard's postmodern critics, Shylock's words would have resonated as an echo of the Gospel: "Then answered all the people, and said, His blood be on us, and on our children."[1] Here Shylock is clearly placing himself in the role of the scribes and the Pharisees during the Crucifixion of Christ, a fact that is reinforced later in the same scene by Shylock's preference for Barabbas over any Christian:

[1] Matthew 27:25.

> I have a daughter—
> Would any of the stock of Barrabas
> Had been her husband rather than a Christian! (4.1.295–97)

Implicit in the usurer's barbed words is his belief that Jesus should have been crucified. If Shylock would rather his daughter had married "any of the stock of Barrabas ... rather than a Christian", it is evident that he prefers Barabbas over Christ. He is placing himself with the mob baying for the blood of Jesus and demanding the release of the terrorist Barabbas. And like the mob, he is content that his deeds be upon his head.

The foregoing illustrates plainly enough that Shylock is not someone with whom Shakespeare intends his audience to sympathize, and this is something we must bear in mind as we witness the usurer's downfall. And yet, in spite of Shakespeare's best efforts to make us see the courtroom scene as he sees it, many of the Bard's critics, and many contemporary producers of the play, invariably paint Shylock as a victim of what they deem to be Portia's hypocritical lack of mercy. One notable and noble exception is Daniel H. Lowenstein, professor of law at the UCLA School of Law, whose masterful analysis of the legal intricacies and moral dynamics of the Portia-Shylock engagement is utterly convincing:

> To understand the trial scene, we must understand it as a whole. The scene—as well as the Shylock-Antonio portion of the play generally—is about an act of attempted murder. Critics tend to write as if the scene is really about the bond, with Portia's invocation of the criminal statute treated as if it were an afterthought. Only by bearing in mind the attempted murder question while reading or watching the scene can we understand Portia's conduct and the richness of Shakespeare's writing.[2]

Lowenstein reminds us that Shylock had repeatedly and publicly declared his intention to enforce the bond and take a pound of Antonio's flesh, even before the trial began, and that he had confirmed these malicious intentions by bringing the enforcement proceedings and having Antonio arrested. He had refused in open court to accept twice the sum owed in lieu of his bond and had declared, rhetorically, that he

---

[2] Daniel H. Lowenstein, "Law and Mercy in *The Merchant of Venice*", in *The Merchant of Venice*, ed. Joseph Pearce, Ignatius Critical Editions (San Francisco: Ignatius Press: 2009), p. 225.

would reject twelve times the amount owed (4.1.84–87). "These actions are easily sufficient to constitute 'direct or indirect attempts' to take Antonio's life", Lowenstein states, indicating that Shylock was already guilty of the offense prior to Portia's arrival. Since this is so, it is wrong to assume that Portia is trapping him. "He has already walked into the trap. Portia's most strenuous endeavor in the trial is to induce him to walk out before the trap springs shut."[3]

Lowenstein then looks at the crucial significance of the short exchange between Portia and Shylock that immediately precedes Portia's "quality of mercy" speech:

> *Portia.*  Do you confess the bond?
> *Antonio.* I do.
> *Portia.*  Then must the Jew be merciful.
> *Shylock.* On what compulsion must I? tell me that.
> *Portia.* The quality of mercy is not strain'd. . . .

Why does Portia seemingly contradict herself in stating on the one hand that Shylock *must* be merciful and on the other that mercy is not *strained*, i.e., compelled? The reason for her seeming contradiction is an earnest desire on her part to save Shylock from the trap he is setting for himself. Lowenstein again:

> Shylock is guilty of a serious crime and will face a severe punishment, but because Antonio is still alive and unharmed, it is still possible for Shylock to extricate himself by voluntarily sparing his adversary. Thus, he "must" be merciful in the sense that if he is not, he will be punished. Yet the mercy cannot be "strain'd", because once he is informed of his plight, his abandonment of the bond will no longer be voluntary and his guilt will be unexpunged. Far from trapping Shylock, Portia essays some of the most eloquent words ever uttered in the English language to induce him to abandon his fatal course.[4]

Portia's most famous speech is infused with dramatic irony. It is not merely *about* mercy; it is itself an act *of* mercy. She has saved her most eloquent words not for the gaining of a lover but for the saving of a sinner. The sinner, however, will not be saved. Given one last chance to walk out of the trap that he has made for himself, Shylock remains resolute in his demands for a pound of Antonio's flesh. "The trap closes

---

[3] Ibid.
[4] Ibid., p. 226.

in on him", writes Lowenstein. "He has himself to blame, not Portia, who has done her best to save him." [5]

But is Portia not somewhat sadistic in her apparent refusal to show Shylock the mercy that she has been espousing? Is she not being a hypocrite in the apparently merciless way in which she applies the "justice" of the bond? Although she is often accused of committing these wrongs against Shylock, she is, in fact, guilty of neither charge. On the contrary, she is acting entirely dispassionately and in conformity with the merciful justice she has been preaching. She had warned Shylock of the dangers of insisting on justice in the absence of mercy and had used her considerable rhetorical gifts to persuade him to change his ways. Shylock must be merciful because in the course of justice without mercy, none of us would see salvation. He had been warned, but the warning went unheeded. Indeed, he had responded by insisting that his deeds be upon his head, i.e., that he should be judged according to the way in which he had judged. Shylock gets what he wants. Indeed, as Portia reminds him, he gets what he demands:

> For as thou urgest justice, be assur'd
> Thou shalt have justice more than thou desir'st. (4.1.315–16)

She is not punishing him more than he deserves in giving him more than he desires; she is simply stating that in demanding merciless justice, he is getting more than he bargained for. Thus, when Shylock tries to cut his losses by accepting the earlier offer of receiving thrice the payment due on the bond, he is reminded that he can have only the justice that he had demanded. He can have the pound of flesh nominated in the bond and nothing more. Although Bassanio remains content to pay Shylock thrice the price of the forfeiture, such payment is not in the bond and is therefore not strictly just. To pay Shylock the money would be an act of mercy, an act of kindness beyond the strict letter of the law. Shylock had sought justice without mercy, and that is precisely what he receives. In justice he can have no complaints. Similarly, when Shylock asks simply for the principal on the loan, Bassanio is willing to pay but is prevented by Portia from doing so:

> He hath refus'd it in the open court;
> He shall have merely justice and his bond.

[5] Ibid.

Finally she raises the issue of the attempted murder:

> The law hath yet another hold on you.
> It is enacted in the laws of Venice,
> If it be proved against an alien,
> That by direct or indirect attempts
> He seek the life of any citizen,
> The party 'gainst the which he doth contrive
> Shall seize one half his goods; the other half
> Comes to the privy coffer of the state,
> And the offender's life lies in the mercy
> Of the Duke only, 'gainst all other voice:
> In which predicament I say thou stand'st,
> For it appears, by manifest proceeding,
> That indirectly, and directly too,
> Thou hast contrived against the very life
> Of the defendant; and thou hast incurr'd
> The danger formerly by me rehears'd.
> Down therefore, and beg mercy of the Duke. (4.1.347–63)

Before Shylock has the opportunity to request the mercy he had refused to Antonio, he is granted it by the Duke:

> That thou shalt see the difference of our spirit,
> I pardon thee thy life before thou ask it. (4.1.368–69)

Throughout the second half of the trial, the uncharitable voice of Gratiano has been baying for Shylock's blood in much the same way as Shylock had been baying for the blood of Antonio earlier in the trial. Gratiano's is the voice of merciless justice, indicating the punishment that Shylock really warrants according to the old law. The fact that his vengeful voice is not heeded represents the triumph of the new law over the old.

There is, however, one remaining aspect of the trial scene that continues to elicit sympathy for Shylock and that seems to suggest a reprehensible crassness on the part of his enemies. The ultimatum given by the Duke that he will "recant" his pardon if Shylock refuses to become a Christian is an action that no reader of the play can sanction without grievous misgivings. For Catholic Christians, the very notion of a forced conversion is anathema, and is explicitly forbidden. According to the *Catechism of the Catholic Church*, man "must not be forced to act contrary to his conscience. Nor must he be prevented from acting according to his conscience, especially in religious matters." [6] Contrary to such teaching, and even though there is no indication that he would have done so in conscience, Shylock is forced to become a Christian, on pain of death. The quality of such mercy is indeed dubious, and there seems little doubt that the Duke's ultimatum effectively nullifies his earlier show of mercy in sparing Shylock's life. But even if this is so, it would be wrong to see in the Duke's action, and in Antonio's earlier insistence that Shylock "become a Christian", an example of mere sadistic cruelty on their part. Though we may regard the sentence as cruel, it does not follow that Antonio and the Duke have a cruel purpose in inflicting it. Most of us believe, and some in Shakespeare's audience may have thought, that a forced religious conversion is an oxymoron, in every important sense. But there is no reason for us to imagine that Antonio and the Duke believe this. Antonio, who is still under the impression that he is wiped out financially, is entitled under the law to half of Shylock's wealth. In consideration for Shylock's conversion to Christianity, Antonio either renounces his entitlement entirely or accepts a restriction on it (4.1.381–82). If the sentence is assumed to be cruel, Antonio and the Duke may fairly be charged with insensitivity but not with hypocrisy or malice.

And yet the insensitivity of his enemies does not transform the consistently vengeful Shylock into the tragic hero that he seems to have become to modern and postmodern readers of the play. The fact is that Shylock fails his final test when he states that he is "content" with the decision of the court that he should convert. If he had refused conversion and accepted death as the price of his religious conscience, he would have become a tragic hero. In such a circumstance, his refusal to convert would paradoxically have illustrated his genuine conversion from being a spiteful and vengeful villain to being a man of religious conscience and conviction.[7] As it is, his own flesh is not only more

---

[6] Paragraph 1782.

[7] Several critics have sought to argue that Shylock's conversion to Christianity is genuine, citing the Duke's and Antonio's generosity and mercy in sparing him his life and in refraining from stripping him of all his worldly possessions, as was their right in law. Believing that he was about to be executed for attempted murder, Shylock "found himself spared and treated generously by his own intended victim, his bitterest enemy, shattering his conviction that Christians who are wronged seek only revenge" (Lowenstein, "Law and Mercy", p. 229).

valuable to him than Antonio's; it is more valuable to him than his religious faith. He fails the first test in refusing to die to himself in choosing the death of another. He fails the second test in renouncing his faith to save his flesh. In both tests he shows himself to be the antithesis of a tragic hero. If there is a tragedy, it is in the absence of any conversion. Shylock is what he has always been. He remains a worldly chooser, a vengeful villain, a venal Venetian.

Considering that Shakespeare and his audience were Christians, it is certainly possible that we are meant to assume that Shylock receives an infusion of grace in these climactic moments, a deus ex machina that sticks in the craw of our materialistic age but which was accepted as part of supernatural reality by Shakespeare's audience. Ultimately, the present writer finds this reading too textually tenuous and contrived to be accepted. *Pace* the postmodernists, it is nonetheless true that Shylock becomes less of a monster if we accept that his soul was capable of catharsis or conversion. Shylock the convert is more amicably human than Shylock the thwarted and embittered loser.

# THE TESTING OF BASSANIO

No sooner has Shakespeare led us through the drama and the climax of the testing of Shylock, the second of the play's pivotal tests, than he leads us directly into the play's third and climactic test, the trial of the rings. This final test, in which Bassanio and Gratiano are both found wanting, is often seen as an anticlimactic descent into mere flippancy, as little more than an unimportant appendage that offers light relief after the intensity of the trial scene. According to this interpretation of the play's final act, *The Merchant of Venice* does not end with a bang but a whimper, or, more precisely, it does not end with a moral but a snigger. Yet this plunging of the plot from the heights of drama to the depths of banality does violence to the formal structure of the entire work and contradicts the clear morality of all that precedes it. It is evident, therefore, that such a reading must be awry and that we should expect to find more than mere banality in the play's conclusion. In light of these expectations, it is important that we treat the test of the rings with the same seriousness and solemnity with which we treated the test of the caskets and the testing of Shylock. When we do so, we discover that the final test is perhaps the most important test of all.

The seeds of the final test are found in the fruit of the first, in which Bassanio has promised to hazard all he has in return for Portia's love. After Bassanio successfully passes this test, Portia offers herself in complete self-sacrifice to him, who is now "her lord, her governor, her king", and she gives him a ring that serves as a sign of the covenant between them:

> Myself, and what is mine, to you and yours
> Is now converted. But now I was the lord
> Of this fair mansion, master of my servants,
> Queen o'er myself; and even now, but now,
> This house, these servants, and this same myself

> Are yours—my lord's!—I give them with this ring,
> Which when you part from, lose, or give away,
> Let it presage the ruin of your love,
> And be my vantage to exclaim on you. (3.2.165–74)

It is curious that the lines in which Portia gives Bassanio the ring and warns him of the consequences of his failure to guard it with life-long diligence are often glossed by modern critics with the direction that they should be "spoken playfully".[1] There is no textual reason for such an assertion except for the mistaken assumption that the final test is a mere meaningless folly. A more accurate reading would treat Portia's words with the same solemnity with which Bassanio had approached the casket test. If her successful suitor had just hazarded everything to win his prize, is it likely that Portia would treat the significance of the ring with such frivolity? Is it not far more likely, and far more in keeping with the dignity of the drama, that Portia sees the ring as the very sign and seal of the covenant of love between husband and wife and that she enunciates these words with utter earnestness? The fact that such a seal is not to be taken lightly is emphasized by Bassanio himself in his acceptance of the ring:

> But when this ring
> Parts from this finger, then parts life from hence;
> O then be bold to say Bassanio's dead! (3.2.183–85)

The ring is clearly no mere plaything but is, on the contrary, a matter of life and death, and something to be guarded until death do the espoused couple part. This is a lesson that Bassanio, for all his promises to hazard his very life for his love, has not yet learned. And this is the very lesson that Portia teaches him in the play's final test. "Beneath the music, poetry, and comedy of the last act", writes Daniel Lowenstein, "is Portia's serious business of impressing Bassanio with the gravity of the marriage oath and of the ring that symbolizes that oath...."[2]

Portia first becomes aware of Bassanio's tendency to put pragmatism over principle during the trial scene, when Bassanio urges the Duke to employ evil means to a good end:

---

[1] See, for instance, the Signet Classic edition, edited by Kenneth Myrick (1998).

[2] Daniel Lowenstein, "Law and Mercy in *The Merchant of Venice*", in *The Merchant of Venice*, ed. Joseph Pearce, Ignatius Critical Editions (San Francisco: Ignatius Press, 2009), p. 229.

And I beseech you,
Wrest once the law to your authority:
To do a great right, do a little wrong,
And curb this cruel devil of his will. (4.1.214–17)

Portia is all too aware that principles must not be compromised and that the law must not be sacrificed on the altar of opportunism. As a Christian, she knows that the Devil cannot be defeated by using the Devil's own methods. A "great right" can never be served by doing a "little wrong"; nor can evil be defeated by evil. It is, therefore, inevitable that her reply to Bassanio would be uncompromising:

It must not be, there is no power in Venice
Can alter a decree established.
'Twill be recorded for a precedent,
And many an error by the same example
Will rush into the state. It cannot be. (4.1.218–22)

At issue here is not simply the integrity of the law but the very acceptance of the existence of pure principle and absolute truth. In the war between the objective morality insisted upon by the Church and the subjective opportunism touted by Machiavelli and his followers, Portia comes down firmly on the side of the Church's moral teaching. She is affirming once again her belief in realism over relativism. Her husband, on the other hand, is prone to sacrifice his principles and his wife to the needs of the moment. This is made manifest during the trial scene, in which Bassanio forgets the principle by which he had won the hand of Portia in the casket test and the promise he had made to her when she gave him the ring:

Antonio, I am married to a wife
Which is as dear to me as life itself,
But life itself, my wife, and all the world,
Are not with me esteem'd above thy life.
I would lose all, ay, sacrifice them all
Here to this devil, to deliver you. (4.1.282–87)

The illegitimacy of Bassanio's reasoning is evident from the fact that the sacrifice he is willing to make is to the "devil". He has broken his promise to hazard all he has for his wife and has promised to sacrifice her to the Devil to deliver his friend from the Devil's clutches. Once again he is succumbing to the evil of committing evil in order to combat evil. He is making the deadly mistake, the mortal sin, of using evil means to a good end. It is no wonder that Portia, disguised and not recognized by her treacherous husband, is unhappy with his words:

> Your wife would give you little thanks for that
> If she were by to hear you make the offer. (4.1.288–89)

It is likely, therefore, that Portia devises the final test of the ring to teach her husband a lesson about the dangers inherent in allowing pragmatism to prevail over principle. She had already witnessed Bassanio's willingness to do "a little wrong", and she had seen him betray his promise of lifelong fidelity to her in his willingness to sacrifice her to the "devil". It was, therefore, almost predictable that he could be persuaded to part with the ring, the very seal and symbol of his promise of lifelong fidelity and sacrifice. When he does so, offering it as a gift to Balthazar, oblivious that the young lawyer is, in fact, his wife in disguise, he betrays not only his wife but his own "hazardous" promise to her. In passing the first test, Bassanio had shown himself worthy in theory; in failing the third test, he shows himself unworthy in practice, his moral relativism rendering him incapable of fulfilling the promise that he would hazard all he had for his wife. This is the situation in which we find ourselves at the commencement of the last act.

# 12

# LIGHT AND LIGHTHEARTEDNESS

The playful exchange between Lorenzo and Jessica at the commencement of the final act is more than a mere curtain raiser to the play's climactic action. It sets the tone and the theme of the drama that will follow and even contains an allusive and synoptic foreshadowing of the deepest meaning in the exchanges between Portia and Bassanio, and between Nerissa and Gratiano, that follow shortly afterward. As such, to view Lorenzo's and Jessica's exchange as merely vacuous and devoid of deeper meaning is to miss Shakespeare's point entirely. Their poetic dialogue, reminiscent of Virgil's *Eclogues*, does not merely serve as a catalog of some of literature's most illustrious lovers, the most faithful and the most faithless, but serves to point us in the direction of the present drama's most illustrious lovers, Portia and Bassanio. As Lorenzo and Jessica wax lyrical about the legendary lovers of the past, we come to realize that the legends, and even Lorenzo and Jessica themselves, are serving as types to which the love between Portia and Bassanio is the archetype. As we are introduced to the faithful Troilus and the faithless Cressida, we are reminded of the faithful Portia and the faithless Bassanio. Allusions to the tragically thwarted loves of Thisbe and Dido are suggestive of the potential tragedy of Portia's thwarted love for her faithless suitor. In the reference to Medea, who was betrayed by Jason, we are again reminded of Portia's betrayal by Bassanio. By extension, the mentioning of Medea's renewing of Aeson, Jason's father, might be seen as an allusion to Portia's saving of Antonio, Bassanio's surrogate father. And as the dialogue returns to the present with the two lovers, Jessica and Lorenzo, playfully goading each other about the genuineness of their own love, we see that they have also become types of Portia and Bassanio:

> *Jessica.*                 In such a night
>     Did young Lorenzo swear he lov'd her well,

> Stealing her soul with many vows of faith,
> And ne'er a true one.
> *Lorenzo.*                    In such a night
> Did pretty Jessica (like a little shrow)
> Slander her love, and he forgave it her. (5.1.17–22)

Jessica's complaints about the falsity of Lorenzo's "vows of faith" foreshadow Portia's similar complaints about Bassanio's broken vows and faithlessness, and Lorenzo's riposte that he would forgive Jessica for her slandering of his love foreshadows Portia's forgiveness of Bassanio. It can be seen, therefore, that this short dialogue is more than a mere curtain raiser for what follows. It is actually an allusive premonition, in microcosm, of the remainder of the play.

The dialogue between Jessica and Lorenzo is interrupted by the announcement of Portia's impending arrival, and we are not surprised to learn that Portia, on her way home, is kneeling and praying at "holy crosses", i.e., at wayside shrines, for "happy wedlock hours". She has no one with her except "a holy hermit and her maid" (5.1.31–33). As we await the heroine's return, we are presented with a musical interlude in which Shakespeare, through the words of Lorenzo, sings a hymn of praise to the order and harmony of God's creation and the workings of his providence:

> How sweet the moonlight sleeps upon this bank!
> Here will we sit, and let the sounds of music
> Creep in our ears. Soft stillness and the night
> Become the touches of sweet harmony.
> Sit, Jessica. Look how the floor of heaven
> Is thick inlaid with patens of bright gold.
> There's not the smallest orb which thou behold'st
> But in his motion like an angel sings,
> Still quiring to the young-ey'd cherubins;
> Such harmony is in immortal souls,
> But whilst this muddy vesture of decay
> Doth grossly close it in, we cannot hear it. (5.1.54–65)

In these sublimely beautiful lines we witness the metaphysics that Shakespeare upholds throughout his plays, and we witness also how this metaphysical concept of reality has placed a chasm between the profoundly Christian Bard and his profanely "post-Christian" critics. For

Shakespeare, the cosmos is neither the mere mechanism of the scientists nor the meaningless mess of the deconstructionists but is, on the contrary, an ordered creation that communicates the "sweet harmony" of God's goodness and the ordered presence of his purpose:

> There's not the smallest orb which thou behold'st
> But in his motion like an angel sings,
> Still quiring to the young-ey'd cherubins. . . .

The music of the cosmos, like the music of the angels, has its *essential* existence in eternity and is therefore not measurable in purely material terms. The song of angels cannot be heard by human ears, nor can the music of the spheres, because such music speaks to the spirit and not to the senses. It is the music of God moving through his creation, the music of his image in his creatures. It is the Divine Presence. And it is present in human souls as it is present in the singing of angels and the harmony of the cosmos, even if our mortality and our sinfulness make us deaf to its promptings:

> Such harmony is in immortal souls,
> But whilst this muddy vesture of decay
> Doth grossly close it in, we cannot hear it.

Although each immortal soul is part of the harmony of the spheres, and partakes of its music, the shadow of the Fall has fallen over mortal flesh, "this muddy vesture of decay", and has deafened the soul to the music of which it is part. The vesture of mortality is "muddy" because it masks what truly lies beneath, the glory and beauty of the immortal soul. Here we see that Shakespeare is yet again siding with the medieval scholastics in his understanding of the cosmos and the human soul's place within it. The music of the spheres is the *substance* of reality, that integral order of the universe that is unchanging, whereas the "muddy vesture" of man's mortality is an *accident*, philosophically speaking; i.e., it does not exist except in its relationship of dependence on the substance. In other words, immortality is the real *substance* of man's humanity, whereas his mortality is the "muddy vesture of decay" that "grossly" closes in the immortal soul.[1] The paradox is

---

[1] Lest Shakespeare or the present writer be misunderstood, the distinction being made is between mortality and immortality, not between the soul and the body. Mortal flesh decays, but immortal flesh does not.

that man's mortality is mortal. It dies when he dies. Unlike the immortal soul, it is not permanent or unchanging. And this is why the soul is deaf to the harmony of the cosmos only "*whilst* this muddy vesture of decay / Doth grossly close it in" (emphasis added). Once the soul enters its true home in eternity, it will see reality as it *is* and not as it *seems* to be.

It is appropriate that Shakespeare includes a transparent reference to the Blessed Sacrament in the midst of this "heavenly" discourse:

> Look how the floor of heaven
> Is thick inlaid with patens of bright gold.

The paten is the small plate of precious metal upon which the consecrated Host is placed during the sacrifice of the Mass, and therefore its employment as a metaphor for the stars in heaven is suggestive of God's hidden but real presence in the cosmos and, by way of analogy, of his hidden but Real Presence in the Eucharist. As such, these two lines emerge distinctly as an indication of Shakespeare's Catholic faith; and in his eloquent portrayal of the music of the spheres, he is placing himself not only firmly on the side of the angels but also on the side of Catholic tradition in the face of the skepticism of the emerging scientism of the embryonic Enlightenment. Far from siding with the skeptics, Shakespeare aligns himself with his medieval forebears, such as Boethius, who wrote about the *musica universalis* in his *De musica*, and Dante, who employed the music of the spheres with unsurpassed splendor in the *Divine Comedy*.

Having waxed lyrical on the metaphysical dimension of music and harmony, Lorenzo proceeds to employ music as a metaphor for grace:

> Since nought so stockish, hard, and full of rage,
> But music for the time doth change his nature.
> The man that hath no music in himself,
> Nor is not moved with concord of sweet sounds,
> Is fit for treasons, stratagems, and spoils;
> The motions of his spirit are dull as night,
> And his affections dark as [Erebus]:
> Let no such man be trusted. Mark the music. (5.1.81–88)

Lorenzo is speaking of grace and the ordering of man's soul. Music (grace) is a gift of divine order, a gift that orders everything toward the divine. Yet music can work its magic only if the one to whom it is played is attentive to its beauty. The man who cares not for music—i.e., for order, the divine order—is the one prone to evil deeds. He kills the inner harmony of his soul and becomes "dark as Erebus", as black as hell. In refusing to respond to the promptings of music, such a man is fit only "for treasons, stratagems, and spoils". He is not to be trusted.

Remembering that Lorenzo has specifically connected music to the divinely ordered music of the spheres, it is difficult to read these subsequent lines without seeing them as yet another attack on the relativism of nominalism and Machiavellianism. The cosmos is ordered toward its Creator, and those who refuse to conform themselves to this objective reality are at war with the divinely ordained harmony and are, in inevitable consequence, sowers of discord. It is also difficult to read these lines without perceiving an attack on the rising power of the antimusical Puritans, who had sought to minimize the role of music in the Anglican liturgy. The Shakespeare scholar Clare Asquith has even suggested that Lorenzo's anti-Puritan words might have constituted an effort to woo Queen Elizabeth back to Catholicism, conjecturing that Shakespeare is exploiting "one of Elizabeth's chief quarrels with the reformers, for she loved and patronized church music." [2] Asquith also sees the words of Lorenzo upon the arrival of the musicians as a thinly veiled appeal to the queen herself, casting Elizabeth as the chaste moon goddess, Diana, in the hope of flattering her back into the Catholic fold:

> Come ho, and wake Diana with a hymn,
> With sweetest touches pierce your mistress' ear
> And draw her home with music. (5.1.66–68)

Such a supposition, though seemingly feasible, appears to be contradicted by Portia's words a little later:

> [T]he moon sleeps with Endymion,
> And would not be awak'd. (5.1.109–10)

The lines are clearly connected thematically because Lorenzo's words are uttered immediately before the musicians begin to play, and Portia's words are spoken as soon as the music ends. Clearly, if we are to take

---

[2] Clare Asquith, *Shadowplay: The Hidden Beliefs and Coded Politics of William Shakespeare* (New York: Public Affairs, 2005), p. 120.

Diana as a coded reference to the queen, Shakespeare's treatment of her is hardly flattering. She is played the music, which is symbolic of the divine will, but will not be awakened with a hymn of grace, preferring to sleep with her mortal lover and choosing to remain defiantly deaf to the knell of her immortal destiny.

With his unerring sense of dramatic decorum, Shakespeare uses Lorenzo's sublime praise of music and all that it symbolizes as a fanfare to announce the arrival of his heroine. The final words of his speech, "Mark the music", herald the arrival of Portia. She *is* the music, in the sense that she serves as the incarnation of the divine order that the music symbolizes, and we should "mark" what she has to say. The playwright is not merely announcing the arrival of his heroine; he is instructing us to listen to her. This is made manifest a few lines later, when Portia asks Nerissa (and the audience) to hearken to the music—"Music, hark!"—and is told by Nerissa that the music is Portia's: "It is your music, madam, of the house" (5.1.97–98). It is Portia's music to which we should hearken. It is her words that we should mark.

Shakespeare's purpose is plain enough. We are meant to heed Portia's words as intently in the final scene as we had heeded them in the trial scene. We are called to be *attentive* because, as Portia herself tells us at this juncture,

> The crow doth sing as sweetly as the lark
> When neither is attended.... (5.1.102–3)

If we will not "mark the music", we will hear not the beauty of Portia's wisdom, singing sweetly as the lark, but merely the cawing of the crow. We will not ascend, with the lark, to sing the praises of the divine order but will remain earthbound, with the crow, seeing nothing beyond the mundane and the meaningless. The lark ascending, meeting its Muse and making its music, remains unheeded. The crow, picking over the dead flesh of murdered words and mutilated meaning, is inattentive to the music of the lark and is therefore deaf to the music of the spheres, and to the music of the Bard. It is almost as though Shakespeare, with prophetic wisdom, had foreseen the way in which his work would be misread by future generations of critics.

> The man that hath no music in himself,
> Nor is not moved with concord of sweet sounds,
> Is fit for treasons, stratagems, and spoils;

> The motions of his spirit are dull as night,
> And his affections dark as [Erebus]:
> Let no such man be trusted. Mark the music.

And yet Shakespeare had no need of prophetic powers to foresee the mutilation of meaning by those who fail to mark the music. Such men were all around him in Elizabethan England: in the government, in the spy networks, in the fashionable new ideas of Machiavellian *realpolitik*, and in the fashionable new theology of the Reformation. His plays resonate continually with the clash between the "word made flesh" of philosophical realism and the "flesh made word" of nominalism.

Since Portia is the music that we should mark, it is little surprise that she continues the discourse on divine order from where Lorenzo leaves off:

> *Portia.* That light we see is burning in my hall;
>    How far that little candle throws his beams!
>    So shines a good deed in a naughty world.
> *Nerissa.* When the moon shone, we did not see the candle.
> *Portia.* So doth the greater glory dim the less.... (5.1.89–93)

Portia's words echo those of Saint Matthew's Gospel in which Christ speaks of his disciples as "the light of the world":

> Ye are the light of the world. A city that is set on an hill cannot be hid.
> Neither do men light a candle, and put it under a bushel, but on a
> candlestick; and it giveth light unto all that are in the house. Let your
> light so shine before men, that they may see your good works, and glo-
> rify your Father which is in heaven.[3]

In her use of the candle as a metaphor for the shining of good deeds in an evil world, Portia is singing in harmony with Christ himself. Since this is clearly so, Portia's home in Belmont, from which the candle shines and the music plays, must be seen as that very city of which Christ speaks, the city set on a hill that cannot be hid. Nowhere is the allegorical connection between Belmont and the City of God more obviously apparent. It is surely also significant that Portia's lines harmonize with lines taken from the work of the Jesuit martyr Robert Southwell. Nerissa's words and Portia's response ("When the moon shone, we did not see the candle.... So doth the greater glory dim the less")

---

[3] Matthew 5:14–16.

harmonize with Southwell's "seeking the sunne it is ... booteles to borrow the light of a candle."[4] The greater glory dims the less, so sing Southwell and Shakespeare in harmony. The candle is dimmed by the light of the moon, and the moon is dimmed by the light of the sun, and the sun is dimmed by the Light of the World himself, the One Source from whom the celestial firmament receives its light. Once again, Southwell's theme is Shakespeare's, the latter seemingly paying homage to the former.

Portia is developing the theme of Lorenzo, pointing us to the music of the spheres and, therefore, to the Master Musician who is the composer and conductor of this cosmic symphony. It is Christ who orders everything by providence and grace so that it dances to the tune of his Father's will. It is Christ who is the Light of the World from whom the disciples receive the light by which they shine forth their good deeds in a "naughty world", thereby glorifying their Father who is in heaven. As usual, it is Portia who puts the matter most succinctly:

> How many things by season season'd are
> To their right praise and true perfection!
> Peace ho! (5.1.107–9)

With these words Portia brings to an end the music that has been playing and also, simultaneously, the symbolically charged discourse on the music of the spheres, and its theological significance, of which the literal music was but an allegorical figure. At the same time, her words point toward the arrival of Bassanio, who is ripe for the lesson that Portia is about to teach. He has been seasoned by his sins, and, in learning the lessons that they teach, he is ready for conversion. He will be reoriented toward the good, toward "right praise and true perfection", that he may find the "peace" that it brings.

"Let me give light", says Portia upon Bassanio's arrival. "But God sort all!" (5.1.129, 132). Her words reiterate those of the Gospel passage to which she had alluded earlier and affirm her faith and trust that the music of providence will resolve the problem of Bassanio's betrayal of her love.

---

[4] From Robert Southwell, *Marie Magdalens Funeral Teares*, quoted in John Klause, "Catholic and Protestant, Jesuit and Jew: Historical Religion in *The Merchant of Venice*", in *Shakespeare and the Culture of Christianity in Early Modern England*, ed. Dennis Taylor and David N. Beauregard (New York: Fordham University Press, 2003), p. 187.

Everything is now set for the final resolution, in which Portia runs rings around her husband in the delightful comedy of the play's denouement. What follows is a riot of double entendres in which the wives, Portia and Nerissa, lead their husbands, Bassanio and Gratiano, in a merry dance in which pride is healed by the balm of humiliation and in which humor and humility go hand in hand. The husbands are reminded that the rings were their wives' first gift to them and that they had been placed on their fingers as a mark of the indivisibility of their lifelong bond of love. They had been "stuck on with oaths" and "riveted with faith unto [their] flesh" (5.1.168–69). As the scene unfolds, the unfaithful husbands are forgiven by their wives, and they finally come to possess the wisdom that can come only with humility, and the true love that can be forged only in the furnace of fidelity. And so the play ends with Gratiano, speaking on behalf of both husbands, declaring that he has learned his lesson:

> Well, while I live I'll fear no other thing
> So sore, as keeping safe Nerissa's ring. (5.1.306–7)

If, on the purely literal level, the play ends with an unequivocal defense of the indissolubility of Christian marriage, it also ends, on an allegorical level, with an equally unequivocal affirmation of faith in Christ and his Church. Remembering that Shakespeare often employs marriage as a metaphor for the mystical relationship of Christ the Bridegroom with his Bride, the Church, it can be seen that the rings symbolize the indissoluble bond between Christ and his Church. By extension, the rings also symbolize the relationship between Christ and the individual Christian, and the relationship between the individual Christian and the Church. Since Portia serves more comfortably as an image of the Church than as an image of Christ, it could be argued that the last of these allegorical relationships, that between the individual and the Church, is the one at the forefront of the applicable significance of the play's final denouement. If this is so, the constant reminder throughout the play of the fate of Robert Southwell, as a living example of one who was true to his bond even unto torture and death, is particularly powerful. Similarly it could be seen that Bassanio's infidelity to Portia is an image of the average Christian's infidelity to the Church, and Shakespeare's urging of his fellow countrymen to return to the Bride of Christ, to which they are solemnly and indissolubly bound, even if it means hazarding their very lives.

But is not this serious moral meaning negated by the seemingly frivolous form that Shakespeare adopts for the play as a whole and the last
scene in particular? Can a play that culminates in a riot of double entendres and sexual innuendo be taken seriously as a conveyer of any meaningful moral? Does not the farce remove the force of the morality?
Does it not render any apparent moral null and void? Does it not perhaps even invert the moral, turning it into nothing more than an ironic
sneer at convention? Such are the questions raised by some postmodern
critics. The problem is that such questions are asked by those who are
clueless about the real nature of religious belief. Take, for example, the
heady mixture of wit and wisdom with which Portia greets the return
of Bassanio:

> Let me give light, but let me not be light,
> For a light wife doth make a heavy husband,
> And never be Bassanio so for me—
> But God sort all! You are welcome home, my lord. (5.1.129–32)

A passage such as this is often glossed in such a way that the emphasis
is placed on the sexual innuendo embedded in the reference to "a light
wife", i.e., an unchaste wife who gives herself lightly to other men,
thereby making a cuckold of her "heavy husband", whereas the deeper
and far more important connection between "Let me give light" and
the implied allusions to Scripture are usually ignored. Ironically, the
prurience of such a reading is akin to Puritanism in the sense that both
the prurient and puritanical reader fail to see the ease with which Portia blends light and lightheartedness. There is, for Portia, and for Shakespeare, no friction between the light of faith and the lightheartedness of
humor. For the Christian, *joie de vivre* and *joie de foi* go hand in hand.
They are very comfortable bedfellows. It is only the nonplussed nonbeliever who thinks that Christians need to "lighten up", whereas, in
fact, the nonbeliever is far more uptight about the presence of morality
than is the Christian about the presence of bawdy humor. "Angels can
fly because they can take themselves lightly", wrote G. K. Chesterton,
whereas "Satan fell by the force of gravity." [5] Nobody takes himself
more seriously than the Devil, and this diabolical tendency is evident in
those postmodern Shakespeare critics who, knowingly or unknowingly,
are of the Devil's party. Such people take the jokes too seriously and

[5] G. K. Chesterton, *Orthodoxy* (London: John Lane, 1908), pp. 223–24.

the moral not seriously enough. This is a serious flaw that leaves those so afflicted utterly unable to read the Bard objectively.

The tragedy of the postmodern critic is that he cannot rise above the nihilistic sneer that is the nearest that the wingless humor of irony ever gets to laughter. Here we shall leave them, grounded in the gutters of Venice, while the true Shakespearean flies with Portia beyond the bounds of Belmont to the realm of real Comedy, where we join the Bard in the purgatorial heights and the paradisal sphere, in which we will find him in the immortal company of that other great poet, Dante, who is his only literary rival.

# 13

## TO BE OR TO SEEM TO BE:
## THAT IS THE QUESTION

And let me speak to th' yet unknowing world
How these things came about. So shall you hear
Of carnal, bloody, and unnatural acts;
Of accidental judgments, casual slaughters;
Of deaths put on by cunning and forc'd cause;
And, in this upshot, purposes mistook
Fall'n on th' inventors' heads—all this can I
Truly deliver. (5.2.371–78)[1]

The first documentary record of Shakespeare's *Hamlet* is its entry in the Stationers' Register on July 26, 1602, but the play itself seems to have been written and performed as early as 1598.[2] Shakespeare's principal source for the play was an earlier play of the same name, based on an old Norse folktale that scholars now call the *Ur-Hamlet*, meaning "original *Hamlet*", which was probably written by Thomas Kyd, best known for his *Spanish Tragedy* (c. 1589). Although Kyd's play has been lost to posterity, it seems certain that it was performed regularly by the Chamberlain's Men (Shakespeare's acting troupe) during the early 1590s, and as such, it is very likely that Shakespeare acted in it during that period. He would therefore have known the earlier play very well and was evidently prompted to write his own version of it. It is reasonable to conjecture that he chose to do so as a reaction against the tone or content of the original. Shakespeare had already been provoked into writing his play *King John* as a reaction against the anti-Catholic bias of an earlier play entitled *The Troublesome Reign of*

---

[1] All quotations from *Hamlet* are from the edition published by Ignatius Press: *Hamlet*, ed. Joseph Pearce, Ignatius Critical Editions (San Francisco: Ignatius Press, 2008).

[2] The play is mentioned in a marginal note of an edition of Chaucer published in 1598, but allusions in the play itself to events that happened after this date suggest that the final version of the play was not completed until as late as 1602.

*King John*, and a few years later, he would write *King Lear* to counter a similar bias in a play entitled *The True Chronicle History of King Leir and his three daughters*, which was possibly written by George Peele. It seems probable, therefore, that Shakespeare wrote *Hamlet* to counter aspects of the earlier play with which he disapproved and to which he wished to make a literary riposte. Since the *Ur-Hamlet* is no longer extant, it is impossible to know what exactly Shakespeare found objectionable in the earlier version, but the fact that Kyd was tried and imprisoned for atheism in 1593 suggests that Shakespeare sought to "baptize" the drama with his own profoundly Christian imagination.

As for the play itself, it is perhaps the most popular and well known of all Shakespeare's works and is also the longest and arguably the most difficult to understand. It has certainly puzzled generations of critics and continues to confuse and confound its readers with infuriating conundrums. Who exactly is Hamlet? Is he a noble and conscientious young man struggling heroically against "the slings and arrows of outrageous fortune", or is he a hopelessly melancholic procrastinator? And what of the Ghost of Hamlet's father? Is he who he says he is, or is he (or it) a demon hell-bent on bringing murder and anarchy to the kingdom of Denmark? And then there is Ophelia. Does Hamlet love her, or is his love, like his madness, merely feigned? And is Ophelia an innocent lamb who is slaughtered by the sins of others, or is she in some way culpable for her own madness and death? On a panoramic level, does the play present a moral vision of reality signaling the triumph of Christian hope, or does it point to the chasm of nihilistic despair?

These puzzles, according to Peter Milward, "are more than enough to turn *Hamlet* from a revenge tragedy to a problem play. No wonder we are left at the end with a feeling rather of bewilderment than of catharsis! No room is left for tears, as at the end of *King Lear*, but only for scratching of the head."[3] The great Samuel Johnson went beyond merely scratching his head in bewilderment at the conundrums and apparent contradictions of the play to an outright condemnation of what he perceived as its deficiencies:

> The poet is accused of having shewn little regard to poetical justice, and may be charged with equal neglect of poetical probability. The apparition left the regions of the dead to little purpose; the revenge which he demands

---

[3] Peter Milward, *Shakespeare's Meta-drama: "Hamlet" and "Macbeth"* (Tokyo: Renaissance Institute, 2003), p. 18.

is not obtained but by the death of him that was required to take it; and
the gratification which would arise from the destruction of an usurper and
a murderer, is abated by the untimely death of Ophelia, the young, the beautiful, the harmless, and the pious.[4]

Similarly, T. S. Eliot insisted that *Hamlet*, "far from being Shakespeare's masterpiece . . . is most certainly an artistic failure", adding that
"the play is puzzling, and disquieting as is none of the others. . . . We
must simply admit that here Shakespeare tackled a problem which proved
too much for him. Why he attempted it at all is an insoluble puzzle."[5]
It might be considered dangerous, or foolhardy even, to beg to differ
with literary *eminenti* such as Samuel Johnson and T. S. Eliot. Yet Eliot, a
much better practitioner of great poetry than he is a critic of it, is certainly being foolishly audacious in his dismissing of *Hamlet* as an "artistic
failure" and is guilty of a critical non sequitur in apparently connecting
this "failure" with the "puzzling" and "disquieting" aspects of the play.
A play, or a poem, can be both puzzling and disquieting without being a
failure, something of which the author of "The Waste Land" should scarcely
need reminding![6] There is also a hint of arrogance in Eliot's claim that
Shakespeare might have bitten off more than he could chew in tackling
*Hamlet*. Had Shakespeare really "tackled a problem which proved too much
for him", or had he simply tackled a problem that proved too much for
the critic? And as for "insoluble puzzles", it is crucial to remember the
difference between a puzzle that is really, objectively, insoluble—i.e., it has
no solution—from a puzzle that is only insoluble to the individual attempt-
ing to solve it. In the latter case the problem is not with the puzzle but
with the one who is puzzled!

There is no denying that *Hamlet* continues to puzzle the critics, but that
does not mean that the puzzle does not have a solution. A puzzle may *seem*
insoluble to the perplexed and apoplexed critic, but it *is* soluble in spite
of the critic's inability to solve it. "*Seems*, madam!" says Hamlet to his

---

[4] Samuel Johnson, *Johnson on Shakespeare: Essays and Notes Selected and Set Forth with an
Introduction by Walter Raleigh* (London: Oxford University Press, 1908), p. 196.

[5] T. S. Eliot, "Hamlet and His Problems", in *Selected Essays* (New York: Harcourt Brace
Jovanovich, 1950), reprinted in William Shakespeare, *Hamlet*, ed. Cyrus Hoy, 2nd ed. (New
York: W. W. Norton, 1992), pp. 181–84.

[6] I am aware, in fairness, that I am guilty of oversimplifying Eliot's critique of *Hamlet* in
making this juxtaposition, but I think that it highlights the kernel of Eliot's problem in
understanding the play, *viz.*, that since Eliot does not understand the play himself there is,
ipso facto, nothing to understand.

mother. "Nay, it *is*; I know not seems" (1.2.76, emphasis added). And it is perhaps the crucial difference between that which *is* and that which only *seems* to be that holds the key to solving the problem that is *Hamlet* and the equally perplexing problem of who Hamlet is.

> Seems, madam! Nay, it is; I know not seems.
> 'Tis not alone my inky cloak, good mother,
> Nor customary suits of solemn black,
> Nor windy suspiration of forc'd breath,
> No, nor the fruitful river in the eye,
> Nor the dejected haviour of the visage,
> Together with all forms, moods, shapes of grief,
> That can denote me truly. These, indeed, seem,
> For they are actions that a man might play;
> But I have that within which passes show—
> These but the trappings and the suits of woe. (1.2.76–86)

In these few words to his mother, Hamlet is exhibiting a deep understanding of metaphysics. He is echoing Aristotle and Saint Thomas Aquinas in his distinction between the *essence* of things and their *accidental* qualities. At its deepest level of meaning, *Hamlet* works on this metaphysical and ontological level. The play deals with *definitions*, with the meanings of things, and with the distinction between those things that essentially *are* and those that only *seem* to be. It is about what things *mean*, not about what things *seem*. And it is about learning to discover the difference between the two. It is the quest for the definite amid the clouds of unknowing. And this is the seemingly insurmountable problem that many critics face when approaching *Hamlet*. As philosophical materialists who see only the physical facts and not the metaphysical truth, such critics are blinded by their ignorance of classical and medieval philosophy from seeing the depths of truth that emerge in Shakespeare's plays.[7] In order to plumb these depths, we need to understand *Hamlet* as its author understood it, and in order to do that, we need to see the play through the playwright's profoundly Christian eyes. This inescapable truth was understood by the Shakespearean critic E. M. W. Tillyard, who emphasized Shakespeare's breadth of spiritual vision in *Hamlet*:

---

[7] Eliot is doubly damned here, of course, because unlike many of his contemporaries, he was well versed in the classical and medieval ethos and was a disciple of Dante, the medieval par excellence.

I doubt if in any other play of Shakespeare there is so strong an impression of the total range of creation from the angels to the beasts. Maybe in the *Tempest* the lower stretches of the chain of being and the doubtful stretches between man and angel are more fully presented, but the angels and man's variety in his own great stretch of the chain are presented there with less emphasis. This way of looking at creation is powerfully traditional and Christian; and in *Hamlet* if anywhere in Shakespeare we notice the genealogy from the Miracle Plays with their setting of Heaven, Purgatory, and Hell, as for instance in the hero's description of himself as a fellow "crawling between heaven and earth". . . . *Hamlet* is one of the most medieval as well as one of the most acutely modern of Shakespeare's plays. And though the theme of spiritual regeneration may be absent from the plot, the setting includes the religious consciousness most eminently.[8]

The only questionable aspect of Tillyard's otherwise excellent appraisal of the "religious consciousness" of the play is his assertion that "spiritual regeneration may be absent from the plot". This is not the case. Hamlet begins, tempted to suicide, in the Slough of Despond, bogged down by the sins of others more than by his own transgressions, and ends with firm resolution and a serene resignation to the will of God:

Not a whit, we defy augury: there is a special providence in the fall of a sparrow. If it be now, 'tis not to come; if it be not to come, it will be now; if it be not now, yet it will come—the readiness is all. Since no man owes of aught he leaves, what is't to leave betimes? Let be. (5.2.211–16)

Hamlet has come a long way from the near-suicidal despondency of his first soliloquy in act 1 to this willing acceptance in act 5 of the benignity of God's providence and his knowledge that "the readiness is all." In between, he has descended Dante-like into the infernal depths and, like Dante, emerges through purgatorial fire into the gracious acceptance of the love of God. This is "spiritual regeneration" at its most sublime, albeit Shakespeare, unlike Dante, leaves his vision of paradise offstage, apart, that is, from the scantiest of glimpses offered in passing as the plot unfolds.

It is perhaps the "readiness" of Hamlet in the play's final scene that provides the other key to solving the puzzle at the play's beguiling heart. If the quest for true meaning, inherent in the discernment of that which is from that which seems, is the means by which Hamlet finds himself,

[8] E. M. W. Tillyard, *Shakespeare's Problem Plays* (London: University of Toronto Press, 1950), pp. 29–30.

then "the readiness is all" is the ultimate end, the very purpose of the play itself. The play reaches its own readiness, its own ripeness, in the readiness of Hamlet to put his trust in God. Hamlet's conversion of heart makes him ready to meet whatever providence may bring. His "readiness" has made him ripe for the picking—and ripe for the pricking by the envenomed foil. He is ready to meet his Maker and is therefore ready to die. "If it be now", so be it—or "let be", to employ Hamlet's precise words. Since "let be" is most commonly rendered in English usage as "Amen", it elevates these words from the level of mere dialogue with Horatio to the level of prayer, i.e., dialogue with God. Hamlet's words represent a doxology, offering formal praise to God for his revealing to Hamlet of the ultimate truth that makes sense of all the apparent contradictions that have bedeviled the play's unraveling. If, as Hamlet now believes, "there is a special providence in the fall of a sparrow", he knows also, from the following words from Matthew's Gospel, from which these lines are plucked, that he has nothing to fear from death: "Fear ye not therefore, ye are of more value than many sparrows."[9] Hamlet's resolve, his resolution, is the resolution of the problem that the play poses. The resolution of the seemingly insoluble problems of life is to be found in Christ alone.

At this point, one is sure to meet the objection of many that such a solution is not only too simple but too simplistic. What of the questions posed at the outset? What of the apparent bloodlust of Hamlet? What are we to make of the Ghost's own apparent bloodlust? And what of poor Ophelia, canonized so eloquently by Samuel Johnson as "the young, the beautiful, the harmless, and the pious"? And what of Hamlet's relationship with Ophelia, in which Hamlet treats her, in Johnson's judgment, "with so much rudeness, which seems to be useless and wanton cruelty"?[10] If Hamlet is a hero, how are we to account for his murderous hatred and his "wanton cruelty"?

These are good questions that will have to be answered if we are to make sense of the play. Once again, however, we can answer these questions only if we are able to see through the eyes of the playwright himself.

---

[9] Matthew 10:31.
[10] Johnson, *Johnson on Shakespeare*, p. 196.

# 14

# HAMLET AND THE GHOST

Let us begin with Hamlet himself. It has been suggested by many critics that Shakespeare may have sought to "politicize" the drama with his own semiconcealed sympathy for the Earl of Essex, who is believed to have been the model for the character of Hamlet.[1] In 1598, the year in which *Hamlet* was written and first performed, the Earl of Essex had quarreled with the queen and had complained bitterly of his treatment at Elizabeth's hands: "When the vilest of all indignities are done unto me, doth religion enforce me to sue? or doth God require it? Is it impiety not to do it? What, cannot princes err? cannot subjects receive wrong? Is an earthly power or authority infinite?"[2] In the following year, Essex concluded an armistice with the Irish rebel leader Tyrone that promised that Catholic worship in Ireland would be tolerated. The armistice served to further alienate Essex from the queen's favor, and when he returned to England he was placed under house arrest.

Shakespeare's admiration for Essex is not really in question, and it has been suggested that allusions to Essex appear in *The Merchant of Venice*, *King John*, *Troilus and Cressida*, *Henry V*, and Shakespeare's cryptic poem "The Phoenix and the Turtle". It is also significant that Sir Charles Percy and a number of other supporters of Essex arranged for Shakespeare's company to stage a performance of *Richard II* on the eve of the Essex rebellion in the hope that the play's depiction of the deposing of a monarch would incite the people of London to rise up against Elizabeth. It is, however, as the model for Hamlet that the Earl of Essex is most obviously present in the Bard's work, and it will be necessary to discuss this connection, and its implications, more closely if we are to get to grips with this most difficult of Shakespeare's plays. As we look

[1] J. Dover Wilson, in *The Essential Shakespeare* (1932), is the most prominent of those who argue that the Earl of Essex was the model for the characterization of Hamlet.

[2] Alison Weir, *The Life of Elizabeth I* (New York: Random House, 1999), p. 436.

at the play's metadrama, we will see the ghostly presence of Essex looming over the action as palpably as the presence of the Ghost itself.

Although Essex was himself a Protestant, he promised toleration of
Catholicism if his planned rebellion succeeded in deposing the queen.
When, at the beginning of 1601, the rebellion failed, Essex was executed,
and the Earl of Southampton, Shakespeare's patron and one of Essex' closest allies, was imprisoned in the Tower of London. At his trial, Essex was
accused of being a papist, or papist sympathizer, but he went to his death
protesting that he remained a Protestant. Essex can therefore be seen as a
representative of all those subjects of the queen who found themselves alien-
ated from her because of her persecution of them on grounds of politics
or religion. Shakespeare's own father had been fined for his recusancy,[3]
as had many of Shakespeare's closest friends, and his patron, Southampton, was a well-known Catholic with many connections to the Catholic
underground. To speak openly of one's disapproval of the queen was dangerous, possibly deadly, and one can see the parallels between the position of Elizabethan dissidents and those of the despondent and disillusioned
Hamlet in the words of his first soliloquy, particularly perhaps in its final
words: "But break, my heart, for I must hold my tongue" (1.2.159).

Since Shakespeare did not write formal allegories, we cannot say that
Hamlet is a personification of Essex. This is clearly not the case. But
we can say that there is much of Essex and his angst-driven rebellious-
ness against the injustices of the monarch in the characterization of
Hamlet. We can also say that there is much of the plight of the Catholic recusant in Hamlet's sense of alienation and in his anger at the
injustices of the powers that be. And yet Hamlet, like Essex, is not a
Catholic. We are informed on several occasions that he has studied at
Wittenberg, the university at which Martin Luther taught, which is
generally considered to be the birthplace of the Protestant Reformation. Clearly, since Wittenberg is gratuitous to the development of the
plot and is not present in the folk tradition that serves as the play's
source, Shakespeare has deliberately infused an element of contemporary religious controversy into the play. And yet he does so in a way
that suggests that his sympathies are not with the Reformers or, at least,
that he regards them with a marked ambivalence. It could be argued,
and indeed has been argued, that much of Hamlet's angst-driven intro-
spection in the early parts of the play are the result of his grappling

---

[3] Recusants were Catholics who refused, in conscience, to attend Anglican services.

with the inadequacies of Protestant theology, and the pun on the Diet of Worms[4] in Hamlet's description of Polonius' corpse is decidedly distasteful (4.3.20–23). It is true that the good and noble Horatio studied at Wittenberg, but it is equally true that the corrupt and ignoble spies Rosencrantz and Guildenstern were also alumni of the same university.

If Hamlet appears to be a Protestant of sorts, it is curious that the Ghost of his father is indubitably Catholic. We know as much from the Ghost's description of his own death:

> Cut off even in the blossoms of my sin,
> Unhous'led, disappointed, unanel'd;
> No reck'ning made, but sent to my account
> With all my imperfections on my head.
> O, horrible! O, horrible! most horrible! (1.5.76–80)

The archaisms *unhous'led*, *disappointed*, and *unanel'd* refer to the Catholic sacraments of Communion, penance (confession), and extreme unction (last rites, or anointing of the sick), all of which were snatched away from him by his sudden death, leaving him cut off in the blossoms of his sin, with all his imperfections on his head. It is for these unabsolved sins that he is being punished, not for the fact that King Claudius has not been punished for murdering him. It is imperative that this crucial fact be noted and remembered, not least because it saves us from the error of believing that Hamlet has to avenge his father so that his Ghost can rest in peace. This is emphatically not the case. As we shall see below, Hamlet's "vengeance" is demanded by justice, by the moral law, and has nothing to do with his father's punishment for his own sins. The Ghost's sins will be "purg'd away" through suffering regardless of whether Hamlet brings King Claudius to justice.

The other evidence for the Ghost's Catholicism is in his final words to Hamlet at their first meeting: "Adieu, adieu, adieu! Remember me" (1.5.91). This is much more than a mere farewell, a fact to which Hamlet testifies when he repeats these words to himself after the Ghost has departed (1.5.111). The Ghost is saying: "To God, to God, to God! Remember me (in your prayers)." The theologians of the Protestant Reformation had poured scorn upon the practice of praying for the dead, dismissing such

---

[4] The Diet of Worms was a general assembly of the estates of the Holy Roman Empire, held in Worms, a small German town, in 1521, at which Martin Luther famously defended his Ninety-five Theses.

pious practices as "papist superstition". And yet here we see the dead actually requesting the prayers of the living. Furthermore, and this is further evidence of Shakespeare's intimate knowledge of Catholic prayers and practices, Hamlet does as his father's spirit has asked of him when he utters the Latin phrase *hic et ubique*, which is a reference to a Catholic prayer for the dead (1.5.156). Although the phrase is usually glossed in isolation and out of context as meaning simply "here and everywhere", it should be seen in the context of the whole prayer, to which, given the context, it is clearly an allusion: "Pro animabus famulorum, famularumque tuarum, et omnium catholicorum hic et ubique in Christo dormientium, hostiam, Domine, suscipe benignus oblatam: ut hoc sacrificio singulari, vinculis horrendae mortis exuti, vitam mereantur aeternam." (For the souls of your servants, and for all Catholics *here and everywhere* who sleep in Christ, receive this Host, Lord, our kind oblation: that those whose horrible chains have been cast off by your singular sacrifice may, by that same sacrifice, be rewarded with eternal life.) [5]

Such evidence proves not only that the Ghost is a Catholic but, crucially, that Catholicism is objectively true. The Ghost has the eyes of eternity. He sees things as they *are* and not merely as they *seem* from the perspective of those trapped in the tunneled vision of time. The living *believe* that something is true or false; the dead *know* the true from the false. The Ghost is, therefore, our most reliable witness to that which *is*, as opposed to that which merely *seems*. This is made clear from his bloodcurdling intimations of what awaits the sinner after death:

> But that I am forbid
> To tell the secrets of my prison-house,
> I could a tale unfold whose lightest word
> Would harrow up thy soul, freeze thy young blood,
> Make thy two eyes, like stars, start from their spheres,
> Thy knotted and combined locks to part,
> And each particular hair to stand an end,
> Like quills upon the fretful porpentine.
> But this eternal blazon must not be
> To ears of flesh and blood. (1.5.13–22)

---

[5] In this context, *hic et ubique* translates as part of the prayer "to all who *here or elsewhere* sleep in Christ". See "For all who are buried in a cemetery or graveyard", Various Prayers for the Dead, in *The Daily Missal and Liturgical Manual* (London: Baronius Press, 2007), p. 1711.

Clearly the Ghost sees and knows things far beyond the ken of those who have not yet shuffled off this mortal coil. Unless, of course, the Ghost is not what he seems but is a demon from hell. This, then, is another crucial question. Is the play's most reliable witness to the really real really reliable?

Horatio gives us the first clue that the Ghost is genuinely the purgatorial spirit of Hamlet's father when he tells Hamlet that the Ghost had a "countenance more in sorrow than in anger" (1.2.231), suggesting a penitential spirit from purgatory, not a demon loosed from hell—and suggesting also that his desire is for justice, not vengeance. Yet the Ghost could be a liar, a fake father posing as a penitent, and Hamlet himself is unsure whether the Ghost is friend or foe. Mindful of his earlier words to his mother that he knows not "seems"—those "actions that a man might play", i.e., feign—but that he demands to know what something *is*, "that within which passes show", he demands to know of the Ghost whether he is really his father's spirit or whether he is a deceiving demon wearing "but the trappings and the suits of woe":

> Angels and ministers of grace defend us!
> Be thou a spirit of health or goblin damn'd,
> Bring with thee airs from heaven or blasts from hell,
> Be thy intents wicked or charitable,
> Thou com'st in such a questionable shape
> That I will speak to thee. (1.4.39–44)

The Ghost answers that he is "thy father's spirit",

> Doom'd for a certain term to walk the night,
> And for the day confin'd to fast in fires,
> Till the foul crimes done in my days of nature
> Are burnt and purg'd away. (1.5.9–13)

He is, therefore, a soul in purgatory, "a spirit of health" destined for heaven once his sins are purged, and not a "goblin damn'd". But do we believe him? Is he what he seems? What, for instance, are we to make of his demand that Hamlet is to avenge his death? Is it plausible that "a spirit of health" would demand an eye for an eye instead of following Christ's commandment that we love our enemies and turn the other cheek? Is the Ghost guilty of a bloodlustful desire for revenge that exposes him as an infernal impostor posing as Hamlet's father? Or is he merely seeking justice? This is another crucial question.

Although the Ghost uses the word "revenge", he is referring to the fact that there is a cold-blooded murderer on the loose who has escaped the justice of the law. Is the ministration of justice and the desire that the criminal should pay for his crime reprehensible or unchristian? Should King Claudius go unpunished? Is it not Hamlet's duty to unmask the criminal and the crime? Surely there can be no question that he has a duty to expose King Claudius' heinous actions once the Ghost has told him of them.

This follows if, of course, the Ghost is telling the truth. Hamlet is at first convinced that he is, declaring after their first meeting that it is "an honest ghost" (1.5.138). Yet Hamlet is healthily skeptical and devises the staging of a play not only to "catch the conscience of the King" but to test the veracity of the Ghost:

> The spirit that I have seen
> May be a devil; and the devil hath power
> T' assume a pleasing shape; yea, and perhaps
> Out of my weakness and my melancholy,
> As he is very potent with such spirits,
> Abuses me to damn me. I'll have grounds
> More relative than this. The play's the thing
> Wherein I'll catch the conscience of the King. (2.2.594–601)

It is evident from such lines that Hamlet's procrastination and apparent inability to take decisive action are not a damnable weakness on his part but that, on the contrary, they are born of virtuous circumspection and a determination that he must become the minister of justice, not the perpetrator of injustice. His delay is the triumph of prudence over prejudice, of that which *is* over that which *seems*. And lest we forget Shakespeare's purpose in highlighting the reason for Hamlet's tardiness, we are reminded once again that Hamlet must know that the guilty party is indeed King Claudius and not the Ghost before he can act with a clear conscience:

> If his occulted guilt
> Do not itself unkennel in one speech,
> It is a damned ghost that we have seen,
> And my imaginations are as foul
> As Vulcan's stithy. (3.2.78–82)

In the event, of course, the King's guilt is exposed and the Ghost is indeed shown to be "honest".

The very concept of an "honest ghost" places the Ghost of *Hamlet* outside the accepted Protestant understanding of ghosts as set forth most notably and notoriously by King James VI of Scotland, later to become James I of England, in his book *Daemonology*, published in 1597, around the time that Shakespeare was contemplating the writing of *Hamlet*. King James considered ghosts to be evil demons, and it is this view of ghosts that animates Hamlet's doubts about whether the Ghost is really the shade of his dead father or whether it is a "damned" spirit sent to deceive him. The fact that the Ghost emerges as an apparition of the soul of Hamlet's father, who is experiencing the cleansing suffering of purgatory, represents an affirmation of a Catholic understanding of ghosts over its Protestant counterpart.

# 15

## OPHELIA

It is almost time to turn our attention to the unfortunate Ophelia, but before we do so, it is necessary to know more about her father, Polonius, and her brother, Laertes.

Like the Fool in *King Lear*, Polonius is a pragmatist par excellence. His worldly philosophy, as expounded in his advice to his son, is devoid of all supernatural insight and divorced from any Christian concept of virtue. It is, therefore, interesting that Shakespeare exhibits his own contempt for such a philosophy through his incarnation of it in such a disreputable character. The "few precepts" that Polonius gives to Laertes are all designed to further his son's worldly advancement and are summarized in the phrase "This above all—to thine own self be true" (1.3.78). Such a phrase, imbued with the fashionable humanism of the late Renaissance, has little to do with the Christian humanism of Shakespeare or Saint Thomas More and more to do with the secular humanism of Niccolò Machiavelli. Indeed, it could be argued that Hamlet, who has an almost obsessive desire to do what is morally right and just in the face of "outrageous fortune", is Shakespeare's riposte to Machiavelli's "Prince", incarnate in *Hamlet* as King Claudius, who would resort to any means, however treacherous, to maintain his authority. Machiavelli's *Prince*, published in 1532, was condemned by Pope Clement VIII, and Shakespeare's agreement with the pope's position is evident in his condemnation of Machiavellianism in many of his finest plays.

If Polonius is clearly depicted as one of the play's villains, his son, Laertes, is an altogether more complex character. In contrast to the banality of Polonius' precepts, Laertes' advice to his sister with regard to her relationship with Hamlet is full of astute political philosophy:

> Perhaps he loves you now,
> And now no soil nor cautel doth besmirch
> The virtue of his will; but you must fear,

His greatness weigh'd, his will is not his own;
For he himself is subject to his birth:
He may not, as unvalued persons do,
Carve for himself; for on his choice depends
The sanity and health of this whole state;
And therefore must his choice be circumscrib'd
Unto the voice and yielding of that body
Whereof he is the head. Then if he says he loves you,
It fits your wisdom so far to believe it
As he in his particular act and place
May give his saying deed; which is no further
Than the main voice of Denmark goes withal. (1.3.14–28)

Laertes is fearful of his sister's relationship with Hamlet and urges her to share his fear: "Fear it, Ophelia, fear it, my dear sister" (1.3.33). He knows that as prince and heir to the realm, Hamlet must always put his duty before his desire. Answerable, ultimately, to his duties to the state of Denmark, Hamlet is not in a position to allow his heart to rule his head. Since Ophelia is not of royal lineage, she should not expect that Hamlet will marry her, and as such, she should preserve her honor by distancing herself from the relationship. These words are painful for Ophelia, but she sees the wisdom that they convey and reluctantly agrees to heed her brother's advice:

I shall the effect of this good lesson keep
As watchman to my heart. (1.3.45–46)

There seems to be a great prescience in Laertes' words. Hamlet does indeed seem to forsake his love for Ophelia as soon as his duty to his father and to Denmark becomes apparent to him. And yet how genuine was Hamlet's love for Ophelia? Laertes seems willing to give Hamlet the benefit of the doubt, believing that perhaps Hamlet does love Ophelia and that the "virtue of his will" is not tainted by unhealthy desires. Polonius, on the other hand, sees nothing but lustful cynicism in the prince's courting of his daughter and calls her a fool to have been taken in by his amorous advances. Ever the cynic himself, Polonius is quick to see cynical desires in others. Stung by his rebuke, Ophelia protests that Hamlet's motives had always appeared honorable:

My lord, he hath importun'd me with love
In honourable fashion.

. . . . . . . . . . . . . . . . . . . . .

And hath given countenance to his speech, my lord,
With almost all the holy vows of heaven. (1.3.110–11, 113–14)

Who is right? Polonius or Ophelia? The worldly cynic who sees only
worldly cynicism in Hamlet's motives? Or the naïve romantic who sees
only true, honorable love, fortified with "the holy vows of heaven"?
The issue continues to confound the critics, even the best of them,
such as A. C. Bradley, who confessed that he was filled with doubt concerning the nature of Hamlet's love for Ophelia:

> I am unable to arrive at a conviction as to the meaning of some of his
> words and deeds, and I question whether from the mere text of the play
> a sure interpretation of them can be drawn. . . .
>   On two points no reasonable doubt can, I think, be felt. (1) Hamlet
> was at one time sincerely and ardently in love with Ophelia. For she
> herself says that he had importuned her with love in honourable fashion,
> and had given countenance to his speech with almost all the holy vows
> of heaven. . . . (2) When at Ophelia's grave, he declared,
>
>> I loved Ophelia; forty thousand brothers
>> Could not, with all their quantity of love,
>> Make up my sum,
>
> He must have spoken sincerely; and, further, we may take it for granted
> that he used the past tense, "loved," merely because Ophelia was dead,
> and not to imply that he had once loved her but no longer did so.[1]

Perhaps Bradley is himself guilty of naïve credulity in accepting at face
value Hamlet's wooing of Ophelia, but he is surely on safer ground in his
insistence that Hamlet spoke sincerely at Ophelia's grave. We can, therefore, assume fairly safely that Hamlet's love for Ophelia was genuine and
was not, like his madness, merely feigned for ulterior motives. And yet
his love, if genuine, prompts further questions. Bearing in mind his duties
to the state of Denmark, was his dallying with a love that he could presumably never consummate in marriage an act of reprehensible folly? Was
his relationship with Ophelia always doomed to end in his beloved's broken heart? If so, it accentuates the aspect of spiritual regeneration in Hamlet's character as the play progresses toward its purposed end. He begins

[1] A. C. Bradley, *Shakespearean Tragedy: Lectures on "Hamlet", "Othello", "King Lear", "Macbeth"* (London: Macmillan, 1952), p. 153.

as a self-centered, self-absorbed wooer of women whom he can never marry
and ends with a serene acceptance of his place in God's providence.

But what of poor Ophelia? Is she really "the young, the beautiful,
the harmless, and the pious" icon that Samuel Johnson makes of her?
And what of Hamlet's treatment of her "with so much rudeness . . . and
wanton cruelty"? Is Ophelia an innocent lamb slaughtered on the altar
of other men's sins? Or does she share some measure of blame for her
own fate?

Taking her father's and her brother's advice, Ophelia distances herself
from Hamlet's advances, thereby adding to his sense of desolation. She
is, however, scarcely to blame for heeding the advice and warnings of
her own family or for being obedient to her father's wishes, especially
if Laertes is correct in his assessment that Hamlet can never marry her.
But let us see things from Hamlet's perspective. His troubled state of
mind as he enters what has become known as the nunnery scene is
made apparent by the near-suicidal depths to which he plunges in his
famous soliloquy:

> To be, or not to be—that is the question;
> Whether 'tis nobler in the mind to suffer
> The slings and arrows of outrageous fortune,
> Or to take arms against a sea of troubles,
> And by opposing end them? (3.1.56–60)

This is Hamlet at his closest to the disgraced and disgruntled Earl of
Essex, weighing the options of suffering the injustices heaped upon him
or of rising in rebellion against them. It is also Hamlet at his closest to
the English recusants who must suffer the slings and arrows of outrageous persecution for their Catholic faith or take up arms in the hope
of overthrowing their persecutors. We need to remember that Shakespeare was not only sympathetic to the Earl of Essex but that all the
evidence suggests that he was himself a Catholic. Furthermore, several
members of his mother's family were involved in taking up arms against
Queen Elizabeth's government in various "papist plots" and were subsequently executed for their involvement. The questions that Hamlet
agonizes over in the famous soliloquy are an exact echo of the questions over which England's Catholics agonized: to be a Catholic and
suffer temporal persecution, or not to be a Catholic and suffer the possibility of eternal punishment for the sin of apostasy. And for those who
choose the former of these two options, a further dilemma arises: to

suffer in stoic silence, or to rise up in anger against the tyrants. That is
the question.

> For who would bear the whips and scorns of time,
> Th' oppressor's wrong, the proud man's contumely,
> The pangs of despis'd love, the law's delay,
> The insolence of office, and the spurns
> That patient merit of th' unworthy takes,
> When he himself might his quietus make
> With a bare bodkin? (3.1.70–76)

Hamlet's predicament has brought him to the brink of suicide, and
we should note that the "pangs of despis'd love" are included among
the list of those burdens weighing heavily on his mind. It seems, therefore, that Ophelia's spurning of him has added to his other cares. It is
only Hamlet's Christian conscience, or at any rate his fear of hell, that
keeps him from acting upon his desire to end his own life:

> Who would these fardels bear,
> To grunt and sweat under a weary life,
> But that the dread of something after death—
> The undiscover'd country, from whose bourn
> No traveller returns—puzzles the will,
> And makes us rather bear those ills we have
> Than fly to others that we know not of? (3.1.76–82)

It is from these depths of despondency that Hamlet first sees Ophelia,
reading a book of prayers, and his initial reaction is anything but cruel:

> The fair Ophelia.—Nymph, in thy orisons [prayers]
> Be all my sins rememb'red. (3.1.88–89)

And yet almost immediately, his mood changes. The (feigned) madness
comes upon him, and he speaks in most unkind riddles to his former
love. Surely this is nothing but "wanton cruelty". Yet his crime of cruelty, though real, is a *crime passionel*, a crime of passion, especially if he
suspects or knows that Ophelia is now working against him as a spy,
gathering information on her father's and King Claudius' behalf. Does
Hamlet know that Polonius and King Claudius are listening to their
conversation? In the absence of stage directions, it is difficult to know
for certain, but the text itself offers tantalizing clues that Hamlet does
indeed know that Ophelia has betrayed him to his enemies. "Ha, ha!

Are you honest?" he asks suddenly, prompting a nervous response from Ophelia, who has perhaps given herself away as a very unconvincing spy. Later he asks, suddenly and for no apparent reason, "Where's your father?" prompting another nervous and lying response from Ophelia. In this context, Hamlet's cruel words to Ophelia take on new life:

> I have heard of your paintings too, well enough; God hath given you one face, and you make yourselves another. You jig and amble, and you lisp, and nickname God's creatures, and make your wantonness your ignorance. (3.1.142–46)

It is also in this context that Hamlet's repeated insistence that Ophelia enter a nunnery takes on new significance. It is not simply that he will not marry her and that therefore she might as well resign herself to celibacy; it is that she would be better off in a convent than in the damnable intrigues and treacheries of the King's court. Better to live the religious life than to stand condemned as a spy in the service of a murderer.

Having looked at the relationship from Hamlet's perspective, let us now see it from Ophelia's:

> Consider for a moment how matters looked to *her*. She knows nothing about the Ghost and its disclosures. She has undergone for some time the pain of repelling her lover and appearing to have turned against him. She sees him, or hears of him, sinking daily into deeper gloom, and so transformed from what he was that he is considered to be out of his mind. She hears the question constantly discussed what the cause of this sad change can be; and her heart tells her—how can it fail to tell her?— that her unkindness is the chief cause. . . .
>
> Still, we are told, it was ridiculously weak in her to lose her reason. And here again her critics seem hardly to realize the situation, hardly to put themselves in the place of a girl whose love, estranged from her, goes mad and kills her father. They seem to forget also that Ophelia must have believed that these frightful calamities were not mere calamities, but followed from *her* action in repelling her lover. Nor do they realize the utter loneliness that must have fallen on her. Of the three persons who were all the world to her, her father has been killed, Hamlet has been sent out of the country insane, and her brother is abroad.[2]

2 Ibid., pp. 162–64.

A. C. Bradley's masterful treatment of Ophelia's perspective needs no further elucidation.

Having seen the relationship from Hamlet's perspective and from Ophelia's, let us look at it from Shakespeare's own perspective. How does the playwright himself view the relationship of his two lovers? Again, Bradley says all that is needed:

> Now it was essential to Shakespeare's purpose that too great an interest should not be aroused in the love-story; essential, therefore, that Ophelia should be merely one of the subordinate characters; and necessary, accordingly, that she should not be the equal, in spirit, power or intelligence, of his famous heroines. If she had been an Imogen, a Cordelia, even a Portia or a Juliet, the story must have taken another shape.... Ophelia, therefore, was made a character who could not help Hamlet, and for whom on the other hand he would not naturally feel a passion so vehement or profound as to interfere with the main motive of the play. And in the love and the fate of Ophelia herself there was introduced an element, not of deep tragedy, but of pathetic beauty, which makes the analysis of her character seem almost a desecration.[3]

Ignoring Bradley's parting injunction that we are desecrating the beauty of Ophelia if we analyze her too closely, we can conclude perhaps that her character is defined by her weakness. It was her weakness that led her to respond to Hamlet's wooing of her, forgetful of the fact that it was very unlikely that he would ever marry her; it was weakness that led her to betray Hamlet through her role as the bait that enabled King Claudius and Polonius to eavesdrop on their conversation; and perhaps, *pace* Bradley, it was weakness that led to her final loss of reason. She is certainly a great tragic figure, but as Bradley reminds us, we should not allow her tragic beauty to distract us from the deeper elements of the play. Hamlet does not allow himself to be distracted by her beauty, and nor should we. He is intent on answering the deeper questions at the dark heart of the drama, and so should we be.

[3] Ibid., p. 160.

# 16

## LIES, SPIES, AND FISHMONGERS

The deeper elements, indeed the deepest elements, of the play are to be found, as we have seen, in the difference between that which *is* and that which only *seems* to be. It is the difference between those who choose to be and those who choose not to be. This is the question to which we must now return.

Immediately after Hamlet exits from the nunnery scene, Ophelia refers to him as "[t]h' observ'd of all observers" (3.1.154), a reference to his popularity and to his being the model of courtliness and scholarship that others observed in order to emulate. He is the "glass of fashion" (3.1.153). The reader, however, sees the irony in her words because, of course, Hamlet's every word and movement in the preceding conversation has been observed from behind the arras by King Claudius and Polonius. The fact is, and as Hamlet knows, the whole of King Claudius' court is a network of spies, making it difficult to discern those who *are* who they say they are—the honest, genuine, or real—from those who are *not* who they say they are—those who only *seem* to be honest, genuine, or real. It is Hamlet's suspicion that Ophelia belongs in the latter group that fuels his anger against her.

In his almost obsessive pursuit of truth and justice, i.e., the things that truly *are* because they are rooted in an immutable moral law, Hamlet is confronted by those who are living a lie and are dealing in deceit. This conflict between the moral object and the morally objectionable is particularly evident in act 2, which is dominated by spies and espionage.

The second act begins with Polonius sending the aptly named Reynaldo[1] to spy on Laertes. He offers Reynaldo elaborate advice on the art of espionage, telling him how to deceive with deftness and dexterity and how to subvert with subtlety and suggestiveness. By the time that

---

[1]Although "Reynaldo" is derived from "king" and is unrelated etymologically to *renard* (French for "fox"), the pun is surely intentional.

Reynaldo leaves on his mission to spy on Polonius' own son, we have lost any vestiges of sympathy for Polonius. We see him for what he is, a master of intrigue who will even betray his own children in order to achieve his goals. Indeed, no sooner has Reynaldo left to spy on Laertes than Polonius begins to hatch the scheme to use his own daughter as bait, enabling him and the King to spy on Hamlet. Here we see, once again and most strikingly, the connection between the volatile action of the play and the equally volatile times in which Shakespeare was himself living. It is, in fact, almost inescapable that we should see Hamlet as the Earl of Essex or as a Catholic recusant, surrounded by spies on every side, and that we should see Polonius as William Cecil, Elizabeth's spymaster, who employed an army of spies to infiltrate England's persecuted Catholic community, intent on betraying priests to their death. Cecil, also known as Lord Burghley, was one of the most loathed figures in England, particularly among the country's Catholics, and one can sense the vitriol that the Catholic Shakespeare pours forth against Cecil in his characterization of Polonius. One senses also that Hamlet's voice is the voice of the playwright in his scathing if cryptic condemnation of Polonius:

> *Polonius.* Do you know me, my lord?
> *Hamlet.* Excellent well; you are a fish-monger.
> *Polonius.* Not I, my lord.
> *Hamlet.* Then I would you were so honest a man.
> *Polonius.* Honest, my lord!
> *Hamlet.* Ay, sir; to be honest, as this world goes, is to be one man pick'd out of ten thousand.
> *Polonius.* That's very true, my lord.
> *Hamlet.* For if the sun breed maggots in a dead dog, being a good kissing carrion—Have you a daughter?
> *Polonius.* I have, my lord.
> *Hamlet.* Let her not walk i' th' sun. Conception is a blessing. But as your daughter may conceive—friend, look to't. (2.2.172–85)

Not surprisingly perhaps, Polonius has no idea what Hamlet is talking about and takes his apparently meaningless rambling as further evidence of the prince's madness. And yet the reader of Shakespeare knows that there is often "reason in madness" to be found in the words of so-called fools and madmen. It is, for instance, impossible to read *King Lear* on any meaningful level if one fails to heed the moral lessons to be

derived from the words of the Fool or, even more so, from the words
of Poor Tom. Such "reason in madness", consisting of "matter and imper-
tinency mixed",[2] is the literary device employed by Shakespeare to elude
the unwanted attention of the state censor. In Elizabeth's England, which
was, in effect, a sort of prototype of the secularist police state, spies,
informers, and censorship were the means by which the government
kept the dissidents under control. Shakespeare, therefore, used all his
ingenuity to sidestep the censorship and make his point, however cryp-
tically. The fact that he is doing so in the above passage is hinted at by
the playwright himself when he has Polonius proclaim that there is
method in Hamlet's madness: "Though this be madness, yet there is
method in't" (2.2.203–4). And lest we do not take the playwright's first
hint, he gives us another immediately afterward:

> How pregnant sometimes his replies are! a happiness that often madness
> hits on, which reason and sanity could not so prosperously be delivered
> of. (2.2.207–10)

Clearly we are meant to take the hint and return to look at Hamlet's
words more closely. If his replies are "pregnant", we are called to act as
midwives of reason, playing our part responsibly in assisting in the birth
of the hidden meaning that they contain. In doing so, we note that a
fishmonger is not all that he seems. Indeed—and to abuse a line from
another of the Bard's plays—a fishmonger by another name would smell
even less sweet. We discover that "fishmonger" is slang for one who
procures prostitutes for another's use. Polonius is a fishmonger: one who
procures spies (prostitutes in the sense that they sell themselves into
sin) for King Claudius. And by extension, of course, William Cecil is a
"fishmonger" who procures spies for Queen Elizabeth.

There is little doubt that the playwright is venting his spleen against
the spymaster, and one senses that he "stages" the latter's death as a
vicarious way of enacting his own desired revenge on the man who was
responsible for putting his friends to death. We should not forget, for
instance, that Burghley's spy network was responsible for the capture
and subsequent torture and execution of the priests Robert Southwell
and Robert Dibdale, both of whom it seems likely that Shakespeare

---

[2] *The Tragedy of King Lear*, ed. Joseph Pearce, Ignatius Critical Editions (San Francisco:
Ignatius Press, 2008), 4.6.176–77.

knew as friends. The events of the play were, therefore, drawn far more closely from life than most of Shakespeare's critics seem to realize.[3]

Returning to the enigmatic "fishmonger" passage, we see Hamlet complain that only one man in ten thousand is "honest", i.e., that only a very small number of men *are* what they *seem*, whereas the rest, living a lie, are *not* what they *seem*. To be or not to be. That is the question. But what of the conundrum about breeding maggots in a dead dog? And why is Ophelia dragged into the conversation? Hamlet is obviously referring to the corruption and decadence of King Claudius' court and of the "fishmongers" who prosper therein. The "dead dog" is Denmark, the "something rotten" to which Marcellus refers in the opening act (1.4.90), and the maggots are presumably the sort of people who thrive amid such corruption, particularly the omnipresent spies but also perhaps the sort of fawning sycophant epitomized by Osric in act 5, whom Hamlet dismisses contemptuously as the type that this "drossy age dotes on" (5.2.184). But what of Ophelia? His introduction of her into the conversation, immediately following the graphic description, pregnant with allegorical applicability, of maggots and "good kissing carrion", suggests that Hamlet already suspects that the fishmonger, Polonius, had procured his daughter's services for the king as a spy. If this reading is correct, it makes sense of the punning on "conception" as meaning both "understanding" and "becoming pregnant". If Polonius lets his daughter "walk i' th' sun", i.e., serve that power that breeds maggots in a dead dog, Polonius may conceive, i.e., gain the knowledge that he wants, but in doing so, his daughter might also conceive, i.e., be defiled by her involvement in "kissing carrion".

King Claudius plays the spymaster himself in act 2, employing the services of Rosencrantz and Guildenstern to spy on Hamlet. The prince's discovery that his two trusted friends from Wittenberg had sold their souls to his murdering uncle adds to Hamlet's angst-ridden sense of foreboding. If his own friends prove false, whom can he trust?

At Hamlet's first meeting with Rosencrantz and Guildenstern, we suspect that he already suspects that they are in the service of King Claudius. His banter with them is awash with punning double entendres connecting their role as spies with that of a prostitute. Fortune "is

---

[3] For a detailed discussion of Shakespeare's probable friendship with Southwell and Dibdale, see Joseph Pearce, *The Quest for Shakespeare* (San Francisco: Ignatius Press, 2008), chapters 4, 5, and 9 *et passim*.

a strumpet", and Rosencrantz and Guildenstern "live about her waist" in her "secret parts" (2.2.231–35). In the same dialogue with them, he effectively calls them liars when they claim that "the world's grown honest", responding that "your news is not true." He then proclaims that "Denmark's a prison ... in which there are many confines, wards, and dungeons" (2.2.236–46). Knowing of Shakespeare's friendship with martyred priests, such as Robert Southwell, who were confined in wards, i.e., cells and dungeons, and were tortured repeatedly in the Tower of London, it seems inescapable that the playwright is using "Denmark" as a euphemism for "England", bringing the drama close to home, or as close to home as he dare. Later in the play, speaking of Rosencrantz and Guildenstern, Hamlet decries the whole business of espionage and denounces those who prostitute themselves to it:

> Why, man, they did make love to this employment;
> They are not near my conscience; their defeat
> Does by their own insinuation grow:
> 'Tis dangerous when the baser nature comes
> Between the pass and fell incensed points
> Of mighty opposites. (5.2.57–62)

Once again, we sense in these words that Hamlet's voice is Shakespeare's own, denouncing the spies who were plaguing Elizabethan England and opining that such spies deserve no sympathy when they fall victim to the treachery that they themselves employ. One wonders, in fact, if Shakespeare had the killing of Christopher Marlowe in mind as he wrote these words.[4]

If the "honesty" of spies is not what it seems, nor is the "madness" of Hamlet. Many of his most incisive observations are made under cover of such madness, and seeing the sagacity amid the folly is part of the secret to understanding the play. Not only is Hamlet perfectly sane, even when he is at his most distraught, but it almost seems on occasion that he is the only sane character among a menagerie of moral misfits. Take, for instance, his response to Polonius' supercilious comment that he will use the newly arrived players "according to their desert":

> God's bodykins, man, much better. Use every man after his desert, and who shall scape whipping? Use them after your own honour and dignity: the

---

[4] For details of Marlowe's employment as a spy and his subsequent violent death, see Pearce, *Quest for Shakespeare*, chapter 8.

less they deserve, the more merit is in your bounty. Take them in.
(2.2.521–27)

Here we see that Hamlet's sanity is rooted in a profoundly Christian understanding of the dignity of the human person and in the love and mercy of God. These are not the words of a madman but of a man maddened by the moral madness that surrounds him. "The time is out of joint", he laments at the end of act 1, adding with resentful anger that he "was born to set it right" (1.5.189–90). His sanity is the antidote to the poison that courses through the sin-cankered plot of the play. Without his heroic struggle to make sense of the madness surrounding him, nothing would make sense at all. Everything would be madness.

## 17

## TRUE MIRRORS AND DECEITFUL CLOUDS

Act 2 concludes with a soliloquy by Hamlet in which he hatches a plan to stage a play reenacting the alleged murder of his father in order to ascertain whether King Claudius was indeed the murderer:

> I have heard
> That guilty creatures, sitting at a play,
> Have by the very cunning of the scene
> Been struck so to the soul that presently
> They have proclaimed their malefactions....
>
> .  .  .  .  .  .  .  .  .  .  .  .  .  .  .  .  .  .  .
>
> The play's the thing
> Wherein I'll catch the conscience of the King. (2.2.584–88, 600–1)

In these lines, not only do we have the scene being set for the play-within-a-play in the following act, but we have an invaluable insight into Shakespeare's philosophy of art and an inkling of his own purpose in writing the play itself.

It is clear that Hamlet perceives that art has a moral purpose and function and that it can prick the conscience of those who experience it. He says much the same thing a little later when he lectures the Players on the art of acting and its purpose, "whose end, both at the first and now, was and is to hold, as 'twere, the mirror up to nature; to show virtue her own feature, scorn her own image, and the very age and body of the time his form and pressure" (3.2.21–25). Again, there is no reason to doubt that Hamlet is here the mouthpiece for Shakespeare himself and that we are seeing Shakespeare's own purpose in writing *Hamlet*—and his other plays—being elucidated. In short, Shakespeare is telling us that the purpose of his plays is to tell it like it is. His work is a mirror that shows us our virtues and our vices and that shows us the times in which we live. Since Shakespeare "is not for an age but for all time", as Ben Jonson famously remarked, he shows us ourselves and our own age through the prism of the timeless Christian morality that informs his work, but he also shows us himself and his own age as he sees it. And since "all the world's a stage", as Shakespeare tells us in *As You Like It*, his plays are themselves plays-within-a-play, serving some purpose in mirroring the plot of which they are a part but also, and crucially, capable of altering the plot profoundly, as does the staging of the play-within-a-play in act 3 of *Hamlet*. Clearly, by implication and by extension, Shakespeare hoped that his own plays would "catch the conscience of the King" (or queen) or, at any rate, that they might expose the crimes of the king (or queen). His plays, therefore, can and should be read, on one level, as a social and religious commentary on Elizabethan and Jacobean England.

In the same scene in which we are given a priceless insight into Shakespeare's vision of the meaning and purpose of his own work, the author, *in persona* Hamlet, reminds us yet again that we should pay careful attention to the "reason in madness", i.e., the wisdom, to be gleaned from the words of his so-called fools and madmen: "And let those that play your clowns speak no more than is set down for them; for there be of them that will themselves laugh, to set on some quantity of barren spectators to laugh too, though in the meantime some necessary question of the play be then to be considered" (3.2.37–43). In other words, actors should not ad lib simply because they are in a comic scene, nor should the spectator let his concentration stray during such moments of light relief, because the words being uttered under cover of folly might contain something crucial, "some necessary question", which must be understood if the play itself is to be understood properly.

Take, for example, the scene between Polonius and the apparently "mad" Hamlet in act 3, scene 2:

*Hamlet*. Do you see yonder cloud that's almost in shape of a camel?
*Polonius*. By th' mass, and 'tis like a camel indeed.
*Hamlet*. Methinks it is like a weasel.
*Polonius*. It is back'd like a weasel.
*Hamlet*. Or like a whale?
*Polonius*. Very like a whale. (3.2.366–72)

Does this apparently flippant scene have anything of value to contribute to the play, or are we tempted to laugh at the comic absurdity of the dialogue, becoming "barren spectators" blinded by our jocularity, "though in the meantime some necessary question of the play be then to be considered"? There is, of course, nothing wrong with laughter, as long as the laughter does not have the last laugh at our own critical expense, but we must not allow the folly to mask the deeper meaning.

We know, because Shakespeare has told us, that folly is often a mask in his plays, and it is necessary, therefore, to remove the mask, or at least to see beyond it. On one level, of course, the absurd dialogue shows Polonius simply humoring the "mad" Hamlet; on another level, it serves to show Polonius as a simpering sycophant; on a deeper level still, it exposes the duplicitous nature of Polonius' relationship with Hamlet, fawning in his presence and yet conspiring against him behind his back. Yet none of these levels of meaning go deep enough to make of this exchange "some necessary question ... to be considered".

At the deepest level, Hamlet is returning to his initial riposte to his mother: "Seems, madam! Nay, it is; I know not seems." Polonius, having devoted his life to spying and conspiring, and to flattery and pragmatism, no longer knows the difference between that which *is* and that which *seems* to be. Living a lie, which is the very "stuff" of spying, and training others to do so, has left him unable to see or discern the truth. It is not that Polonius really believes that the cloud is in the shape of a camel, or a weasel, or a whale. He does not. On the literal level, he is simply humoring and flattering Hamlet; it is on the metaphorical level that the "necessary question to be considered" emerges.

Polonius, as a secular humanist whose philosophy was expounded in his advice to his son, is a relativist who does not perceive the objective correlative at the root of reality. He does not understand the difference between truth and mere opinion because "truth" *is* mere opinion: you have your truth and I have my truth and nobody has the right to insist that your truth is better than mine. Polonius, as a relativist, is the antitype of Hamlet, as his philosophy is the antithesis of Hamlet's. "This above all—to thine own self be true" translates in practice to "Is, madam! Nay, it seems; I know not is."

It is easy to see that a cloud is a natural metaphor for such an unnatural creed, and indeed, G. K. Chesterton employed this selfsame metaphor to describe relativism as "something that changes completely and entirely in every part, at every minute, like a cloud".[1] A camel is a camel; a weasel is a weasel; and a whale is a whale—but a cloud can

[1] G. K. Chesterton, "Of Sentimentalism and the Head and Heart", *Church Socialist Quarterly*, January 1909.

*seem* to be any of these things while in objective reality being none of them. Shakespeare is saying, through the "madness" of Hamlet, that Christian philosophy is rooted in an acceptance of objective reality, whereas the rootless "precepts" of Polonius have lost touch with all that really *is*.[2] Polonius' practical and pragmatic precepts cannot disguise the fact that, philosophically speaking, he has his head in the clouds.

And we need to remember that since Polonius may be modeled on Elizabeth's spymaster, William Cecil, Shakespeare's "reason in madness" is designed as an attack on those who put the practical and pragmatic precepts of Machiavellian *realpolitik* before the unchanging principles of religious truth. As well as being a timeless critique of relativism, it was a timely attack on the secular humanism of Shakespeare's own day and the persecution of Catholicism that was its bitter and deadly fruit.

If Shakespeare lampoons the folly of relativism in moments of comic relief, he is deadly serious about the presentation of orthodox theology. Nowhere is this more apparent than in King Claudius' angst- and conscience-driven soliloquy in act 3. The King is profoundly orthodox in his understanding of the eternal consequences of sin, the power of prayer, the possibility of forgiveness, and the worldly cost to himself of obtaining that forgiveness. If he will obtain forgiveness, he must confess his sin, not merely to a priest but to his wife and to the world, and he must relinquish all his ill-gotten gains—"My crown, mine own ambition, and my queen" (3.3.55). Hamlet arrives just as the King sinks to his knees in an attempt at prayer, and sees, in this unguarded moment, his opportunity to have his revenge:

> Now might I do it pat, now 'a is a-praying;
> And now I'll do't.... (3.3.73–74)

And yet, of course, he does not do it. Once again he delays. Is this another example of Hamlet's endless procrastination, his inability to act?

---

[2] Christian philosophy is rooted in *realism*, the assertion that universals have real existence, as opposed to the opposite view of *nominalism*, the assertion that universals have no real existence but are merely names. The former view, embraced by Christian orthodoxy, was held by Socrates, Plato, and Aristotle and was affirmed by the great Christian philosophers, such as Augustine and Thomas Aquinas; the latter view was held by William of Ockham and would later be championed by Thomas Hobbes. Shakespeare is clearly aware of the philosophical controversy between realism and nominalism that had been raging for five hundred years by the time that *Hamlet* was written. As an orthodox Christian, Shakespeare defended the realist position, whereas the nominalist position, which he condemned, became the source of much of the relativism that was growing in influence in Elizabethan England.

Or is it, rather, a further example of his ponderous circumspection, his praiseworthy ability to think clearly before acting decisively? His words clearly indicate the latter. If he kills the King while he is at prayer, he will send him to heaven. Is this fit "revenge" for his crimes, for his cold-blooded murder of Hamlet's father?

> A villain kills my father; and for that,
> I, his sole son, do this same villain send
> To heaven.
> Why, this is hire and salary, not revenge. (3.3.76–79)

At this point there is nothing particularly reprehensible in Hamlet's train of thought. Whether or not he is justified in taking the King's life for the murder of his father, we are not surprised to find that he loses the appetite to do so as soon as he realizes that he could be doing the King a great favor in so doing. His next words, however, are not so easy to justify:

> When he is drunk asleep, or in his rage;
> Or in th' incestuous pleasure of his bed;
> At game, a-swearing, or about some act
> That has no relish of salvation in't—
> Then trip him, that his heels may kick at heaven,
> And that his soul may be as damn'd and black
> As hell, whereto it goes. (3.3.89–95)

"This speech," wrote Samuel Johnson, "in which Hamlet, represented as a virtuous character, is not content with taking blood for blood, but contrives damnation for the man that he would punish, is too horrible to be read or to be uttered." [3]

The speech is indeed horrible, but we should employ a degree of circumspection, worthy of Hamlet himself, before we condemn the speaker too harshly. We need to remind ourselves that the man of whom he speaks has murdered Hamlet's father and has subsequently wedded his mother. This is enough to awaken hellish thoughts in the best of men, even if it is not enough to justify them. And we should remember that Hamlet is not a static character throughout the unfolding of

---

[3] Samuel Johnson, *Johnson on Shakespeare: Essays and Notes Selected and Set Forth with an Introduction by Walter Raleigh* (London: Oxford University Press, 1908), p. 193.

the play. He begins in a state of near-suicidal melancholy and experiences the "slings and arrows of outrageous fortune" with passionate circumspection until he arrives at the settled serenity and sagacious resignation of the final act. He is on a journey, a pilgrim en route from a close encounter with hell, via purgatory, to a glimpse of the heaven that beckons offstage. In the midst of this journey, we should not expect our hero to behave impeccably, without a blemish on his character. He is, as he says of himself, "very proud, revengeful, ambitious; with more offences at my beck than I have thoughts to put them in, imagination to give them shape, or time to act them in" (3.1.125–28). He is a miserable sinner, though more sinned against than sinning, who finds himself "crawling between earth and heaven" (3.1.127–28). He is, in fact, very much like the rest of us, except perhaps that he has more reason than most of us for being angry with the situation in which he finds himself. The key point, however, is that even at his most earthy, he never loses sight of heaven. He knows right from wrong, and virtue from vice, and tries to do what a good and virtuous man is called to do. He does not always succeed, and occasionally, as in the speech just cited, he allows imprudent passion to overpower his usual prudent circumspection. Such moments are, however, the exception and not the rule.

Hamlet knows that unbridled passion is wrong, whether it be in the service of lust, as in the case of the "incestuous" relationship between his mother and King Claudius, or whether it be in the service of hatred, as in the case of his thoughts and words in the offending and offensive speech just discussed. This is made abundantly plain in his complaint to his mother that "reason panders will" (3.4.88), i.e., that reason panders our desires instead of our desires being governed by reason. Once again, we see the recurring conflict between that which is and that which only seems to be. If our desires are governed by reason, we are subjecting the subjective to the objective, and in so doing, we ensure that that which *seems* to be is mastered by that which *is*. If, on the other hand, "reason panders will", we are subjecting the objective to the subjective, and in so doing, that which *is* is sacrificed to that which *seems* to be. Put plainly, there is a natural moral law, not invented by man, that transcends and trumps our desires. Something is right or wrong, whether we like it or not. We can be fooled by our desires into believing that what we want is good for us, whereas in fact it is harmful. It *seems* to be good, but it *is* in fact harmful. The whole of *Hamlet* turns on this inescapable distinction between reason and will, between that which is and that which seems to be, and the test of success is the extent to which the protagonists conform their will to reason. This is Hamlet's struggle throughout the play, and we see at the end that he succeeds.

It is intriguing that Hamlet makes this distinction between reason and will, with all that it implies, during his impassioned meeting with his mother, and even more so in the context of the reappearance of the Ghost. Why is it that Hamlet can see the Ghost but his mother cannot? It is not because the Ghost is only a figment of Hamlet's imagination, as his mother believes, because we know that Horatio, Bernardo, and Marcellus have also seen it. Is it because Hamlet's mother is blind to the spiritual truth that the Ghost represents? Has her disordered will usurped her reason to the extent that she no longer perceives the spiritual basis of reality? In losing her reason, has she lost her faith?

Again we see the perennial conflict between realism and nominalism, or Christianity and relativism, which animates the very heart of the action. The Ghost is indubitably a believing Catholic, as we have seen, and is suffering in purgatory for his sins. As such, the Ghost represents Catholic truth and the necessity of the Christian soul to repent of its sins. Hamlet's mother is unable to see either the truth or the necessity of repentance. Her disordered will has made her blind. There are, after all, none so blind as those who *will* not see. Her response is to believe that the Ghost does not exist, even though we know that independent witnesses testify to its objective existence; furthermore, she believes that the one who sees it is mad. "Alas, he's mad!" she exclaims when Hamlet sees the arrival of the Ghost (3.4.105). Hamlet's response to her blindness and misperception is unequivocal:

> It is not madness
> That I have utt'red. . . .
> .   .   .   .   .   .   .   .   .   .   .   .   .   .   .   .   .
> Mother, for love of grace,
> Lay not that flattering unction to your soul,
> That not your trespass but my madness speaks:
> .   .   .   .   .   .   .   .   .   .   .   .   .   .   .   .
> Confess yourself to heaven;
> Repent what's past; avoid what is to come;
> And do not spread the compost on the weeds,

To make them ranker. Forgive me this my virtue;
For in the fatness of these pursy times
Virtue itself of vice must pardon beg,
Yea, curb and woo for leave to do him good. (3.4.141–42, 144–46,
149–55)

The conclusion that must be drawn from this exchange between mother and son is apparent enough. The Ghost exists, whether we like it or not, and in spite of any belief to the contrary by those who have made themselves morally blind through a pandering of the will. Furthermore, if the Ghost exists, so does purgatory, in which the Ghost is confined. And if purgatory exists, so does the necessity to "repent what's past".

# 18

## INVERSION AND PERVERSION

In act 4 we see what might be termed an infernal inversion of the plot as Laertes emerges as an anti-Hamlet and King Claudius is revealed as an anti-Ghost.

When Laertes returns from France intent on avenging the death of his father, we are presented with a parallel between his own role and that of Hamlet. Yet Shakespeare does not employ this dramatic parallel to highlight their similarities but to emphasize their differences. This is apparent from the way in which Laertes responds to his father's death:

> How came he dead? I'll not be juggled with.
> To hell, allegiance! Vows, to the blackest devil!
> Conscience and grace, to the profoundest pit!
> I dare damnation. To this point I stand,
> That both the worlds I give to negligence,
> Let come what comes; only I'll be reveng'd
> Most thoroughly for my father. (4.5.127–33)

This expression of outrage differs to a shocking degree from Hamlet's reaction to the news of his own father's murder. Whereas Hamlet goes to great pains to ensure that his father's spirit is an "honest ghost" and not a demon intent on deceiving him into sinful acts, Laertes proclaims his hellish allegiance to the "blackest devil" if it will assist him in his desire for vengeance. And why not? He had been taught by his father that the one axiomatic truth was to be true to himself above all else. Why should Laertes allow anything, even the threat of hell itself, to come between him and his desire to be true to his own lust for revenge? His words follow logically from the "precepts" he had received from his father. He has not inherited the precept of the Our Father that "*thy* will be done, on earth as it is in heaven" but the unchristian precept of his own father that "*my* will be done on earth, and to hell with heaven."

Shakespeare's grasp of Christian theology and philosophy is unerring, and he shows us the dangers of erring in the direction of an anthropocentric view of reality. Hamlet, as a good Christian, goes to enormous lengths to ensure that his own passions do not get the better of his better judgment, i.e., that he never loses his grasp of a Christian understanding of good and evil; Laertes, a secular humanist, is a slave to his passions because he knows no judgment other than his own. The fact that Hamlet is aware of the inherent weakness and danger of Laertes' philosophy is made clear in his words to Horatio about the spies Rosencrantz and Guildenstern:

> 'Tis dangerous when the baser nature comes
> Between the pass and fell incensed points
> Of mighty opposites. (5.2.60–62)

The "baser nature" is sin, or the self-centeredness (pride) that is the father of sin, and the "mighty opposites" are the forces of good and evil. Hamlet knows that it is dangerous to allow our pride (our "own self above all") to blur our knowledge of the "mighty opposites". Laertes, however, toys with such danger in his self-centered daring of damnation, seemingly oblivious to the fact that it is not possible to remain neutral or aloof in the war between the mighty opposites. *Pace* Nietzsche, one cannot go "beyond good and evil" but must serve the one or be enslaved by the other. If in serving our "own self" we fail to serve the good beyond the self, we will invariably be serving evil. This is precisely what happens to Laertes once he dares damnation. Almost immediately, he becomes a pawn in King Claudius' plot to kill Hamlet.

Taking Laertes into his confidence, the King takes on the same role with Polonius' son as the Ghost has taken with Hamlet, urging "revenge" for the death of the father:

> Now must your conscience my acquittance seal,
> And you must put me in your heart for friend,
> Sith you have heard, and with a knowing ear,
> That he which hath your noble father slain
> Pursu'd my life. (4.7.1–4)

Again, however, Shakespeare does not employ the dramatic parallel between the Ghost and King Claudius to highlight their similarities but to dramatize their differences. Whereas the spirit of Hamlet's father is

an "honest ghost", telling the truth to his son and revealing King Claudius' hideous secret, King Claudius is thoroughly dishonest in his dealings with Laertes and conceals the hideous secret. It is not that he is
lying to Laertes in what he says to him; the lie is in what he fails to say.
He does not say that he had murdered Hamlet's father, nor does he let
Laertes know that Hamlet had killed Polonius in error, in the mistaken
belief that it was he, the King, who was concealed behind the arras
when Hamlet had struck the fatal blow. It is not in the King's interest
to tell the whole truth, so he resorts to the half-truth instead, and the
half-truth is tantamount to a lie. The fate of Laertes, and the fate of
others, is not sealed by what Laertes has "heard, and with a knowing
ear"; it is sealed by what he has not heard in his unknowing ear. The
King has poisoned Laertes' ear as surely as he had poisoned the ear of
Hamlet's father, and with equally fatal results.

The connection between sin and poison is reinforced later in the
same scene when King Claudius fabricates a story in which he claims
that a report of Laertes' prowess with the rapier had aroused Hamlet's
envy:

> Sir, this report of his
> Did Hamlet so envenom with his envy
> That he could nothing do but wish and beg
> Your sudden coming o'er, to play with you. (4.7.102–5)

This juxtaposition of poison and sin, venom and envy, serves as a fitting
prelude to the King's hatching of the scheme in which he and Laertes
will conspire to murder Hamlet with poison. Before he unfolds his
plan, however, the King reveals his fundamental relativism[1] in a short
speech that reminds us inescapably of Polonius' "precepts":

*King.* Laertes, was your father dear to you?

. . . . . . . . . . . . . . . . . . . .

*Laertes.*                    Why ask you this?

---

[1]Shakespeare is not contradicting himself in making the King's failed effort at prayer and
repentance in act 3 thoroughly orthodox in its understanding of theology whereas his words
to Polonius in the following act appear to be totally relativist. It is a common enough psychological twist to find that one unwilling to repent begins to justify the sin by believing
that it is in fact not sinful. It is the switch from an uncomfortable objective reality to a
comfortable subjective substitute "reality". The King will not live virtuously, so he makes a
virtue out of his vice in an act of self-justification. He has passed from what *is* to what *seems*
to be.

*King.* Not that I think you did not love your father;
But that I know love is begun by time,
And that I see, in passages of proof,
Time qualifies the spark and fire of it.
There lives within the very flame of love
A kind of wick or snuff that will abate it;
And nothing is at a like goodness still;
For goodness, growing to a pleurisy,
Dies in his own too much. That we would do,
We should do when we would; for this "would" changes,
And hath abatements and delays as many
As there are tongues, are hands, are accidents;
And then this "should" is like a spend-thrift's sigh
That hurts by easing. But to the quick of th' ulcer:
Hamlet comes back; what would you undertake
To show yourself in deed your father's son
More than in words?
*Laertes.*                    To cut his throat i' th' church.
*King.* No place, indeed, should murder sanctuarize;
Revenge should have no bounds. (4.7.107, 109–28)

The King's words are pregnant with import, and they promise, if we read them with the careful attention they warrant, to give birth to a profound knowledge of the whole play. The speech represents a two-edged sword, both edges of which are envenomed, cutting the cosmos with the cold pragmatism of the Machiavel and the slippery philosophy of the sophist.

Love, according to the King, is not as the Christian sees it. It is not something eternal that has its existence in the heart of God himself, from whom it springs and to whom it returns; on the contrary, it is something that is "begun by time". It is not an absolute that is unconquerable and transcendent but is a mere subject of temporal forces: "Time qualifies the spark and fire of it." The "very flame of love" is not the Holy Spirit, omnipresent, omnipotent, omniscient, and undying; it is, rather, something that contains within itself the self-destructive seeds of entropy. Similarly, goodness, according to the King, is not as the Christian perceives it. It is not something that has its source in the Absolute Goodness of God, a goodness without limits; it is something finite that "dies in his own too much". From this sophistry in the service of a relativism and materialism that denies the existence of an all-loving God and all principles of metaphysics, the King proceeds to a principle of pragmatic fundamentalism that makes action the touch-stone of virtue:

> That we would do,
> We should do when we would; for this "would" changes,
> And hath abatements and delays as many
> As there are tongues, are hands, are accidents;
> And then this "should" is like a spend-thrift's sigh
> That hurts by easing.

Apart from serving the King's Machiavellian purpose of inciting Laertes to take instant vengeful action against Hamlet, these words also contain an implicit and presumably unwitting[2] critique and condemnation of Hamlet's procrastination and circumspection. Hamlet had apparently dith-ered and delayed for the entire duration of the play, vacillating with soliloquized "spendthrift sighs" between what he "would do" and what he "should do". He had hesitated to take his own life during his moment of deepest despondency and had hesitated to take the King's life during many moments of introspective circumspection. Yet, as we have seen, his delay was virtuous, avoiding the temptation to suicide in the knowl-edge that it was a sin, punishable after death, and avoiding the killing of the King until he was sure that the Ghost was "honest" and that the King was indeed guilty of cold-blooded murder. The King, on the other hand, is employing rhetoric to tempt Laertes to rash judgments and to the instant gratification of his lust for revenge. When Laertes discovers later that what he "would do" he should not have done, because he did not know all the facts necessary to make a sound judgment, it will be too late to rectify the wrong done. Hamlet will be mortally wounded, and the King will have obtained his desire at Hamlet's and Laertes' expense.

The fact that we are meant to be horrified by the King's line of reasoning is evident from the response that it elicits from the hotheaded Laertes. In stating that he would willingly cut Hamlet's throat "i' th' church", Laertes is adding the sacrilegious to the murderous, thereby holding God in as much scorn as Hamlet. As if to confirm Shakes-peare's intention that we should utterly condemn the King for his Lucifer-like tempting of Laertes' lowest passions, the King echoes Laertes' sacrilege:

---

[2] I.e., unwitting to the King, not to the playwright.

No place, indeed, should murder sanctuarize;
Revenge should have no bounds.

The King's words are doubly damnable: first, because they are stating that revenge has no bounds, that it has rights that not even the love of God or the laws of religion can mitigate; and second, because we know what Laertes does not know, that the King is himself a murderer. The King, as an unholy ghost, is pouring the poison of infernal rhetoric into Laertes' unknowing ear, killing him with the venom of his words as surely as the envenomed sword will kill him later.

# 19

# A *MEMENTO MORI*

The King is busy plotting the death of others but is seemingly unmindful that he himself must die and face the judgment of his sins. It is his own sins, and their consequences, that should animate the King, not the real or alleged sins of others. Since, however, the King seems to have forgotten his own death, Shakespeare reminds us of the dangers inherent in his forgetfulness by setting the very next scene in a graveyard with two rustics digging a grave. And not only are they digging a grave, but they are talking about death and decomposition. The scene is thus set for Hamlet to take up the theme of mortality as he waxes threnodic, skull in hand, about the reality of death. And, ironically, all of this is introduced as comic relief! "Then comes the comic relief," wrote C. S. Lewis, "surely the strangest comic relief ever written— comic relief beside an open grave, with a further discussion of suicide, a detailed inquiry into the rate of decomposition, a few clutches of skulls, and then 'Alas, poor Yorick!'." [1]

"The subject of *Hamlet* is death", Lewis continues, reminding us of its ubiquitous presence throughout the entirety of the play but particularly in this one scene:

> In *Hamlet* we are kept thinking about it all the time, whether in terms of the soul's destiny or of the body's. Purgatory, Hell, Heaven, the wounded name, the rights—or wrongs—of Ophelia's burial, and the staying-power of a tanner's corpse. . . . [2]

It is intriguing, and surely significant, that Shakespeare employs this long *memento mori* at the dramatically strategic point between the scene in which the evil King, heedless of his own death, is plotting the death

[1] C. S. Lewis, "Hamlet: The Prince or the Poem?" in *Selected Literary Essays*, ed. Walter Hooper (Cambridge: Cambridge University Press, 1969), p. 98.
[2] Ibid., pp. 98–99.

of others, and the play's final scene in which the King, the Queen, Hamlet, and Laertes meet their deaths. The graveyard scene is sandwiched between one scene in which the specter of death looms large and ominous, like a death cloud, over the poisonous plans of King Claudius, and the catastrophic cataclysm of the play's climactic scene in which death rains down on, and reigns over, all and sundry.

The churchyard scene is, therefore, much more than mere comic relief. It contains much that Shakespeare seeks to convey, and as such, it warrants our close attention.

First and foremost, and as we have stated, the scene serves as a *memento mori*, a reminder of death and the fact that we all must die, which was a popular literary and artistic motif in medieval times. In the visual arts, it often consisted of a skull positioned appropriately within the composition, and clearly Shakespeare is following this tradition with the abundance of skulls that appear in this scene, most particularly that of the deceased Yorick. It is present in literature also, such as in the epitaph to Shakespeare's contemporary Thomas Gooding, carved into the wall of Norwich Cathedral:

> All you that do this place pass bye
> Remember death for you must dye.
> As you are now even so was I
> And as I am so shall you be.
> Thomas Gooding here do staye
> Waiting for God's judgement daye.

Within Catholic tradition, the *memento mori* serves the purpose of reminding us of the Four Last Things: death, judgment, heaven, and hell. A Catholic, such as Shakespeare, cannot think of death without thinking, at the same time, of the three other Last Things. King Claudius and Laertes are clearly forgetful of the Four Last Things in their hellish exchange in the previous scene, whereas Hamlet is always mindful of them. From the early soliloquy in which the fear of judgment after death deflects the morbid Hamlet from thoughts of suicide, to his musings over the skulls of the deceased in the play's penultimate scene, the play's principal protagonist is never far in thought from death, judgment, heaven, and hell. And, of course, the Ghost is nothing less than a walking, talking *memento mori*, reminding Hamlet, and us, of our ultimate destiny.

In the short exchange with Horatio that follows the famous scene with the skull of Yorick, we see not merely a *memento mori* but clear and present evidence of Shakespeare's friendship with the Jesuit martyr Saint Robert Southwell:

> *Hamlet.* Let me see. [*Takes the skull.*] Alas, poor Yorick! I knew him, Horatio: a fellow of infinite jest, of most excellent fancy; he hath borne me on his back a thousand times. And now how abhorred in my imagination it is! My gorge rises at it. Here hung those lips that I have kiss'd I know not how oft. Where be your gibes now, your gambols, your songs, your flashes of merriment that were wont to set the table on a roar? Not one now to mock your own grinning—quite chap-fall'n? Now get you to my lady's chamber, and tell her, let her paint an inch thick, to this favour she must come; make her laugh at that. Prithee, Horatio, tell me one thing.
> *Horatio.* What's that, my lord?
> *Hamlet.* Dost thou think Alexander look'd a this fashion i' th' earth?
> *Horatio.* E'en so.
> *Hamlet.* And smelt so? Pah!
>
> [*Throws down the skull.*]
>
> *Horatio.* E'en so, my lord.
> *Hamlet.* To what base uses we may return, Horatio! Why may not imagination trace the noble dust of Alexander till 'a find it stopping a bung-hole?
> *Horatio.* 'Twere to consider too curiously to consider so.
> *Hamlet.* No, faith, not a jot; but to follow him thither with modesty enough, and likelihood to lead it, as thus: Alexander died, Alexander was buried, Alexander returneth to dust; the dust is earth; of earth we make loam; and why of that loam whereto he was converted might they not stop a beer-barrel?
>
> Imperious Caesar, dead and turned to clay,
> Might stop a hole to keep the wind away.
> O, that that earth which kept the world in awe
> Should patch a wall t' expel the winter's flaw!
> But soft! but soft! awhile. Here comes the King. (5.1.179–211)

Many of Shakespeare's contemporaries must have seen the obvious allusion in Hamlet's discussion of Alexander and Caesar, within the context of a *memento mori*, with a verse from Robert Southwell's own famous poetic *memento mori*, "Upon the Image of Death", published shortly after the Jesuit's death in 1595:

Though all the East did quake to hear
Of Alexander's dreadful name,
And all the West did likewise fear,
To hear of Julius Caesar's fame,
Yet both by death in dust now lie,
Who then can scape but he must die?[3]

Once the first obvious allusion is noted, the diligent reader is alerted to the presence of others. The Clown's claim that "thou dost ill to say the gallows is built stronger than the church" (5.1.46–47) appears unavoidably connected to the plight of the English martyrs, such as Saint Robert Southwell, who were hanged, drawn, and quartered for the "crime" of being Catholic priests in Elizabeth's England. Which of the "mighty opposites" would prove stronger: the gallows or the Church? The hangman or the martyr? Machiavellian *realpolitik* or Christian principle? The "own self above all" secular politics of King Claudius, Polonius, Elizabeth, and William Cecil or the Christian convictions of Hamlet, Shakespeare, and Southwell?

There is also a probable negative portrayal of Queen Elizabeth in Hamlet's words to the skull of Yorick: "Now get you to my lady's chamber, and tell her, let her paint an inch thick, to this favour [i.e., death] she must come. . . ." On the literal level, these words refer, presumably, to the vanity of the character of the Queen in the play, or, perhaps, to the "frailty" that is woman in general, but it is hard to avoid the suspicion that it is a subtle sideswipe at Elizabeth's own "majesty". Elizabeth was known to daub cosmetics onto her face in ever-increasing quantities as she got older, hiding her aging (mortal) face in a mask of youth. A description of Elizabeth at the end of 1600, at around the time that Shakespeare was working on *Hamlet*, paints a lurid picture of her painted features that parallels Hamlet's allusion to the lady: "It was commonly observed this Christmas that her Majesty when she came to be seen was continuously painted, not only all over her face, but her very neck and breast also, and that the same was in some places near half an inch thick."[4]

Once our critical eye has become accustomed to the presence of half-concealed allusions to the political and religious situation in Elizabeth's

[3] For the full text of this poem, see Joseph Pearce, *Flowers of Heaven: A Thousand Years of Christian Verse* (San Francisco: Ignatius Press, 2005), pp. 73–74.

[4] G. B. Harrison, ed., *Elizabethan and Jacobean Journals, 1591–1610* (London: Routledge, 1999), 3:132.

England, our eyebrows are raised by the jocular banter about the "madness" of England. "[T]here the men are as mad as he", quips the Clown in reference to Hamlet (5.1.149–50). To a recusant Catholic, forced to practice his faith in secret, fearful of arrest, and fined for his refusal to attend the services of the state religion, England must indeed have seemed to have "gone mad".

# 20

# THE TRIUMPH OF SANITY

The scene in the churchyard ends on the theme of madness. The King and Queen both accuse Hamlet of madness, echoing the earlier judgment of the Clown: "O, he is mad", exclaims the King (5.1.266); "This is mere madness", laments the Queen (5.1.278). Yet who is really "mad"? The King and Laertes have plotted, in open defiance of heaven, to murder Hamlet in an act of poisonous treachery; the Queen, blinded by her own vanity, painted "an inch thick", is unaware of the monster she has married; and poor Ophelia, driven to distraction by events, is lying dead in her grave. In this company of madmen, Hamlet and his trusted friend Horatio are the only ones who are not mad.

As if to emphasize the irony of the situation, the following scene commences with a confirmation of Hamlet's, and Horatio's, sanity:

> *Hamlet.* Our indiscretion sometimes serve us well,
> When our deep plots do pall; and that should learn us
> There's a divinity that shapes our ends,
> Rough-hew them how we will.
> *Horatio.*                    That is most certain. (5.2.8–11)

These words of Hamlet, confirmed with the utmost certainty by the ever-honest and trustworthy Horatio, are among the most important in the whole play. Throughout the preceding four acts, each of the main characters has battled to achieve the triumph of his respective will. King Claudius and Polonius have plotted and spied in a series of cynical Machiavellian machinations to achieve their designs; Laertes, upon his return from France, has sought satisfaction of his desire to avenge his father's death; and Hamlet has meandered unceasingly around the problem of how he may fulfill his promise to his father to bring the King to justice. And yet now, in the final scene, Hamlet comes to the realization that the unfolding drama is governed by the will of God. It is the omnipotent hand of divine providence that is directing the play, as surely and as unerringly as Prospero directs events in *The Tempest*. Try as they will, they will not defeat the will of God. Defy and deny the heavens, the heavens will not be denied. In these words of Hamlet, our eyes are suddenly opened. We need to reread the play all over again in order to see it from the perspective of eternity. How does the divine author of things shape the ends of the characters in spite of their rough-hewing of his will? How does this divine author achieve his end by bringing matters to an end?

Hamlet's words about providence are much more than mere words. He is not simply talking about providence; his words are providential. They are prophetic. They not only look back over the events that we have witnessed in a way that makes sense of them; they look forward to the play's impending climax. We are made aware that we are about to see the hand of providence shape the ends of each of the characters. We are being forewarned that the approaching coup de theatre will be a veritable coup de grace.

And lest we forget the importance of Hamlet's prophetic words about the omnipotence of providence, Hamlet himself reminds us of them in his final words before the entry of the King and the Queen:

> Not a whit, we defy augury: there is a special providence in the fall of a sparrow. If it be now, 'tis not to come; if it be not to come, it will be now; if it be not now, yet it will come—the readiness is all. Since no man owes of aught he leaves, what is't to leave betimes? Let be. (5.2.211–16)

Again, there is so much in these few lines of crucial importance to our understanding of the play. In the first instance, we are once more being reminded by Hamlet of the hidden hand of providence, and we are witnessing, perhaps for the first time, a real serenity on Hamlet's part, a true peace that arises from his knowledge and acceptance of providence. He is now ready for what follows, whatever it might be, and, as he tells us, the readiness is all.

As we discussed earlier, it is perhaps the "readiness" of Hamlet that helps us solve the puzzle at the play's mysterious heart. Hamlet's "readiness" is the ultimate end and the very purpose of the play itself. The play reaches its own readiness, its own ripeness, in the readiness of Hamlet to put his trust in God.

We have already looked at some of the clues embedded in the words from Matthew's Gospel, "there is a special providence in the fall of a sparrow", that Hamlet chooses to quote at this crucial juncture. We have seen that the words that follow this line in the Gospel offer reassurance that Hamlet has nothing to fear from death: "Fear ye not therefore, ye are of more value than many sparrows."[1] Yet an even closer scrutiny of the biblical clue that Shakespeare presents to us offers further solutions to the problems that have confused and confounded so many critics in their efforts to get to grips with this most enigmatic of plays.

Since it seems inescapable that Shakespeare had selected this particular passage from Scripture at such a key moment in the drama for a specific purpose, it will help to quote the following verses to see where the playwright is leading us:

> Fear ye not therefore, ye are of more value than many sparrows. Whosoever therefore shall confess me before men, him will I confess also before my Father which is in heaven. But whosoever shall deny me before men, him will I also deny before my Father which is in heaven. Think not that I am· come to send peace on earth: I come not to send peace, but a sword. For I am come to set a man at variance against his father, and the daughter against her mother, and the daughter in law against her mother in law. And a man's foes shall be they of his own household. He that loveth father or mother more than me is not worthy of me; and he that loveth son and daughter more than me is not worthy of me. And he that taketh not his cross and followeth after me, is not worthy of me. He that findeth his life shall lose it: and he that loseth his life for my sake shall find it.[2]

Clearly Hamlet's mention of the scriptural "sparrow" is a bird–sign pointing us to the passage from which it is plucked. When we follow the sign, we discover one of the most controversial passages from Scripture and one that sheds new light on the meaning of the play. Those who confess the Christian creed before men, i.e., in the practice of their lives, have nothing to fear in death. Hamlet, who has always grappled with the dilemmas of the drama from an orthodox perspective and has sought always to do what *is* right and not what merely *seems* to be right, has reached the point of serenity at which he knows he has nothing to fear from his impending death. This is his "readiness". He is mindful of the Four Last Things and is "ready" for death and judgment, and the promise of heaven. King Claudius, however, in the light

---

[1] Matthew 10:31.

[2] Matthew 10:31–39.

of this passage of Scripture, has everything to fear in death. He is emphatically "unready". Having denied Christ in the abominations of his life
and in the heresy of his words, he can expect to be denied by Christ
after his death. He had been unmindful of the Four Last Things and is
unready for death and judgment, and the prospect of hell.

And then there are the shocking words of Christ that he does not
come to bring peace on earth. His peace, like his kingdom, is not of
this world; it is not to be found in the hearts of the worldly, of those
who place their trust in temporal power and pleasures. It is not to be
found in the heart of King Claudius. But nor does it seem to be found
in those who are trying to do what is right. Hamlet cannot be said to
have had "peace" throughout the play. On the contrary, we have seen
him plunged into the very depths of despondency and to the very edge
of despair. And yet he did not despair. His circumspection, his prudence, and his temperance have brought him finally to the point of
*peaceful* resignation to the will of God, to a trust in the "divinity that
shapes our ends". He has faced the "slings and arrows of outrageous
fortune" by taking up his cross and following his Christian conscience.
In doing so, he has been found "worthy" and is "ready" for what he is
about to face. And what is it that he is about to face? He is about to
face the ultimate paradox, with which Christ ends the passage of Scripture to which Shakespeare has led us: "He that findeth his life shall lose
it: and he that loseth his life for my sake shall find it." Death, for the
Christian, is not the end but the beginning.

It can be seen, therefore, that Shakespeare has guided us through a
hidden passage of Scripture to the place where the real heart of his
meaning resides. There is to be no peace on this earth, in this vale of
tears, only suffering and the promise of a cross that we must bear. But
what of the *sword* that Christ promises? Where is the sword to be found,
and what does it mean? On the literal and most obvious level, the sword
is to be found in the final scene as the instrument of Hamlet's and
Laertes' death. If it is God's will that the play should end thus, and
Hamlet clearly thinks that it is, Christ has brought the sword that brings
the drama to an end. But there is another highly significant sword at
the beginning of the drama that warrants further attention, not least
because it crosses swords allegorically with the other sword that will be
the instrument of Hamlet's death. At the end of the first act, Hamlet
goes to considerable lengths to insist that Horatio and Marcellus swear
an oath upon his sword:

*Hamlet.* Never make known what you have seen to-night.
*Both.* My lord, we will not.
*Hamlet.*                              Nay, but swear't.
*Horatio.*                                                      In faith,
   My lord, not I.
*Marcellus.*          Nor I, my lord, in faith.
*Hamlet.* Upon my sword.
*Marcellus.*                      We have sworn, my lord, already.
*Hamlet.* Indeed, upon my sword, indeed.
*Ghost.* [*Cries under the stage.*] Swear.
*Hamlet.* Ha, ha, boy! say'st thou so? Art thou there, truepenny?
   Come on. You hear this fellow in the cellarage:
   Consent to swear.
*Horatio.*                  Propose the oath, my lord.
*Hamlet.* Never to speak of this that you have seen,
   Swear by my sword.
*Ghost.* [*Beneath*] Swear.
*Hamlet.* Hic et ubique? Then we'll shift our ground.
   Come hither, gentlemen,
   And lay your hands again upon my sword.
   Swear by my sword
   Never to speak of this that you have heard.
*Ghost.* [*Beneath*] Swear, by his sword. (1.5.144–61)

Why does Hamlet go to such trouble to insist that his friends swear upon his sword? Five times he or the Ghost insist upon it. Commenting on this scene, Samuel Johnson, citing the Shakespearean actor and producer David Garrick as his authority, wrote that "it was common to swear upon the sword, that is, upon the cross which the old swords had upon the hilt." [3] This practice, which dates back until at least the Crusades, not only makes the sword synonymous with the cross, thus connecting it to the key passage from Matthew's Gospel, but makes of the whole drama something of a crusade. Hamlet and his confreres are swearing upon the cross because they are at war with the infidel. King Claudius and Polonius, and the company of spies with which they surround themselves, are at war with the cross, a fact that is further highlighted by the pun in act 3 in which King Claudius is likened to a "moor", i.e., a Muslim (3.4.67).

---

[3] Samuel Johnson, *Johnson on Shakespeare: Essays and Notes Selected and Set Forth with an Introduction by Walter Raleigh* (London: Oxford University Press, 1908), p. 190.

It is also interesting that Hamlet insists that swearing in faith alone is not enough, an insistence that resonates powerfully with the religious controversies of the Reformation. Horatio and Marcellus both swear "in faith" that they will not divulge what they have seen, but Hamlet and the Ghost both demand that they swear upon the sword. The reappearance of the Ghost at this stage reinforces the importance of this scene, suggesting that Hamlet's insistence is sanctioned by the supernatural powers of heaven. (The Ghost is in purgatory and is therefore destined for heaven, he is saved, and Hamlet reminds us of the Ghost's honesty by referring to him as a "truepenny", i.e., an honest person, not a forgery.) In insisting that "faith alone" is not sufficient, Hamlet and the Ghost are taking the Catholic side in the dispute between the Protestant belief in *sola fide* (by faith alone) and the Catholic doctrine of *fide et operibus* (by faith and works). Here the sword represents the need to *work* for salvation; merely believing that we are saved is not enough. The sword qua sword shows that we must *fight* for what we believe in, and the sword qua cross shows that we must live self-sacrificially by taking up our cross and following Christ. In both cases, suffering cannot be avoided. It is, therefore, little wonder that Hamlet suffers greatly throughout the play.

Once we have established a symbolic connection between the sword and the cross, we can view the whole bloody climax of the play in a new anagogical setting. Indeed, once this connection is made, the whole anagnorisis is anagogical. The poisoned sword is the cross upon which Hamlet, the faithful Christian, is crucified. He is killed not so much by the sword (cross) itself but by the poison (sin) upon it. And once the poison-sin metaphor is established, we can see Laertes as the Good Thief of Scripture, justly killed by the poison (sin) on the sword (cross), asking for forgiveness and obtaining it before he dies. King Claudius emerges as a figure of Satan, or the satanic, whose treachery becomes apparent at the moment of climax (the symbolic crucifixion) and who discovers to his horror that he is destroyed by the power of his own poison.

But is this not all a little too easy, a little contrived? Does it not leave too many unanswered questions? Many critics, including *eminenti* such as Samuel Johnson, clearly think so. Let us return to the passage we quoted from Johnson at the beginning of our discussion of *Hamlet*:

> The catastrophe is not very happily produced; the exchange of weapons is rather an expedient of necessity, than a stroke of art. A scheme might

easily have been formed, to kill Hamlet with the dagger, and Laertes with the bowl.

The poet is accused of having shewn little regard to poetical justice, and may be charged with equal neglect of poetical probability. The apparition left the regions of the dead to little purpose; the revenge which he demands is not obtained but by the death of him that was required to take it; and the gratification which would arise from the destruction of an usurper and a murderer, is abated by the untimely death of Ophelia, the young, the beautiful, the harmless, and the pious.[4]

The problem is that Johnson is not seeing the play as Shakespeare means him to see it. He is seeing it from a worldly and not an otherworldly perspective. He is not meant to see as man sees but as God sees. He is meant to see the drama through the eye of the needle of paradox. He must understand that we must lose our life in order to gain it and that the first shall be last, and the last first. This is madness to the eyes of the world, but to those who have the eyes of faith, it is the beginning of wisdom. As Hamlet himself insists, there is a divinity that shapes our ends, and since this is so, we have to learn to see the events that shape our ends from the perspective of the divine. The question is not so much "What would Jesus do?" as "What has Jesus done?" Where is his hand in the events that shape our lives? This is the question.

If we look at Johnson's critique from the perspective of paradox and providence, the play will make much more sense than he imagines. From the perspective of providence, it is providential, and therefore artistically necessary, for Laertes to be killed by the poison of his own sword, i.e., his own treachery, and not through the mere *accident* of drinking from the bowl. From the perspective of providence, the apparition most certainly did not leave the regions of the dead to little purpose. If it had not been for the intervention of the "honest ghost", Hamlet would never have known of the King's treachery and murder; he would never have known that any justice was necessary. The Ghost, who can be nothing but "honest" because he comes from the eternal realm, where everything *is* and nothing merely *seems* to be, is absolutely necessary to inject a healthy dose of supernatural objectivity into the picture. As a soul in eternity, and therefore closer to the presence of God, he is the most *real* character in the whole play. He sees more than anyone else because he sees what *is* and not what *seems* to be. His very

[4] Johnson, *Johnson on Shakespeare*, p. 196.

presence tears apart the petty Machiavellian schemes of relativists, such
as King Claudius and Polonius, ripping their *seems* to the seams. He
shines forth the heavenly light of purgatory into the twilight zone of
lies, half-truths, and deception into which Denmark had fallen. No,
and with the greatest of respect to the great Dr. Johnson, the Ghost did
not appear "to little purpose".

But what of Hamlet's death? And what of Ophelia's? Can we really
be satisfied by their destruction? Perhaps not. In an ideal world, the
innocent would not fall victim to the sins of others. But we live not in
an ideal world but in a fallen one, and this is the world in which Shakespeare and all his characters reside. Shakespeare is not writing Christian
fantasy but Christian realism, and this entails martyrdom and suffering
on the part of the innocent. This is the real world in which Shakespeare found himself, a world in which people he knew were brutally
executed merely for being Catholic priests. Why would the playwright
whitewash such grim realities from his plays? And why would we want
him to? *Hamlet* is not a fairy story, or at least not the sort that Johnson
seems to desire. There is no guaranteed "happy ending" in this life, and
if we are indeed to live "happily ever after", it is in the next life, not in
this one. "Happily ever after" happens offstage, after the final curtain
has fallen, and Shakespeare's great gift is the way in which he is always
pointing offstage to the deeper reality that is beyond it.

# 21

## "AND FLIGHTS OF ANGELS SING THEE
## TO THY REST"

So, at last, we come to Hamlet's death and the promise of his resurrection.

The honorable Horatio is, appropriately, the first person to speak following the death of the prince whom he had served so loyally:

> Now cracks a noble heart. Good night, sweet prince,
> And flights of angels sing thee to thy rest! (5.2.351–52)

Horatio's words, ending in a *requiem* for Hamlet, are a translation, with only a minor alteration, from the Latin of the *In paradisum*, the antiphon of the burial service following the Requiem Mass: "In paradisum deducant te angeli.... Chorus angelorum te suscipiat, et cum Lazaro quondam paupere aeternam habeas requiem." (May the angels lead thee into paradise.... May the choir of angels receive thee, and may thou have eternal rest with Lazarus, who once was poor.) It is surely no coincidence that Hamlet's own last words, uttered immediately before these, are "[T]he rest is silence", in which "rest" quite clearly signifies both *cetera* and *requies*.[1] Thus Shakespeare ends his play by offering a Requiem Mass for the "noble heart" of his hero, giving his heroic prince the Catholic burial service that was now illegal in the "rotten" and "mad" state of England.

---

[1] Gerard Kilroy, "Requiem for a Prince: Rites of Memory in *Hamlet*", unpublished manuscript.

22

# LOVE'S SILENCE

The story of King Lear did not originate with Shakespeare. It had been told by Geoffrey of Monmouth in the twelfth century and reemerged in book 2 of Edmund Spenser's *Faerie Queene*, published in 1590, and also in Sir Philip Sidney's *Arcadia*, first published in 1590 and republished in a more complete edition in 1598. Although Shakespeare was undoubtedly aware of these versions of the story, it is likely that his principal sources were the *Chronicles* of Holinshed, published in 1577, and, perhaps most influential of all, a dramatized version of the story entitled *The True Chronicle History of King Leir and his three daughters*. This play, possibly written by George Peele, had been in the repertoire of the Queen's Men since the 1580s, though it was not published until late in 1605, around the time that Shakespeare is thought to have started work on his own version of the story.

It seems inescapable that Shakespeare would have known the earlier dramatized version and may even have acted in it. It is, however, a rather frivolous, whimsical work, climaxed with a happy ending, and is very different from the play that Shakespeare would write. Michael Wood, in his biography of Shakespeare, has us imagine the Bard browsing in John Wright's shop near London's Newgate Market in the autumn of 1605: "There, in a freshly inked pile of quartos on the flap board of the shop, lay his old favourite, now available for the first time in print: 'The True Chronicle History of King Leir and his three daughters ... As it hath been divers and sundry times lately acted'. Given his long fascination with the tale, Shakespeare could not have resisted it." [1] In fact, *pace* Wood, there is no evidence that the earlier "Leir" was ever a "favourite", and Shakespeare's decision to write a new version of the play as soon as he became aware of a published edition of the earlier version suggests that he was initially inspired by a desire to write

---

[1] Michael Wood, *Shakespeare* (New York: Basic Books, 2003), p. 274.

something very different. It might not have been so much "fascination" with the earlier play as provocation by it. Peter Milward, in *Shakespeare's Meta-drama: Othello and King Lear*, writes that the earlier play had been "savagely torn to pieces and . . . thoroughly rewritten" by Shakespeare, expurgating its "clearly Protestant, anti-Papist bias". Milward concludes that Shakespeare "was, no doubt, put off by the protestant bias of the old play, just as he had already undertaken in his play of *King John* to modify a similar bias in *The Troublesome Reign of King John*." [2]

Milward unearths further fascinating evidence to suggest a possible source for Shakespeare's inspiration for the writing of *Lear*. In 1603 Sir Brian Annesley, a knight at the court of Queen Elizabeth, died, leaving behind three daughters. Prior to his death, the two elder daughters had tried to have him certified as insane in order to profit from his estate. They were prevented in their efforts by his youngest daughter, Cordelia, who had a monument erected to her parents "against the ungrateful nature of oblivious time". Cordelia Annesley became the second wife of Sir William Harvey, almost certainly an acquaintance of Shakespeare, and it is possible that it was from Sir William that Shakespeare learned of this curious parallel to the story of Lear and his daughters. Further evidence that this might be the case is suggested by the fact that there is no mention of Lear's madness in the original tale and also from the fact that Shakespeare uses the spelling "Cordelia" for Lear's youngest daughter, whereas it is rendered as "Cordella" in the earlier version of the play.

Regardless of the source of his inspiration for writing a new version of the story, or his motivation for doing so, it would clearly be woefully inadequate to limit our discussion of the play to the likely seeds from which it grew without paying due attention to the abundant fruits of Shakespeare's own inimitable imagination. *King Lear*, possibly his greatest work, surpasses and transcends in literary quality and philosophical depth all the earlier versions of the story. The play is, in fact, not one story but two. It interweaves the story of Lear and his daughters with the parallel story of Gloucester and his sons, the latter of which is probably derived from "The Tale of the Blind King of Paphlagonia" in Sidney's *Arcadia*, in such a way that we cannot truly speak of plot and subplot but only of co-plots woven together with majestic skill.

---

[2] Peter Milward, S.J., *Shakespeare's Meta-drama: "Othello" and "King Lear"* (Tokyo: Renaissance Institute, 2003), p. 104.

The co-plots parallel each other on the literal level. Lear is betrayed by the deception of his self-serving daughters, Regan and Goneril; Gloucester, by the deception of his illegitimate son, Edmund. Cordelia, the loyal and faithful daughter of Lear, suffers the hardships of exile because of her father's blind arrogance; Edgar, the loyal and legitimate son of Gloucester, suffers the hardships of exile through his father's blind ignorance. Lear and Gloucester lose everything in the worldly sense but, in the process, gain the wisdom they were lacking. The overarching and most obvious moral theme resonates with the Christian paradox that one must lose one's life in order to gain it, or with the words of Christ that there is no greater love than to lay down one's life for one's friends. Lear and Gloucester embody the truth of the former; Cordelia and Edgar (and Kent), the truth of the latter.

Apart from this overarching moral dimension that should be obvious to all, there is another dimension to Shakespeare's work, rooted in the politics of his day but relevant to the politics of all ages. This dimension, arising from the creative interaction of Shakespeare's Catholic sensibilities with an environment hostile to Catholicism, is discovered in what Peter Milward calls the "metadrama" of the plays or what Clare Asquith has referred to as the "shadowplays" within the plays.

In *King Lear* the metadrama is present from the very first scene, when the King promises political power to those who "love us most" (1.1.53).[3] Lear, symbolic of the state, demands all. There can be no room for other loves. Immediately, his self-serving daughters, Goneril and Regan, outdo each other in sycophantic promises of absolute allegiance. It is left to Cordelia, the youngest daughter, to "[l]ove, and be silent" (1.1.64). She loves her father but cannot "heave [her] heart into [her] mouth" (1.1.93–94), uttering platitudes to curry favor beyond that which her conscious dictates is decorous. Unlike the feigned or affected affection of her sisters, her love is "[m]ore ponderous than [her] tongue" (1.1.80); it is genuine and will not debase itself with falsehood or flattery. She will love the King "[a]ccording to [her] bond, no more nor less" (1.1.95). She cannot offer the King (or state) any allegiance beyond that which her conscience dictates is appropriate morally. The parallels with the position that Catholics found themselves in during the reign of Henry VIII,

---

[3] All quotations from *King Lear* are from the edition published by Ignatius Press: *The Tragedy of King Lear*, ed. Joseph Pearce, Ignatius Critical Editions (San Francisco: Ignatius Press, 2008).

and in Shakespeare's time under Elizabeth and James, is patently obvious. When Henry VIII declared himself supreme head of the Church of England, effectively making religion subject to the state, his subjects were forced to choose between conforming to his wishes, and thereby gaining his favor, or defying his will and incurring his wrath. Only the most courageous chose conscience before concupiscence; most chose to please the king and ignore their conscience. There are always more Gonerils and Regans than there are Cordelias.

The metadramatic element is made even more apparent in Cordelia's justification for her refusal to kowtow:

> Good my lord,
> You have begot me, bred me, loved me. I
> Return those duties back as are right fit,
> Obey you, love you, and most honor you.
> Why have my sisters husbands, if they say
> They love you all? Haply, when I shall wed,
> That lord whose hand must take my plight shall carry
> Half my love with him, half my care and duty.
> Sure I shall never marry like my sisters,
> To love my father all. (1.1.97–106)

On the literal level, Cordelia proclaims that her future husband has rights over her love that she is not at liberty, in conscience, to dispense with, even to her father. On a deeper level, Shakespeare may have been employing marriage as a metaphor for the relationship of the individual believer with Christ. Catholic ecclesiology is rooted in the belief, itself rooted in Scripture, that Christ is the Bridegroom and the Church his Bride. Cordelia's "husband" is Christ, and she is not at liberty to render unto Caesar that which belongs to Christ. The allegory and its applicability are clear. Catholics are not permitted, in conscience, to offer all their love to their father or mother, or to their king or country. They can love only as Cordelia loves, according to their bond. Our parents and our country have begotten us, bred us, loved us, and we should "return those duties back as are right fit" in obedience, love, and honor. This is "right fit", but it goes beyond our bond, beyond the bounds of a good conscience, to obey, love, and honor father or mother, king or country, as gods. The worship of our parents or the worship of the state is a mark of disordered love that presages evil.

"But goes thy heart with this?" asks Lear, following Cordelia's sagacious discourse. "Ay, my good lord", she replies. "So young, and so untender?" says Lear. "So young, my lord, and true", says Cordelia (1.1.107–9). The exchange is tellingly poignant. Cordelia is not merely being true to her heart, to her conscience (and to her God); she is being true to Lear. He is wrong, and she is right to tell him so. It is for his good as much as it is for hers. It is no wonder that it has been suggested that the very name of Cordelia is a punning reference to *coeur de Lear* (French for "Lear's heart") with echoes of *coeur de lion* ("lionheart"). Cordelia has the heart of a lion, and she is the heart of Lear. When Lear loses Cordelia, he loses his heart and his way.

## 23

## THE WISDOM OF FOOLS AND
## THE SANITY OF MADMEN

Apart from the obvious parallels with the secular politics of Elizabethan and Jacobean England, with its persecution of Catholics and other "nonconformist" dissidents, the other major metadramatic element revolves around the nature and meaning of "wisdom". It is often said that the Fool can be seen as the personification of Lear's conscience, the voice of (self-)criticism that informs Lear of the folly of his actions and the seriousness of the predicament in which his folly has left him. This, however, is only half the story—and the less important half. The more important half of the story begins only once the Fool disappears without trace. It is only once Edgar takes his place as "Fool" that the deeper wisdom is revealed.

Why does the Fool disappear? Why does a character who has played such an important and integral part in the play, declaiming many of its best and wittiest lines, suddenly disappear into thin air, having declared, as an apparent riposte to Lear, that "I'll go to bed at noon" (3.6.84)? Superficially, it might appear that this is a formal faux pas on Shakespeare's part. If lesser playwrights allow characters to disappear, leaving apparent loose ends, without so much as a "by your leave", it would be seen as a fatal flaw in their literary abilities. Are we to assume, therefore, that the Fool's disappearance is evidence of a flaw in Shakespeare's literary abilities? Although we might be tempted to make such an assumption, we do so at our peril. Only the most arrogant literary critics would presume to know more about the art of playwriting than the world's greatest playwright. It is, therefore, much safer to assume that Shakespeare had some deeper meaning in mind for the Fool's sudden and unannounced departure. Let us explore further.

As already stated, it is often assumed that the Fool serves as the King's conscience. As a "fool", a character devoid of discernible family connections and without roots or destiny beyond his function within the drama, he is ideally suited for employment as a personified abstraction conveying allegorical significance. "But where's my Fool?" asks Lear. "I have not seen him this two days" (1.4.72–73). We know therefore that the Fool (Lear's conscience) was significantly absent when Lear made the rash decision to hand his kingdom to Goneril and Regan (who may be said, within the context of this allegorical reading, to represent false love or secular ambition) while banishing Cordelia (representing true, self-sacrificial love and perhaps also, as Lear's "heart", Lear's own capacity to love truly and self-sacrificially). Equally significant is the Knight's response to Lear's complaint about the Fool's absence: "Since my young lady's going into France, sir, the Fool hath much pined away" (1.4.74–75). Cordelia's banishment has led to the pining away of Lear's conscience. It can be deduced, therefore, on a psychological level, that his injustice toward Cordelia has left him feeling guilty and that the witticisms of the Fool represent the incessant nagging of the King's conscience.

The Fool first enters the play in person as Lear receives the first of the snubs from his disloyal "loving" daughters, via Oswald, Goneril's steward. As Lear begins to perceive that he might have been foolish in handing over power to his two unworthy daughters while banishing the worthy one, the Fool emerges for the first time to rebuke him for the foolishness of his action. When Lear threatens him with "the whip" for daring to speak so candidly, the Fool responds with words of salient and sapient indignation: "Truth's a dog must to kennel; he must be whipped out, when Lady the Brach may stand by th' fire and stink" (1.4.113–16). Such words must have resonated powerfully among those members of Shakespeare's audience who feared being persecuted by the secular powers (Lady the Brach) for adhering to religious truths that had been made illegal. The adherents of Truth were suffering, left out in the cold, while those whose iniquities stank to high heaven could warm themselves by the fire (before ultimately being cast into it!).

"Dost thou call me fool, boy?" Lear asks in response to the Fool's nagging witticisms and criticisms. The Fool quips, "All thy other titles thou hast given away; that thou wast born with" (1.4.152–54). Literally, the Fool is indeed calling the King a fool, and a fool he is; yet, since "foolishness" is being used as a metaphor for "conscience" and the wisdom it serves, the Fool is also saying that Lear is left with nothing but his conscience. All the other titles, all the other worldly accretions with which he had been robed, have been removed; he is left naked except for his "foolish" conscience, a metaphysical nakedness that is itself a foreshadowing of Lear's physical nakedness in the pivotal scene in act 3.

It is, however, a common mistake to assume that the words of the Fool encompass and encapsulate the wisdom that Shakespeare wishes to convey in the play. In fact, and on the contrary, he shows that the wisdom of the Fool is insufficient. It is itself naked. Conscience can be informed only by the "wisdom" it serves, and the "wisdom" of the Fool is very much a worldly wisdom. It understands politics; it understands *realpolitik*; it is Machiavellian, albeit in an apparently benign way (unlike the "wisdom" of Edmund, who epitomizes Machiavellianism at its most base and ugly). "Thou hadst little wit in thy bald crown when thou gav'st thy golden one away" (1.4.166–67). This is the limit and the summit, the crowning moment, of the Fool's wisdom. The King is foolish, in the eyes of the Fool, for losing his kingdom, for losing his power, for exchanging the comforts of his crown for the discomforts of his crownlessness. The Fool would not understand the wisdom of Kent, speaking from the discomfort and humiliation of the stocks, into which he has been placed for defying the secular power, that "[n]othing almost sees miracles / But misery" (2.2.168–69). This, for the Fool, would be folly. Yet this is, for Shakespeare, as for Kent, the beginning of wisdom. The deepest insights in *King Lear* come from those who come to wisdom through suffering, who perceive, furthermore, that the *acceptance* of suffering is the beginning of wisdom. For the Fool, who seems to believe that wisdom is connected with the pursuit of comfort, or the elimination of suffering, such words would be foolish.

Shakespeare's intention in showing the necessity of suffering for the attainment of wisdom is made manifest in his juxtaposition of Kent's words of wisdom with those of Edgar. The second scene of act 2 ends with Kent's proclamation that "[n]othing almost sees miracles / But misery"; the following scene has Edgar, now an outlaw forced to adopt the guise of madness as Poor Tom, proclaiming that "Edgar I nothing am" (2.4.21). Edgar is "nothing" in his "misery" and is fit to see miracles, or fit to be the means by which others may see them. He will "with presented nakedness outface / The winds and persecutions of the sky" (2.4.11–12) and, in his own nakedness, will inspire Lear to do likewise.

Edgar, disguised as Poor Tom (a "madman"), becomes the voice of sanity and wisdom in the second half of the play, in much the same way that the Fool is the voice of sanity and wisdom in the first half. The difference is that Poor Tom's wisdom is spiritual, unlike the worldliness of the Fool, and, indeed, is avowedly Christian. The Fool greets Poor Tom's arrival with fear: "Come not in here, Nuncle, here's a spirit. Help me, help me!" And again, the Fool repeats: "A spirit, a spirit. He says his name's Poor Tom" (3.4.39–40, 42). Edgar enters, reciting a line from a ballad about the Franciscans ("Through the sharp hawthorn blows the cold wind") and bemoaning how the Devil, "the foul fiend", had led him "through fire and through flame" (3.4.45–46, 51). The Franciscan connection is apposite and surely not accidental since Saint Francis was known as the *jongleur de Dieu*—God's juggler, or a "fool for Christ"—who famously stripped himself naked in public and, "with presented nakedness", witnessed to his "houseless poverty" (3.4.26). Edgar, as Poor Tom, plays the Franciscan part to perfection and begins to eclipse the Fool as the voice of sanity and to replace him in the role as Lear's conscience. Compare, for instance, the pragmatic worldliness of the Fool's "wisdom" with Poor Tom's allusion to the Ten Commandments followed by his candid confession of sin:

> *Fool.* This cold night will turn us all to fools and mad-men.
> *Edgar.* Take heed o' th' foul fiend; obey thy parents; keep thy word's justice; swear not; commit not with man's sworn spouse; set not thy sweet heart on proud array. Tom's a-cold.
> *Lear.* What hast thou been?
> *Edgar.* A servingman, proud in heart and mind; that curled my hair, wore gloves in my cap; served the lust of my mistress' heart, and did the act of darkness with her; swore as many oaths as I spake words, and broke them in the sweet face of heaven. One that slept in the contriving of lust, and waked to do it. Wine loved I deeply, dice dearly; and in woman out-paramoured the Turk. False of heart, light of ear, bloody of hand; hog in sloth, fox in stealth, wolf in greediness, dog in madness, lion in prey. Let not the creaking of shoes nor the rustling of silks betray thy poor heart to woman. Keep thy foot out of brothels, thy hand out of plackets, thy pen from lenders' books, and defy the foul fiend. Still through the hawthorn blows the cold wind.... (3.4.78–100)

"Tom's a-cold." Sanity, seen as madness by the worldly, is out in the cold, confessing its sins, and gaining wisdom through suffering. (Meanwhile, insanity, "Lady the Brach", is in the warmth of Gloucester's castle, standing by the fire in the stench of its own iniquity, corrupted by the pursuit of comfort.) Tom repeats the refrain from the Franciscan ballad, and Lear, pricked with the hawthorn of conscience more than by the cold wind, emulates Poor Tom's example, and the example of Saint Francis, by tearing off his clothes and proclaiming, "Off, off, you lendings!" (3.4.111). This is the pivotal moment of the play, the point on which the drama turns, the moment when Lear finally goes "mad". It is the "madness" of religious conversion. His conscience is baptized, and the Fool makes way for Edgar. From this moment, the Fool fades from view (so much so that his disappearance is hardly noticed) and Edgar emerges in his place as Lear's *Christian* conscience. "The Prince of Darkness is a gentleman", Poor Tom proclaims, and when Lear asks him, "What is your study?" he answers: "How to prevent the fiend, and to kill vermin" (3.4.146, 161–62). To Lear's unbaptized conscience, these words would have appeared foolish. He would have seen the poverty-stricken surface of the tramp and not the depths of his wisdom; he would have perceived that the vermin were fleas or lice, not sins and vice. Now, however, he refers to Poor Tom as "this philosopher" or as this "learnèd Theban" (3.4.157, 160), the latter reminiscent of the famous Tiresias, the blind seer of Greek legend whose eyeless vision is far better than those with eyes to see. The parallel with Poor Tom, who sees more in the "blindness" of his "madness" than the world sees in its "sanity", and who in his poverty is richer than kings, is clear enough.

## 24

## "WHEN MADMEN LEAD THE BLIND ..."

Once one perceives the importance and profundity of Edgar's role and purpose, one begins to see that even his "nonsense" makes sense, albeit in the coded way in which a riddle makes sense. Take, for instance, the words with which Edgar brings this pivotal scene to a close:

> Child Rowland to the dark tower came;
> His word was still, "Fie, foh, and fum,
> I smell the blood of a British man."

Rowland, the nephew of Charlemagne, the Holy Roman Emperor, and the hero of the medieval classic *The Song of Roland*, is a symbol of Christian resistance to the infidels; he is also a symbol of Christian martyrdom. The juxtaposition of Roland with the nursery tale of Jack the Giant-Killer, or Jack and the Beanstalk, is intriguing. This nursery tale, a great favorite of G. K. Chesterton, who perceived it as a perennial reminder of the struggle of the righteous underdog against the encroachments of iniquitous power, appears to be an allusion to the play's own inner struggle between the Machiavellian giants of infidel iniquity and the righteous underdogs, stripped of power but gaining thereby in faith and wisdom. As with *The Song of Roland*, Shakespeare's *Lear* recounts the struggle between the Christian underdog and the infidel hordes; and, as with Jack the Giant-Killer, it is a struggle between the Giant Might of the State and the plight of powerless dissidents. The recitation of the Giant's ominous chant, "Fie, foh, and fum, / I smell the blood of a British man", seems to evoke the martyrdom of Catholics in Shakespeare's own time at the hands of the Giant power of the state and conjures the shadow of the looming presence of the play's own malicious giants, Goneril, Regan, and Edmund, who crave the blood of their powerless enemies.

The use of the crime of "treason" as the justification for the persecution and execution of Catholics in Elizabethan and Jacobean England is evoked in the use of the charge of treason by Cornwall and Regan against the innocent Gloucester. The word "traitor" is employed no fewer than four times by Cornwall and Regan in the space of only sixteen lines (3.7.23–38), a repetition that must have resonated potently with the highly charged politics of Shakespeare's England.

Edgar's words at the beginning of act 4, coming immediately after the horrific punishment carried out by Cornwall and Regan against the "traitor" Gloucester (Edgar's father), and immediately before Edgar sees Gloucester in his pitiable blinded state, are particularly powerful and singularly apt:

> Yet better thus, and known to be contemned,
> Than still contemned and flattered. To be worst,
> The lowest and most dejected thing of fortune,
> Stands still in esperance, lives not in fear:
> The lamentable change is from the best,
> The worst returns to laughter. (4.1.1–6)

It is "better" to be "known to be contemned" (by the state), Edgar insists, "[t]han still contemned [by God] and flattered". The one whose conscience is clean "stands still in esperance [hope]" (of salvation) and "lives not in fear" (of final damnation). The words about the "lamentable change" being "from the best" while the "worst returns to laughter" reminds us of *The Consolation of Philosophy* by Boethius, as do the words of Kent from the "misery" of the stocks: "Fortune, good night; / Smile once more, turn thy wheel" (2.3.175–76).

The arrival of Gloucester allows Shakespeare to play with the axiomatic paradoxes at the heart of the play: the blind seer, the wise fool, and the sane madman. "I stumbled when I saw" (4.1.19), says Gloucester, alluding to his "blindness" (when he still had his sight) in believing the treachery of Edmund and in condemning the innocent Edgar. "Bad is the trade that must play fool to sorrow" (4.1.43), says Edgar, possibly a coded allusion to Shakespeare's own position as a "closet dissident" daring to speak out against the injustices of the time only in the metadramatic language of blind men, madmen, and fools. " 'Tis the times' plague, when madmen lead the blind" (4.1.46), says Gloucester, his double-edged sharpness serving as an implicit metadramatic indictment of the status quo in Jacobean England. Seeing more clearly now that he is blind, Gloucester speaks disdainfully of "the superfluous and lust-dieted man" who "will not see / Because he does not feel" (4.1.69–71). Physical blindness is as nothing compared to the metaphysical blindness of those who succumb to the comfortable numbness of secular ambition and the materialism it serves.

The same axiomatic paradox prevails in the following scene, in which Albany becomes Goneril's "fool". "My fool usurps my body" (4.2.28), says Goneril, expressing her contempt for her husband. As ever, however, the "fool" in *Lear* is more than it seems. Though, no doubt, Goneril is referring to her husband, it is Edmund who is "usurping" her body. We have just learned of Goneril's adulterous relationship with him, or at least her adulterous intentions toward him. In this sense, Shakespeare is saying that Goneril, being a fool, sees her husband as a fool, whereas, in fact, Edmund is the fool, morally speaking, through his lack of virtue. One might even say that Goneril's own lustful passion, her sin, is the "fool" that usurps her body. Legitimacy, in the Christian understanding of marriage, is the love, conjugal and otherwise, between husband and wife; illegitimacy is lust and adultery, both of which can be said to usurp the legitimate bounds of marriage. In this context, Edmund's own illegitimacy seems to accentuate the deeper meanings of "foolishness" being presented to us.

If Albany is Goneril's "fool", we should not be surprised that he fulfils the same function as Lear's Fool and Lear's "madman", Edgar. Throughout the scene, he is the conveyer of wisdom, though Goneril, unlike Lear, is not disposed to listen to the promptings of her "conscience". "O Goneril!" Albany exclaims upon entering the scene, immediately after Goneril has proclaimed him her "fool":

> You are not worth the dust which the rude wind
> Blows in your face. I fear your disposition:
> That nature which contemns its origin
> Cannot be bordered certain in itself;
> She that herself will sliver and disbranch
> From her material sap perforce must wither
> And come to deadly use. (4.2.29–36)

On the literal level of the drama, the virtuous Albany is warning his wife that her sinfulness and her evil disposition will have evil consequences; on the deeper level of the metadrama, it is difficult to avoid the conclusion that Shakespeare, the Catholic, is referring to the Anglican church, and its anomalous position, when he speaks of the "nature which contemns its origin" not being able to "be bordered certain in itself" (that which breaks with tradition will not have the authority to define doctrine) and "will sliver and disbranch / From her material sap" (will become separated from the living tradition and sacramental life of the Church) and thus "perforce must wither / And come to deadly use." Albany's words echo the "prophecy" of the Fool in act 3:

> When priests are more in word than matter;
> When brewers mar their malt with water;
> When nobles are their tailors' tutors,
> No heretics burned, but wenches' suitors ...
>
> . . . . . . . . . . . . . . . . .
>
> Then shall the realm of Albion
> Come to great confusion. (3.2.81–84, 91–92)

On the most obvious level, the reference to priests being "more in word than matter" alludes to hypocritical clergy failing to practice what they preach. Shakespeare may, however, have had more in mind than a merely Chaucerian condemnation of bad clergy. By Shakespeare's time, the speculation of many Catholics toward Anglicanism was such that it was commonly believed that the Anglican clergy were not validly ordained and that, therefore, they were priests "more in word than matter".[1]

Goneril responds to her husband's reproach with contempt, telling him that "the text is foolish" upon which his sermon is based. Albany replies, "Wisdom and goodness to the vile seem vile: / Filths savor but themselves" (4.2.37–39). The riposte is incisive. Goneril considers Albany's Christian approach to virtue "foolish" because her lack of virtue makes her blind to "wisdom and goodness". Albany is a "fool" to the eyes of the blind. Goneril's contempt for Christianity is made manifest when she calls her husband a "[m]ilk-livered man" who "bear'st a cheek for blows" (4.2.50–51), indicating her disdain for anyone who "turns the other cheek". She, like Edmund, her partner in adultery, is a disciple of Machiavelli, not of Christ.

---

[1] The invalidity of Anglican orders was not formally promulgated by the Catholic Church until *Apostolicae curae* in the reign of Pope Leo XIII (1878–1903), but because of the changes to the consecration of bishops in the Edwardian Ordinal, during the short reign of King Edward VI (1547–1553), speculation had already begun with regard to the validity, or otherwise, of Anglican orders.

## 25

## REASON IN MADNESS

The denouement begins in earnest when Edgar heals his father of his suicidal despair: "Why I do trifle thus with his despair / Is done to cure it" (4.6.33–34). "Thy life's a miracle", Edgar tells Gloucester after the latter's failed "suicide" attempt, adding that the "fiend" (despair) has parted from him (4.6.55, 72). Gloucester's recovery of hope is connected to his embrace and acceptance of suffering:

> [H]enceforth I'll bear
> Affliction till it do cry out itself
> "Enough, enough," and die. (4.6.75–77)

"Bear free and patient thoughts" (4.6.80), counsels Edgar, reminding Gloucester that true freedom is connected to patience, particularly patience under crosses, patience in the face of adversity and suffering. He who loses such patience loses his freedom and becomes a slave to his appetites, a slave to sin.

As Edgar utters these words of perennial wisdom to his father, King Lear enters "fantastically dressed in wild flowers". It is now that Shakespeare's genius really excels. Lear, the epitome of "madness", emerges as a figure of Christ, the epitome of sanity. "No, they cannot touch me for coining", Lear proclaims; "I am the King himself" (4.6.83–84). This is the first clue to the figurative appearance of Christ, though it becomes more obvious later. Lear is not a counterfeit king; he is "the King himself", the True King from whom all other kings derive their authority. Edgar alludes to the Christ connection immediately by heralding Lear's appearance with the exclamation "O thou side-piercing sight!" (4.6.85), a phrase that encapsulates both the tragedy and the comedy of Lear's "madness". His flower-clad appearance is side-piercingly comic, yet Edgar's words also remind us of the piercing of Christ's side after his death on the Cross. No doubt, to the eyes of the blind, the sight of the "King of the Jews" wearing a crown of thorns would have been side-piercingly comic. Lear declares that he is "cut to th' brains" (4.6.195), referring to a presumably imaginary head wound and also to his "madness". His words remind us of the crown of thorns piercing the head of Christ. Lear's purgatorially purified imagination is now fit to receive the stigmata, the very wounds of Christ, echoing the Franciscan "madness" of Edgar (Saint Francis having famously received the stigmata). Immediately afterward, we are given an even clearer indication of the juxtaposition of Lear's suffering with the suffering of Christ:

> *Lear.* No seconds? all myself?
> Why, this would make a man a man of salt,
> To use his eyes for garden water-pots,
> Ay, and laying autumn's dust.
> *Gentleman.* Good sir—
> *Lear.* I will die bravely, like a smug bridegroom. What!
> I will be jovial: come, come; I am a king;
> Masters, know you that? (4.6.196–203)

The imagery in these few lines is awash with references to the Agony in the Garden. "No seconds? all myself?" alludes to the fact that Christ is left alone in his Agony. After he had beseeched his disciples, his "seconds", to stay awake, they had fallen asleep. This weakness on the part of his closest companions "would make a man a man of salt, / To use his eyes for garden water-pots". The tears of saltwater fall to the ground, watering the Garden. Ultimately, Christ's Passion and subsequent Resurrection ("Then there's life in 't" [4.6.205], says Lear at the end of this Passion-coded discourse) would water "autumn's dust", the dust of the Fall. He "will die bravely" on the following day, "like a smug bridegroom". Christ, of course, referred to himself, through his parables, as the Bridegroom, and he is, of course, "a king", though many denied his Kingship and were scandalized by it: "I am a king; / Masters, know you that?" The faithful know it; the infidels do not.

Why, one wonders, is Shakespeare so intent on equating Lear with Christ? He is indicating that, having shown contrition and having taken up his own cross, Lear has mystically united himself with the suffering of Christ. In so doing, Christ's very presence will be mystically united with the one who takes up his cross and follows him. Lear is one with Christ.

The profundities now come thick and fast. "Nature's above art in that respect" (4.6.86), proclaims Lear, an allusion to the popular

Renaissance debate concerning the relative importance of nature ("gift", talent or inspiration) and art (training). In insisting on the primacy of God-given talent and inspiration over artfulness and cunning, Lear is really encapsulating the inherent dynamic of the whole play. On one side are the "sheep" who come to an acceptance of God's grace, and the virtue that is its fruit (Lear, Cordelia, Edgar, Kent, Gloucester, Albany); on the other are the "goats" who refuse God's grace and rely on their own artfulness and cunning (Goneril, Regan, Edmund, Cornwall).

Lear now swaps roles with Edgar, espousing seemingly delirious "reason in madness", or, rather, reason in riddles. In the sense that Edgar was a figurative representation of Lear's Christian conscience, Lear *becomes* Edgar as soon as he becomes one with his conscience. Referring to the words of flattery of Goneril and Regan, he remarks with humility that "they told me I was everything; 'tis a lie, I am not ague-proof" (4.6.105–7). When Gloucester asks to kiss his hand, he responds: "Let me wipe it first; it smells of mortality" (4.6.135). Cured of his pride, he denounces the harlotry of his daughters with the same shrill sanity that had characterized Edgar's earlier denunciation of the "fiend":

> Behold yond simp'ring dame,
> Whose face between her forks presages snow,
> That minces virtue and does shake the head
> To hear of pleasure's name.
> The fitchew, nor the soilèd horse, goes to 't
> With a more riotous appetite.
> Down from the waist they are Centaurs,
> Though women all above:
> But to the girdle do the gods inherit,
> Beneath is all the fiend's.
> There's hell, there's darkness, there is the sulphurous pit,
> Burning, scalding, stench, consumption; fie, fie, fie! (4.6.120–31)

Having regained the "madness" of humility, Lear is now ready to be reunited with Cordelia.

"Ripeness is all" (5.2.11), Edgar reminds his father, and Lear is now ripe enough in wisdom and virtue to meet the daughter he had wronged and beg forgiveness, just as Gloucester had ripened through suffering to be reconciled with the son he had wronged. Having been reunited with his heart (*coeur de Lear*), the king is now ready to suffer whatever fortune throws at him. Even the prospect of prison is desirable if it means being united with Cordelia:

> Come, let's away to prison:
> We two alone will sing like birds i' th' cage:
> When thou dost ask me blessing, I'll kneel down
> And ask of thee forgiveness: so we'll live,
> And pray, and sing, and tell old tales, and laugh
> At gilded butterflies, and hear poor rogues
> Talk of court news; and we'll talk with them too,
> Who loses and who wins, who's in, who's out;
> And take upon's the mystery of things,
> As if we were God's spies: and we'll wear out,
> In a walled prison, packs and sects of great ones
> That ebb and flow by th' moon. (5.3.8–19)

Lear gets his desire instantly, as Edmund orders them to be taken to prison. His response is one of joy: "Upon such sacrifices, my Cordelia, / The gods themselves throw incense" (5.3.20–21). It is difficult to read these lines of Lear without the ghostly presence of martyred Catholics coming to mind. There is circumstantial evidence to suggest that the young Shakespeare had known the Jesuit martyr Edmund Campion, and even stronger evidence to suggest that he had known Robert Southwell, the Jesuit poet and martyr who had ministered secretly to London's beleaguered Catholics in the early 1590s.[1] The Jesuits were "traitors" in the eyes of Elizabethan and Jacobean law but were "God's spies" in the eyes of England's Catholics. If caught, they were imprisoned and tortured before being publicly executed. Since it seems likely that Shakespeare had known Southwell, and since it is even possible that Shakespeare might have been among the large crowd that witnessed Southwell being executed, the words of Lear resonate with potent poignancy: "Upon such sacrifices ... [t]he gods themselves throw incense." Within this context, the repetition of the word "traitor" four times in only sixteen lines by Regan and Cornwall during their interrogation of Gloucester has perhaps an added significance. It is also significant perhaps that Edmund declares himself a disciple of the new secular creed of Machiavelli almost immediately after these words of Lear are spoken. "[K]now thou this, that men / Are as the time is" (5.3.31–32), he declares, implicitly

---

[1] See Joseph Pearce, *The Quest for Shakespeare* (San Francisco: Ignatius Press, 2008).

deriding the "madness" of Lear's faith-driven words in favor of relativism and self-serving *realpolitik*. Lear himself had criticized the Machiavellian worldliness of Edmund and his ilk in his stated desire that he and Cordelia, from the sanity and sanctity of their prison cell, should "laugh at gilded butterflies", those elaborately attired courtiers fluttering over nothing but fads and fashions, "and hear poor rogues / Talk of court news", in the knowledge that they as "God's spies" will outlast, even in "a walled prison", the "packs and sects of great ones / That ebb and flow by th' moon". Fashions come and go, Lear seems to be saying, but the Truth remains. He also seems to be implying, through his reference to the moon, that it is Edmund and the play's other "gilded butterflies" and "poor rogues" who are the real lunatics, trading the promise of virtue's eternal reward for life's transient pleasures, trading sanity for the madness of Machiavelli.

Lear's "reason in madness" culminates in the enigma of his last words, uttered over the dead body of Cordelia:

> Do you see this? Look on her. Look, her lips,
> Look there, look there. (5.3.312–13)

His last vision, moments before his death, is that of Cordelia risen from the dead. He dies, therefore, deliriously happy.

Perhaps G. K. Chesterton had the deliriously happy Lear in mind when he dubbed Shakespeare as "delirious" in comparing him to Chaucer:

> Chaucer was a poet who came at the end of the medieval age and order
> ... the final fruit and inheritor of that order.... [H]e was much more
> sane and cheerful and normal than most of the later writers. He was less
> delirious than Shakespeare, less harsh than Milton, less fanatical than Bun-
> yan, less embittered than Swift.[2]

The fact is that Chaucer could condemn the corruption of his own day through the perspective of a Christian faith that he knew all his compatriots shared. Shakespeare lived at a time of philosophical and theological fragmentation in which the medieval age and order had been broken. He could not condemn the corruption of his age through the perspective of the Christian faith that he shared with Chaucer because the faith of Chaucer was now outlawed. Like Cordelia, he had little

---

[2] G. K. Chesterton, *Chaucer* (London: Faber & Faber, 1932), p. 12.

option but to "[l]ove, and be silent". Shakespeare's delirium was the
delirium of Lear, the delirium of Edgar. It was "reason in madness".
Indeed, one cannot avoid hearing the delirium of Shakespeare in the
words of Edgar as he enunciates the final words of this finest of plays:

> The weight of this sad time we must obey,
> Speak what we feel, not what we ought to say.
> The oldest hath borne most: we that are young
> Shall never see so much, nor live so long. (5.3.325–28)

In Edgar's words we hear a lament for contemporary England, and a
lament, perhaps, for Shakespeare's own recently deceased father, who
had been persecuted for his Catholic faith. We hear also a lament for
the loss of Catholic England and the rise of the modernism of Machiavelli. We hear a swan song for Chaucer's England. Yet there remains
hope, a hope that is enshrined in the play's happy ending. "All friends
shall taste / The wages of their virtue," says Albany, "and all foes / The
cup of their deservings" (5.3.304–6). Justice is done. Edmund, Goneril,
Regan, and Cornwall are dead. Cordelia and Lear are also dead, but
there is an inkling in Lear's final vision that the lips of Cordelia, and
those of Lear himself, are about to "taste / The wages of their virtue".
And, of course, there is sublime hope in the fact that the kingdom is
left in the hands of Edgar, whose baptized Christian conscience had
restored Lear to his sanity. It is the meekness of Edgar that inherits the
earth, not the Machiavellian madness of Edmund or the more benign
secularism of the Fool. As with the climax to all good comedies, all's
well that ends well.

   It is indeed ironic, and paradoxically perplexing, that this most delirious of Shakespeare's plays is usually considered a tragedy, even though,
for those who see with the eyes of Lear, or Edgar, or Cordelia, it has a
happy ending. Perhaps the real tragedy is that so many of those who
read Shakespeare do not possess the eyes of Lear, Edgar, and Cordelia.
In the infernal and purgatorial sufferings of life, it is all too easy to lose
sight of the promise of paradise. If we succumb to this self-inflicted,
self-centered blindness, we will see only a tragedy where we should see
a Divine Comedy.

# EPILOGUE: WHY PROTESTANTS SHOULD NOT BE SCARED OF THE CATHOLIC SHAKESPEARE

Over the previous chapters, we have examined three of Shakespeare's plays, seeking a textual exegesis based upon the overwhelming historical evidence that the Bard was a believing Catholic. If the world's greatest playwright was a "papist", as the documentary evidence of his life suggests,[1] it becomes necessary to read his works objectively in the light of such knowledge. In seeing the plays through the playwright's Catholic eyes, we see an abundance of additional evidence buttressing the solid historical evidence. It is as though the documentary evidence and the textual evidence form two halves of a gothic arch, the one half serving to support the other. Taken together, the case for the Catholic Shakespeare would seem to be impregnable.

What should Shakespeare's numerous Protestant admirers make of such a revelation? Should they feel threatened by the Catholic Shakespeare? Should they run away from him? Should they retreat to a position of denial, in spite of the evidence? Should they become suspicious of his plays? Should they stop reading them (heaven forbid!)?

Of course Protestants should not stop reading the plays, nor should they shy away from their author, not least because there is absolutely nothing to fear. The surprising truth is that the Catholic Shakespeare emerges as someone with whom Protestants can feel very comfortable. Far from being a threat, he emerges as an unexpected ally, whom Protestants should welcome with open arms, open hearts, and open minds. How is this? How can the old enmity be put to one side? How can Protestants see the Catholic Bard as a friend?

The answer lies in the plays themselves. Throughout the plays that we have examined in the preceding pages, and throughout those many plays that have remained beyond the scope of this volume, we see that Shakespeare's Catholicism does not manifest itself primarily in a doctrinal dialectic with Protestantism but in a philosophical dialectic with

---

[1] See appendix A to this volume or read Joseph Pearce, *The Quest for Shakespeare: The Bard of Avon and the Church of Rome* (San Francisco: Ignatius Press, 2008).

the emergent atheism (de facto if not always de jure) of the embryonic Enlightenment. Although allusions to the doctrinal disputes of the Reformation and Counter-Reformation are present in the plays, they are eclipsed by the overarching dialectic with secularism.

Shakespeare's heroes and heroines are invariably adherents of tradition-oriented philosophy and religion, motivated in their choices and their actions by an implicit understanding of Christian orthodoxy and a desire to conduct themselves with traditional virtue. His villains, in contrast, are Machiavels, disciples of the new cynical creed of Machiavelli, who are motivated solely by a self-serving desire to get what they want. Shakespeare's greatest heroines, such as Cordelia, Portia, Desdemona, and Isabella, exhibit a self-sacrificial love emblematic of the Christian saint. His great villains—such as Edmund, Goneril, Regan, and Cornwall in *King Lear*; King Claudius in *Hamlet*; Iago in *Othello*; or the demonically twisted Macbeths—are all philosophical iconoclasts, ripping to shreds Christian philosophy and openly defying orthodox moral theology.

Clearly, Protestants can feel entirely comfortable with the inherent moral dynamic of Christian orthodoxy in the plays, and this is surely one of the reasons that Protestant and Catholic scholars are equally at home in the moral atmosphere that the Bard presents to his audience. Yet why is there such a seemingly curious silence from Shakespeare, for the most part, on the doctrinal differences between Protestantism and Catholicism? Would we not expect to see more of an obvious engagement with the differences between Catholic and Calvinist theology? Is not such comparative silence an argument against the Bard's Catholicism? On the contrary, and paradoxically, the silence is, if anything, further evidence of his "papist" sympathies.

Let us put ourselves in Shakespeare's shoes. As a Catholic in Elizabethan and Jacobean England, his enemy was not primarily the relatively powerless Puritans but the compromisers and equivocators of the Anglican establishment. It was the Anglican ascendancy that was responsible for the systematic, state-sponsored persecution of England's Catholics. This ascendancy, putting its "faith" in expediency and *realpolitik*, epitomized the unprincipled Machiavellianism that is the target of Shakespeare's philosophical and artistic ire. Let us not forget that this same Machiavellian establishment was responsible for persecuting the Puritans at the very same time that it was endeavoring to crush the "papists". Richard Clyfton, the Puritan whose influence on the

Pilgrim Fathers is so well documented, was preaching his separatist beliefs at his parish in Nottinghamshire from 1586 to 1605, i.e., at exactly the same time as Shakespeare was writing his plays in London. The fact is that Puritans and Catholics shared a common disdain for the impositions of the state church and shared in the persecution meted out by the state church against its "nonconformist" enemies. It should be remembered, for instance, that Henry Barrowe and John Greenwood, two of the leaders of Puritan separatism, were executed for sedition in 1593, even as Shakespeare's Jesuit friend Robert Southwell was being tortured in the Tower of London for his own "crimes" of "treachery" and "sedition". Two years later, Southwell would share the same fate as Barrowe and Greenwood, being executed for his refusal to conform to the dictates of the state religion.

Many Puritans, as conscientious objectors to the 1559 Act of Uniformity that made attendance at Anglican services compulsory, were fined for their defiance of the law. In other words, they found themselves in exactly the same onerous position as Shakespeare's father and daughter, both of whom were fined by the state for their refusal to attend the services of the state religion. Is it any wonder that Shakespeare should reserve his rhetorical skills for those who were persecuting his friends and family rather than expending time and effort attacking those who were also being persecuted by the same common Machiavellian foe? It may or may not be true that my enemy's enemy is my friend, but is it certainly true that one is not going to spend valuable time attacking the enemies of one's enemy.

Another intriguing parallel between the plight of Catholics and Puritans is their shared hope that the persecution would end following the death of Elizabeth and the accession to the throne of James I. Catholics had high hopes that a period of tolerance would follow in the wake of James' accession, and the relatively overt Catholicism of Shakespeare's *Measure for Measure*, in which the virtuous heroine is an aspirant to the Franciscan sisterhood, was a measure of Shakespeare's own hopes of a new era of religious liberty for Catholics. Similarly, the Puritans had hoped for religious liberty following James' accession, and as with the Catholics, their hopes would be dashed. At the Hampton Court Conference in 1604, the king and the Anglican establishment united in opposition to Puritan nonconformism, and a new period of persecution was heralded for Catholics and Puritans alike.

In 1606, the year in which Shakespeare's daughter was fined for her Catholic recusancy, the Anglican archbishop of York, Tobias Matthew, began a ruthless campaign against both Catholic recusants and Puritan separatists. Under Matthew's draconian leadership, all nonconformists, whether Catholic or Puritan, were hounded mercilessly. Writing of the treatment of Puritan separatists, William Bradford, one of the most celebrated of the Pilgrim Fathers, described their plight in terms that are indistinguishable from the plight of England's beleaguered Catholics:

> But after these things they could not long continue in any peaceable condition, but were hunted & persecuted on every side, so as their former afflictions were but as flea-bitings in comparison of these which now came upon them. For some were taken & clapt up in prison, others had their houses besett & watcht night and day, & hardly escaped their hands; and ye most were faine to flie & leave their howses & habitations, and the means of their livelehood.... Yet seeing, them selves thus molested ... and that ther was no hope of their continuance ther, by a joynte consente they resolved to goe into yᵉ Low-Countries, wher they heard was freedome of Religion for all men; as also how sundrie from London, & other parts of ye land, had been exiled and persecuted for yᵉ same cause, & were gone thither, and lived at Amsterdam, & in other places of yᵉ land.[2]

Whereas the Puritan exiles found sanctuary in Amsterdam, England's Catholic exiles sought sanctuary in such places as Douai and Rheims in France, at Valladolid in Spain, and of course in Rome; otherwise their plight was essentially the same, being hounded from their country by the Machiavellian machinations of the state and its "established" religion. Again, is it any wonder that Shakespeare's rhetorical spleen is vented against the Machiavels and not against the Calvinists?

The parallels between the plight of England's Catholics and Puritans would eventually find historical expression in the migration of Catholic and Puritan exiles to the New World, to Maryland and New England respectively, and only much later would the two groups fall into political conflict with each other. Since such conflict occurred decades after Shakespeare's death, it forms no part of his imaginative engagement with the two parties. Instead, we have to see the parallel plight of Puritans and Catholics in Shakespeare's own time as the historical context

---

[2] William Bradford, *Bradford's History "Of Plimoth Plantation"*, ed. Ted Hildebrandt (Boston: Wright and Potter, 1898), pp. 14–15.

that serves as the background to his life and work. Once such a context is grasped, Shakespeare emerges paradoxically and surprisingly as an unwitting ally of Protestant nonconformism, albeit by an accident of history rather than by any conscious design or desire on his part. Furthermore, he emerges as a powerful prophet of the times in which orthodox Christians, Catholic and Protestant alike, find themselves today.

Shakespeare writes with unequaled eloquence about the conflict between Christianity and secular fundamentalism. He defends Christian virtue in the characterization of his Christian heroes and heroines and in the cathartically Christian denouements of his dramatic plots. His heroes defy the secular fundamentalism of the Machiavel, even unto death. They are not only Christians but are often martyrs for their virtue and their faith. In plays such as *Hamlet*, he defends the Christian realism of Augustine and Aquinas against the nascent relativism of the late Renaissance. In an age in which Catholics and Evangelicals find themselves increasingly as allies in the defense of life, liberty, and marriage, Shakespeare emerges as a powerful voice for the culture of life against the Machiavellianism of the culture of death and its poisonous relativism. Ultimately, Protestants should not be scared of the Catholic Shakespeare because he is on their side. In an age of diabolical scandal, from in utero infanticide to the destruction of marriage, the Bard of Avon is on the side of the angels.

# APPENDIX A

# SHAKESPEARE'S SHOCKING CATHOLICISM

*Time shall unfold what plighted cunning hides. . . .*

— Cordelia (*King Lear*, 1.1.282)

Could the most famous writer in history have been a Catholic? The very suggestion is enough to throw the liberal literary establishment into an apoplexy of spluttering fury. How could the Bard of Avon, who has been lauded by "queer theorists", feminists, relativists, and atheists as one of their own, be a tradition-oriented Christian? The very thought is unthinkable. And yet it seems that the unthinkable is a reality.

G. K. Chesterton certainly believed that the evidence pointed toward Shakespeare's Catholicism, stating that the "convergent common sense" that led to the belief that the Bard was a Catholic was "supported by the few external and political facts we know".[1] One presumes from this assertion that Chesterton was familiar with the considerable historical and textual evidence for Shakespeare's Catholicism that had been gathered by the nineteenth-century Shakespearian scholar Richard Simpson. Yet Simpson was not the first scholar to conclude that there was sufficient evidence to point to the Bard's Catholicism. In 1801 the French writer François René de Chateaubriand asserted that "if Shakespeare was anything at all, he was a Catholic."[2] Thomas Carlyle wrote that the "Elizabethan era with its Shakespeare, as the outcome and flower-age of all which had preceded it, is itself attributable to the Catholicism

---

[1] G. K. Chesterton, *Chaucer* (1932), reprinted in *G. K. Chesterton: The Collected Works*, vol. 18 (San Francisco: Ignatius Press), p. 333.

[2] Quoted in H. Mutschmann and K. Wentersdorf, *Shakespeare and Catholicism* (New York: Sheed and Ward, 1952), p. vi.

of the Middle Ages".[3] Carlyle's great Victorian contemporary John Henry Newman was even more emphatic about the Catholic dimension, stating that Shakespeare "has so little of a Protestant about him that Catholics have been able, without extravagance, to claim him as their own".[4] Hilaire Belloc, echoing the verdict of Newman, insisted that "the plays of Shakespeare were written by a man plainly Catholic in habit of mind." [5]

These great writers of the Victorian and Edwardian periods had perceived Shakespeare's Catholicism in the moral vision that emerges from the plays. Yet modern "scholars", blind to this moral vision, have habitually misread the plays. Instead of seeing evidence of traditional Christian morality, they see the plays as a reflection of their own secular fundamentalist prejudices. It is, therefore, necessary to discover the real Shakespeare, and the real beliefs that he held, in order to expose this literary abuse of his work. Thankfully, a good deal of solid historical scholarship in recent years has added significantly to the "few external and political facts" known by Chesterton and his contemporaries. In consequence, the claims made by Carol Curt Enos in her book *Shakespeare and the Catholic Religion* are more self-confidently emphatic than those made by Chesterton: "When many of the extant pieces of the puzzle of Shakespeare's life are assembled, it is very difficult to deny his Catholicism." [6] Every piece of the puzzle, placed painstakingly where it belongs, brings us closer to an objectively verifiable picture of the man who wrote the plays. And that man emerges as a believing Catholic at a time when Catholics were persecuted ruthlessly for their faith.

Let us examine the documentary and historical evidence.

The investigation of Shakespeare's life begins with the overwhelming evidence that the faith of his family was defiantly Catholic. Much of the historical scholarship has centered on the spiritual will of John Shakespeare, the poet's father, which clearly demonstrates his Catholic *bona fides* and itemizes his earnest desire to die a Catholic, in good faith and conscience. Item IV is particularly striking for its enunciation of his

[3] Quoted in Peter Ackroyd, *Shakespeare: The Biography* (London: Chatto and Windus, 2005), p. 472.

[4] John Henry Newman, *The Idea of a University* (1873), quoted in Peter Milward, *Shakespeare the Papist* (Naples, Fla.: Sapientia, 2005), p. x.

[5] Hilaire Belloc, *Europe and the Faith* (1920), quoted in Velma Richmond, *Shakespeare, Catholicism, and Romance* (New York: Continuum, 2000), p. 16. ·

[6] Carol Curt Enos, *Shakespeare and the Catholic Religion* (Pittsburgh: Dorrance, 2000), p. 45.

desire that he should receive the last rites of the Church, and his hope that the *desire* for the last rites should suffice should there be no priest to administer the sacrament at his moment of death. In the time of persecution in which John Shakespeare was living, it was a crime, punishable by death, to harbor a priest in one's home. It was, therefore, very possible that no priest would be available for the Catholic *in extremis*. It is in the spirit of this gloom of persecution, with the cloud of unknowing looming overhead, that John Shakespeare's defiant desire for the last rites should be understood.

Other items of the will lamented and repented any "murmuration against god, or the catholic faith" and offered "infinite thanks" to God for all the benefits he had received, including "the holy knowledge of him and his true Catholic faith".[7] The strength of the evidence that John Shakespeare remained a defiant Catholic, in the midst of widespread anti-Catholic persecution by the Elizabethan state, has forced most modern scholars to accept that William Shakespeare was brought up as a believing Catholic. Such evidence is strengthened by the fact that John Shakespeare would later fall foul of the law for his continued commitment to the Catholic resistance, being fined in 1592 for his "recusancy", i.e., his refusal, in conscience, to attend Anglican services. It should be noted also that Shakespeare's mother was a member of the Arden family, one of the most militantly defiant Catholic families in the whole of England.

If the overwhelming weight of the evidence has forced most scholars to accept that Shakespeare was raised in a staunchly Catholic family, they insist that he lost his faith after he came to seek his fortune in London. This is very convenient for the secular scholar because it enables him to see any Catholic influence in the plays as a remnant of a childhood faith that the poet had since rejected. Unfortunately for these scholars, the actual facts of Shakespeare's life suggest that he remained a believing Catholic throughout his years in London and that his Catholic faith informed his works.

Again, let us examine the evidence.

Before his arrival in London, there is evidence that he might have spent some time as a schoolmaster in a militantly Catholic home in Lancashire, and there is also evidence that he was forced to leave his hometown of Stratford in a hurry because of persecution by Sir Thomas

---

[7] See Joseph Pearce, *The Quest for Shakespeare*.

Lucy, a notorious persecutor of Catholics. In London, Shakespeare's patron, the Earl of Southampton, was a well-known Catholic, from a staunchly Catholic family, who had the Jesuit Saint Robert Southwell as his confessor. There is considerable documentary evidence to show that Shakespeare and Southwell were friends before the latter's arrest in 1592. Southwell was tortured repeatedly during his imprisonment in the Tower of London and would be hanged, drawn, and quartered at Tyburn in 1595. He would later be canonized as one of the Forty Martyrs of England and Wales. There is also good circumstantial evidence that the young Shakespeare may have met another Jesuit martyr, Saint Edmund Campion, and it seems likely that he knew the martyred priest Robert Dibdale, who would later be beatified by the Church.

If Shakespeare counted priests among his friends, we know that he counted those who persecuted Catholics among his enemies. Court records show that he found himself embroiled in a legal dispute with William Gardiner, a justice of the peace of singularly disreputable character, "who defrauded his wife's family, his son-in-law and his stepson, oppressed his neighbors and fleeced his tenants".[8] Gardiner and his equally disreputable stepson, William Wayte ("a certain loose person of no reckoning or value, being wholly under the rule and commandment of the said Gardiner"),[9] petitioned the court for protection, securing the issue of a writ craving "sureties of the peace against William Shakespeare, Francis Langley, Dorothy Soer, wife of John Soer, and Anne Lee, for fear of death, and so forth." Although some sources have recorded that Shakespeare was being prosecuted for physically assaulting William Wayte, this is unlikely. There is no evidence that Shakespeare possessed violent tendencies, and the fact that two of his codefendants were married women suggests that any "violence" done against Wayte or Gardiner, justified or otherwise, was executed with the tongue or with the pen, not with any other part of the anatomy or with any other implement. Nonetheless, this curious court case does give us an invaluable insight into the sort of people with whom Shakespeare was choosing to associate and the sort of people whom he chose to call his enemies. It is interesting, for instance, that Anne Lee was the wife of the recusant Roger Lee, whose house had hidden many proscribed priests, and that Anne herself had been denounced in the previous year for attending Mass,

[8] Mutschmann and Wentersdorf, *Shakespeare and Catholicism*, p. 119.
[9] Ibid.

where she apparently helped the Jesuit John Gerard to hide from the authorities. Such are the people whom Shakespeare was counting among his friends in 1596.

Even more intriguing is the character of Shakespeare's enemy, William Gardiner. He is variously accused by his contemporaries of being "unchristian", "irreligious", "unchristianlike", "ungodly", and as "a man inclined to strange opinions". Some considered him an atheist, while others considered him a sorcerer or an alchemist. In a court case in 1588, he had been accused of "witchcraft, sorcery ... and holding of irreligious opinions". There is, however, one belief of which Gardiner was never in danger of being accused. Nobody would ever have accused him of being a Catholic. Whether he was a Puritan, an atheist, or a sorcerer, everyone knew that he was not a papist, not least because he had earned a reputation for persecuting London's Catholic community, of which Shakespeare was now a part.

Gardiner's virulent anti-Catholicism has been preserved for posterity in a report that he sent to Elizabeth's Privy Council in January 1585 documenting a raid on a Catholic home in London. This document exhibits Gardiner's vehement disapproval of "papistry" and gives an invaluable insight into the sort of man whom Shakespeare considered to be his enemy. Shakespeare would take his own revenge on both Gardiner and Wayte, writing them into *The Merry Wives of Windsor* and the second part of *Henry IV* as the characters of Justice Shallow and Slender, respectively. Both plays were first performed in 1597, so it is possible that Justice Gardiner, who died in November of that year, would have been aware that his adversary had "staged" his revenge.

During the final years of Elizabeth's reign, Shakespeare became involved in a controversial play about Saint Thomas More, who had been martyred for his Catholic faith on the orders of the queen's father, Henry VIII, more than sixty years earlier. Not surprisingly, the play was blocked by Sir Edmund Tilney, Master of the Revels, who was Elizabeth's official censor. Quite simply, Thomas More was still a hot potato more than sixty years after his death, touching a raw nerve not only with Elizabeth, whose father had the saint's blood on his hands, but with the Elizabethan state as a whole. Thomas More had been executed by the reigning monarch for refusing to compromise his Catholic conscience on the altar of Machiavellian *realpolitik*, making him an archetype for Campion, Dibdale, Southwell, and many others who had suffered a similar fate in the reign of Elizabeth. As such, any positive depiction of

More could be seen as a dangerous indictment of England's present rulers. The play was written by Anthony Munday, but Shakespeare seems to have become personally involved in the saga surrounding the play. The original manuscript is still in existence and contains amendments to Munday's original text that are generally believed to be by Shakespeare.[10] It seems that Shakespeare had tried to patch up Munday's original work, apparently with the intention of getting it past the censor. Shakespeare's amendments clearly illustrate his sympathy with More and his belief that there were lessons to be learned by his own time from More's holy example.

Further evidence of Shakespeare's admiration for More is discernible in Shakespeare's Sonnet 23, in which the poet employs the same pun on More's name that he had used in his addition to Munday's play. If the middle "more" in the twelfth line of the sonnet is capitalized ("More than that love which More hath more expressed"), the sonnet is transfigured into a moving tribute to the saint, in which Shakespeare contrasts his own "unperfect" love, weakened by "fear" and "rage", with the holy love "which [M]ore hath more expressed". There is also a sublime allusion to the Mass as "the perfect ceremony of love's right", reinforced by the pun on "right"/"rite" and illustrating a deep theological understanding of the Mass as the "perfect ceremony" that re-presents Christ's death for sinners as "love's right" and "love's rite". Unlocking this beguiling sonnet still further, we see that the poet laments that he is not present at this "perfect ceremony" as often as he should be because of "fear of trust", perhaps a reference to the spies who were present at these secret Masses intent on reporting the names of "papists" and on betraying the priests to the authorities. Since he does not have the heroic self-sacrificial love, even unto death, of a Thomas More, the poet desires that his "books" be his "eloquence", the "dumb presagers of my speaking breast". The final two lines are surely addressed to both the poet himself and to his reader, beseeching the latter to "learn to read" in his plays what the poet's love, silent through fear, dare not speak openly. Since they will not *hear* the poet speak his mind openly, his readers must *see* what he means in his plays, hearing with their eyes and using their own "love's fine wit" to discern his deeper meaning.

[10] For an overview of the scholarship that led to the belief that the handwriting is Shakespeare's, see Oscar James Campbell and Edward G. Quinn, eds., *The Reader's Encyclopedia of Shakespeare* (New York: MJF Books, 1966), pp. 799–800.

O learn to read what silent love hath writ,
To hear with eyes belongs to love's fine wit.

Bearing in mind Shakespeare's evident devotion to Thomas More, it is no surprise that he was persuaded to intervene in an effort to get Munday's play past the censor who had written "Perform this at your peril" in the play's margin.

In spite of Shakespeare's best efforts to make the play acceptable, Tilney refused to lift the ban on its performance. It would be a further four hundred years, during the reign of another Elizabeth, before Munday's *Sir Thomas More* would finally be performed. When the Royal Shakespeare Company staged the play at the new Globe Theatre in the summer of 2004, Shakespeare and More were at last united in art as they had always been in creed. The Bard, who in Ben Jonson's memorable tribute "was not of an age, but for all time", had finally been allowed to pay homage to the saint who, as in the title of Robert Bolt's memorable play, was "a man for all seasons".

One of the most convincing pieces of evidence for Shakespeare's Catholicism is to be found in his purchase of the Blackfriars Gatehouse in March 1613. This house was "a notorious center of Catholic activities",[11] which had "sundry backdoors and bye-ways, and many secret vaults and corners" and had been "in time past suspected, and searched for papists".[12] In 1598, acting on a report that the gatehouse was a hive of recusant activity that had "many places of secret conveyance in it" and "secret passages towards the water", i.e., toward the river Thames, from whence priests could make their getaway, the authorities raided the house. John Fortescue, the Catholic owner of the house, was absent during the search, but his wife and daughters were interrogated, admitting that they were recusants but refusing to confess that they had hidden priests in the house. In 1605 the Jesuit John Gerard, the most wanted man in England, appeared in desperation at the gatehouse, wearing a wig and false beard as a disguise and asking for shelter, stating that he did not know where else to hide.

Little is known of the history of the gatehouse in the few years from the time that the Fortescues went into exile until the time that Shakespeare purchased it, but as late as 1610 it was reported in Naples that it

---

[11] Mutschmann and Wentersdorf, *Shakespeare and Catholicism*, p. 136.

[12] T. Wright, ed., *Queen Elizabeth and Her Times: A Series of Original Letters* (London, 1838), 2:249, quoted in Mutschmann and Wentersdorf, *Shakespeare and Catholicism*, p. 137.

was the base for Jesuits plotting to "send the King an embroidered doublet and hose, which are poisoned and will be death to the wearer".[13] As much as such a statement can be dismissed as the product of the idle fantasies of embittered exiles or anti-Catholic spies, it is apparent nonetheless that Shakespeare had chosen to purchase one of the most notorious Catholic houses in the whole of London. This in itself is curious enough, but it is not by any means the end of the story.

Shakespeare chose to lease the gatehouse to John Robinson, an active Catholic whose brother had entered the English College at Rome to train for the priesthood. It is obvious that Shakespeare knew that in leasing the gatehouse to John Robinson he was leaving it in the possession of a recusant Catholic. In consequence, and as Ian Wilson surmised in *Shakespeare: The Evidence*, Robinson was "not so much Shakespeare's tenant in the Gatehouse, as his appointed guardian of one of London's best places of refuge for Catholic priests".[14] Furthermore, John Robinson was not merely a tenant but a valued friend. He visited Shakespeare in Stratford during the poet's retirement and was seemingly the only one of the Bard's London friends who was present during his final illness, signing his will as a witness.

Shakespeare died on Saint George's Day 1616, leaving the bulk of his wealth to his daughter Susanna, who had been listed as a recusant Catholic ten years earlier. Other beneficiaries of his will included several of his recusant Catholic friends. It is clear, therefore, as the Anglican clergyman Richard Davies lamented in the late 1600s, that Shakespeare "dyed a papist". It is equally clear that he lived as a papist, a fact that the English did their best to hide in the centuries after his death, and a fact that modern literary critics are trying to deny today. The news that the Bard of Avon was a passionate member of the Church of Rome is shocking news to those who have built their reputations on fallacious readings of his plays. Hopefully it is a shock from which they will not recover. It is, however, a cause of great joy to Catholics to know that William Shakespeare is on the side of the angels.

---

[13] John Morris, *The Troubles of Our Catholic Forefathers* (London: Burns and Oates, 1972), 1:144.

[14] Ian Wilson, *Shakespeare: The Evidence* (New York: St. Martin's Griffin, 1999), p. 397.

# APPENDIX B

# HOW TO READ SHAKESPEARE (OR ANYONE ELSE)

As with all things, it is best to begin with the basics. Before we can understand how to read Shakespeare properly, we need to know how to read properly; and before we can know how to read properly, we must know how to think properly.

There are two ways of thinking. We can think objectively, or we can think subjectively. Thinking objectively requires an engagement with the reality beyond ourselves in such a way that we understand the necessity of conforming ourselves to that reality. Such thought is centered not in the self but in the other. We come to understand ourselves through an understanding of the other, i.e., the truth that exists outside ourselves. On the other hand, thinking subjectively engages all experience from the perspective of the self and judges it accordingly. Such thought is centered not in the other but in the self. There is no better and more succinct way of expressing these two ways of thinking than through G. K. Chesterton's response to Holbrook Jackson, in which Chesterton is thinking objectively while Jackson is thinking subjectively:

*Jackson.* A lie is that which you do not believe.
*Chesterton.* This is a lie: so perhaps you don't believe it.
*Jackson.* Truth and falsehood in the abstract do not exist.
*Chesterton.* Then nothing else does.
*Jackson.* Truth is one's own conception of things.
*Chesterton.* The Big Blunder. All thought is an attempt to discover if one's own conception is true or not.
*Jackson.* Negations without affirmations are worthless.
*Chesterton.* And impossible.
*Jackson.* Every custom was once an eccentricity; every idea was once an absurdity.
*Chesterton.* No, no, no. Some ideas were always absurdities. This is one of them.

*Jackson.* No opinion matters finally: except your own.
*Chesterton.* Said the man who thought he was a rabbit.[1]

In this exchange, Chesterton is on the side of philosophical *realism*, a belief that metaphysical things such as love, virtue, and beauty are *real*, i.e., that they exist as an independent reality whether we believe it or not, or like it or not. Jackson is on the side of philosophical *nominalism* or *relativism*, a belief that there are no absolute truths or values and that love, virtue, and beauty are not *things* that really exist but are *concepts* constructed and labeled by the human mind to make sense of its experience. Clearly, these two positions are mutually incompatible. They cannot both be true. If one is true, the other is, ipso facto, false.

The present author is definitively and decidedly on the side of philosophical realism, which is to say that he is on the side not only of Chesterton but of Socrates, Plato, Aristotle, Augustine, Aquinas—and Shakespeare! This being so, he will argue definitively and decidedly that to think objectively is to think correctly and realistically, whereas to think subjectively is to think incorrectly and unrealistically. And if this is true of the way we think, it is equally true of the way we read. One must read objectively in order to read correctly and realistically.

Objective reading is, first and foremost, a discipline. In order to read objectively, we must discipline ourselves to avoid all temptations to subjectivity, which is to say we must avoid approaching the text with our own prejudices. A text makes sense before we read it, and its sense does not depend on our reading of it.[2] As such, we do not make sense *of* a text; rather, it should make sense *to* us—and perhaps in the case of really good books, it might not only make sense *to* us, but it might make sense *of* us! It might make us understand ourselves better in the light of the truth that comes from beyond ourselves. This is the greatest fruit of objective reading. It enables us to transcend ourselves, and our selfishness, in our engagement with the great truths of the cosmos. It enables us to grow in the presence of the genius manifested in the text. A subjective reading, on the other hand, working on the prejudiced presumption that "truth is one's own conception of things" or that "no opinion matters except your own", will be unable to transcend the self

---

[1] Chesterton's handwritten responses in his own copy of Jackson's *Platitudes in the Making*, quoted in Joseph Pearce, *Wisdom and Innocence: A Life of G. K. Chesterton* (San Francisco: Ignatius Press, 1996), pp. 172–73.

[2] This presumes, of course, that the text has objective merit and is not nonsense.

in its "making sense" of the book because nothing makes sense except the self! The tragedy is that the subjective reader is unable to grow in the presence of the genius manifested in the text because there is, for the subjective reader, no greater genius than himself![3]

Having discussed the two types of reading, it is necessary to understand that there are essentially two types of books, scientific and artistic. Scientific books deal with facts and facts alone, whereas artistic books engage the creative imagination.[4] In the case of the former, the facts should quite literally speak for themselves. In the case, for instance, of a book on arithmetic, we can read "$25 \times 2 = 50$" in only one way. In other words, there is no room, and no possibility, of reading a scientific text in any way but objectively. In the case of a more advanced work of physics, we might see another equation, "$E = mc^2$". In this case, we might not understand the intricacies of the theory of which the equation is an expression, but we will still know that it must be read objectively. If it does not make sense to us, we know or trust that it still makes sense nonetheless. If we do not understand, we *know* that we do not understand. In the case of artistic books, however, the meaning of the text is not so obvious. How can we read an artistic book objectively when there seems to be so many possible interpretations of its meaning? The only way is to see it, as far as possible, through the eyes of the author, who is not only the "other", enabling us to escape from the confines of our own subjective prejudices, but the "other" who speaks with more authority than all the other "others", i.e., the literary critics.[5]

In order to understand why the author has the authority to speak authoritatively about the text, we need to understand the nature, and supernature, of the creative process. This whole issue and its relationship to the reader's understanding of the work was expressed by J. R. R.

---

[3] Although some subjective readers, i.e., relativists, may balk at the rhetorical sweep of such a generalization, the fact remains that relativism implicitly and de facto places the center of all authority to judge the cosmos into the eye of the beholder.

[4] Although strictly and purely speaking there are only two types of books, many books are a combination of these two types. Books of history, for instance, will deal with facts, hopefully authenticated by annotated sources, but will also be subject to the historian's metahistorical presumptions based on his philosophical understanding of man and society. Since an understanding of history is derived from our philosophical understanding of reality, historians invariably read the same set of facts and come to different conclusions as to their significance. The same is true of other academic arts, mistakenly claiming to be sciences, such as politics or economics.

[5] I am aware of C. S. Lewis' debate with E. M. W. Tillyard in *The Personal Heresy*, but this is not the place to address the issues raised by Lewis in that particular debate.

Tolkien when he wrote that "only one's guardian Angel, or indeed God Himself, could unravel the real relationship between personal facts and an author's works. Not the author himself (though he knows more than any investigator), and certainly not so-called 'psychologists'."[6] In these few words we are given the tools to form a true appraisal of the role and limitations of literary criticism. Let us look closer at what he is saying.

One does not need to share Tolkien's Christian faith in order to recognize, or agree with, his insistence on the transcendent nature of the creative process and its products. The pagan poets invoked the Muse, and even an atheist such as Percy Bysshe Shelley recognized the quasi-mystical forces at work in the creative process, forces that transcend the conscious will of the author (or artist, or musical composer, etc.). In his essay "A Defense of Poetry", Shelley wrote:

> Poetry is not like reasoning, a power to be exerted according to the determination of the will. A man cannot say, "I will compose poetry." The greatest poet even cannot say it; for the mind in creation is as a fading coal which some invisible influence, like an inconstant wind, awakens to transitory brightness; this power arises from within, like the colour of a flower which fades and changes as it is developed, and the conscious portions of our natures are unprophetic either of its approach or its departure. Could this influence be durable in its original purity and force, it is impossible to predict the greatness of the results; but when composition begins, inspiration is already on the decline, and the most glorious poetry that has ever been communicated to the world is probably a feeble shadow of the original conceptions of the poet.

The insistence by Tolkien and Shelley on the transcendent nature of the creative process is crucial to a true understanding of literature and literary criticism. It is, however, the crucial *misunderstanding* of this transcendence that has led to much of the error in modern criticism. The modern misapprehension springs from the assumption that the transcendence negates the validity, and therefore the relevance, of the author's *intention*. Since the author's intention is subject to the mystical power of creativity, we need not take the intention seriously. Furthermore, if the author's intention is relatively worthless, so, ultimately, is the author himself, leaving us only with the text. The problem is that this line of

---

[6] Humphrey Carpenter, ed., *The Letters of J. R. R. Tolkien* (London: George Allen and Unwin, 1981), p. 288.

reasoning arises from a misunderstanding of what Tolkien and Shelley are actually saying. Shelley insists that "the most glorious poetry ... is probably a feeble shadow of the original conceptions of the poet." In other words, the poet is the original conceiver of the poem, and the poem a pale shadow of the poet's conception. The poem is derived from, and dependent on, the poet. It follows, therefore, that we will better understand the conception, i.e., the poem, if we better understand the conceiver, i.e., the poet. T. S. Eliot, in "The Hollow Men", echoes Shelley:

> Between the conception
> And the creation
>
> .   .   .   .   .   .   .   .   .
>
> Falls the Shadow
>
> .   .   .   .   .   .   .   .
>
> Between the potency
> And the existence
>
> .   .   .   .   .   .   .   .
>
> Falls the Shadow

For Eliot, who was on the path to Christianity when he wrote these lines, the fall of the Shadow was the shadow of the Fall, but for the atheist poet and the Christian poet alike, there is a shared understanding that the *existence* of the work cannot be separated from the *potency* that resides in the *personhood* of the poet. It is for this reason that Tolkien insists that the author "knows more than any investigator", even if the author himself cannot grasp the transcendent mystery at the heart of creativity.[7] If for "investigator" we read "critic", it can be seen that

---

[7] The fact is that all transcendent meaning remains subsistent to, and ultimately dependent upon, the fundamental beliefs of the author. Although an author might be astonished by what he has written, feeling the mystical force at work in the creative process, the astonishment is never due to the fact that his work contradicts his own beliefs. He might feel astonished, and hopefully humbled, by the fact that his work has transcended the limitations of his conscious design, but he is never shocked to discover that he has written something with which he is in fundamental disagreement! If the transcendence is due to grace, as Christians believe, such grace does not merely possess the author, working through him as though he were a *tabula rasa* on which the grace does the writing. On the contrary, the work is better understood as an *incarnation* of the mystical relationship between the gift (the grace) and the gifted. Since, for the atheist, the transcendence cannot be a spiritual force from outside, it must be a subconscious force from within. As such, for the Christian and the atheist alike, the product of the creative process remains an incarnation of the personhood of the author, his mystical or subconscious child.

Tolkien, Shelley, and Eliot are insisting that we must understand the solidity of the author and his beliefs before we listen to the opinions and beliefs of the "hollow men". Even if we accept, as we should, that a great work of literature will have a profundity of meaning beyond the conscious design of the author, we still need to see the transcendent beauty through the prism of the *personhood* of the author. If we fail to discipline ourselves to follow this critical modus operandi, we will see literature through the blurred focus of our own inadequate vision, or through the inadequate vision of a critic. Such an approach does not negate the necessity of employing our own judgment, or of giving consideration to the judgment of critics, but it insists that we should subject our judgment, and that of the critics, to the authorial authority of the person from whom, or through whom, the work was given life. This is the literary litmus test. Any literary criticism that fails to take this test, or fails to pass this test, is unworthy of the name.

Let us take some practical examples to illustrate the crucial connection between an author and his work. Shelley could not, and would not, have written Christian allegorical poems such as Samuel Taylor Coleridge's "Rime of the Ancient Mariner" or William Wordsworth's "Resolution and Independence"; Gerard Manley Hopkins' "Wreck of the Deutschland" could not have existed without the potency of the poet's deep Christian faith and his grounding in scholastic philosophy; Tolkien could not have written *The Lord of the Flies* any more than William Golding could have written *The Lord of the Rings*. Without knowledge of Dante's deeply ingrained Thomistic imagination, it is impossible to understand the depth and design of the *Divine Comedy*, which is why most modern critics are stuck in the *Inferno* and cannot see the value, beauty, and profundity of the *Purgatorio* or the *Paradiso*. Without knowledge of Chaucer's orthodox Christian philosophy, it would be difficult to see the Christian realist rebuttal of nominalism in the *Canterbury Tales* and *Troilus and Criseyde*. Without knowledge of the tradition-oriented religious faith of Cervantes or Swift, it is likely that *Don Quixote* and *Gulliver's Travels* will be read and understood through the erroneous eyes of the lampooned protagonists rather than through the sagacious eyes of the authors. Without knowledge of Emily Brontë's deeply held Christian faith, it is tempting to see *Wuthering Heights* as a sympathetic portrayal of unbridled carnal passion rather than as a cautionary tale warning against it. In the case of Cervantes, Swift, and Brontë, therefore, the crucial philosophical distance between the author and his protagonists is the very key to understanding the deepest meaning of the work.

Without knowledge of Eliot's sympathy for the political and cultural philosophy of Charles Maurras, his devotion to Dante, and his trajectory toward Christian conversion, it is tempting to see "The Waste Land" as an expression of nihilism instead of a condemnation of it. Without knowledge of Tolkien's insistence that *The Lord of the Rings* is "of course a fundamentally religious and Catholic work",[8] it is likely that we will miss the deep theology that informs the plot. Without Evelyn Waugh's assertion that the theme of *Brideshead Revisited* is "the operation of divine grace on a group of diverse but closely connected characters",[9] we would perhaps miss the crucial supernatural character of the novel and see it instead as a romantic tale of sexual (i.e., homosexual) and adulterous love.

Surely all of these examples are obvious. Surely it requires a mere modicum of common sense to see the truth that one must see the work, first and foremost, through the eyes of the author, as far as this is possible.

As a means of illustrating this point still further, it is perhaps illuminating to compare the study of literature with the study of history. If we insist on studying history through the prejudices and presumptions of our own day, we will succeed only in misinterpreting the motives and purpose of historical actions. If we do not know what people believed, we will not understand why they behaved and acted as they did. We will not understand what really happened. Our prejudice or our ignorance will have made us blind. In order to understand history, we must understand enough to empathize with, even if we do not sympathize with, the protagonists of the period being studied. And what is true of history is equally true of literature. We must know what the author believed in order to know what he is saying and doing in his work. We must empathize with, even if we do not sympathize with, the author's beliefs. Failure to understand the author's beliefs will lead to a failure to understand the work. Our prejudice or our ignorance will have made us blind. This critical reality was expressed eloquently by T. S. Eliot, writing of his literary hero and mentor, Dante:

---

[8] Carpenter, *Letters of J. R. R. Tolkien*, p. 172.

[9] Evelyn Waugh, preface to the second edition of *Brideshead Revisited*, Everyman's Library edition (New York: Alfred A. Knopf, 1993), p. 1.

You cannot afford to *ignore* Dante's philosophical and theological beliefs, or to skip the passages which express them most clearly; but ... on the other hand you are not called upon to believe them yourself.[10]

What is true of Dante is equally true of Shakespeare. Once we accept that the author–work nexus is axiomatic to a true understanding of literature, it becomes clear that the more we know about Shakespeare, the more we will understand his work. For this reason, the debate over Shakespeare's religious beliefs is sending shockwaves through literature departments around the world. In *Shakespeare and the Culture of Christianity in Early Modern England*, Dennis Taylor, professor of English at Boston College, discusses the way in which the work of historians was impacting the work of Shakespearian criticism:

> In or about 1985, the landscape of Shakespeare and religion studies began to change. In that year, Ernst Honigmann and Gary Taylor, representing mainline Shakespeare criticism, argued for the continuing influence of Shakespeare's Catholic background on his plays. Since 1985, there has been a flood of criticism reconsidering Shakespeare's relation to his Catholic contexts. . . . What we have seen since 1985 is the widespread acceptance of the importance of Shakespeare's Catholic background on both his mother's and his father's side, so much so that Honigman and Taylor's 1985 work—and Peter Milward's *Shakespeare's Religious Background* (1973)— are now routinely cited, with various qualifications, in standard editions and biographies of Shakespeare.[11]

If Shakespeare was a Catholic, and was greatly influenced by the Catholicism of his parents and the persecution that surrounded the practice of Catholicism in his day, it forces us to reread the plays in an entirely new light.[12] The more that historical evidence comes to light, the less able are the doyens of postmodernity to do what they like with the plays. In the past, the lack of knowledge of the personhood of Shakespeare has enabled critics to treat him as a *tabula rasa* upon which they can write their own prejudiced agenda. For the proponents of

---

[10] T. S. Eliot, *Selected Essays, 1917–1932* (New York: Faber and Faber, 1932), p. 218.

[11] Dennis Taylor and David N. Beauregard, eds., *Shakespeare and the Culture of Christianity in Early Modern England* (New York: Fordham University Press, 2003), p. 24.

[12] For the huge body of evidence suggesting that Shakespeare was not only raised a Catholic but that he remained one throughout his life, see Joseph Pearce, *The Quest for Shakespeare: The Bard of Avon and the Church of Rome* (San Francisco: Ignatius Press, 2008). For a condensed summary of the evidence, see appendix A to this volume, "Shakespeare's Shocking Catholicism".

"queer theory", he becomes conveniently homosexual; for secular fundamentalists, he is a protosecularist, ahead of his time; for "post-Christian" agnostics, he becomes a prophet of postmodernity. It was all so easy to mold Shakespeare into our own image when the Bard was a myth, but now that he is emerging as a man, a living person with real beliefs, such distortion becomes more difficult. For "postmodern" Shakespeare scholars, the emergence of tangible evidence for the Catholic Shakespeare is not only a challenge but a threat. If he was a Catholic, he becomes irritatingly antimodern. He would have believed that the practice of homosexuality was a sin, or that the secular state should be subject to the teachings of the Church, or that the religious conformity of the medieval past was superior to the post-Reformation fragmentation of Christian belief. From the perspective of the modernist and postmodernist, Shakespeare emerges as an unenlightened and recalcitrant reactionary. From the perspective of tradition-oriented scholars, the evident clarity of moral vision that they had always perceived in the plays becomes more explicable and more clearly defined.

It is not necessary to agree or sympathize with Shakespeare's Catholicism in order to read his works objectively, but it is necessary to understand his philosophical and theological beliefs and to see the plays in the light of those beliefs' profound influence. There are only two ways of reading Shakespeare, as there are only two ways of reading anyone else. We can read him objectively, by seeing his works through his own eyes, i.e., through the eyes of a Catholic living in Elizabethan and Jacobean England, or we can read him subjectively, seeing his works through the myopia of our own prejudice. Rejecting the fatuousness of the latter, this book has been an effort to read the works objectively, seeing through Shakespeare's eyes.

# SUBJECT INDEX

Ackroyd, Peter, 192n3
Act of Uniformity (1559), 188
Admiral's Men, 15–16
Aeson (father of Jason in Gk. myth), 101
Aix, First Council of (789), 44
Alexander the Great, 154
Anglican establishment in England,
    178–79, 187–88
Annesley, Sir Brian and Cordelia, 167
anti-Semitism attributed to *Merchant of
    Venice*, 15–16, 21–24, 39–41, 82–83,
    85–86
Aquinas. *See* Thomas Aquinas and
    Thomism
*Arcadia* (Sidney), 166, 167
Arden, Mary (Shakespeare's mother) and
    Arden family, 193
*argumentum ad captandum*, 82–83
*argumentum ad hominem*, 82–83
Aristophanes, 44
Aristotle
    on accident, 22n4
    realism of, ·67, 115, 141n2, 200
    Thomist Christian Aristotelianism, 74
    on usury, 44
art versus nature in *King Lear*, 181–82
*As You Like It* (Shakespeare), 139
Asquith, Clare, 42, 105, 168
atheists and atheism
    creative process for, 202, 203n7, 204
    Shakespeare claimed as atheist, 191
    Shakespeare's plays in dialogue with,
        187
    theological perspective of, 10
Augustine of Hippo, 68, 74, 141n2, 190,
    200
author, ultimate authority of, 201–2
avarice of Shylock in *Merchant of Venice*,
    51–55

Bacon, Francis, 67n2
"Ballad of the Crueltie of Geruntus"
    (Anonymous), 21
Bancroft, Richard, 42
Barabbas, 90–91
Barrowe, Henry, 188
Beauregard, David N., 17n4–7, 19n9,
    21n2, 42n3, 108n4, 206n11
being versus seeming. *See* realism
Belloc, Hilaire, 192
Belmont in *Merchant of Venice*
    meaning of name, 32–33
    moral meaning of, 35, 48–49, 62, 63,
        65, 68, 79, 87, 107
    *Il pecorone*, as literary source for, 20
    Venice contrasted with, 40, 63, 65,
        75, 79, 87
Bible. *See* Scripture
Blackfriars Gatehouse, London,
    Shakespeare's purchase of, 197–98
blindness in *King Lear*, 168, 175, 177–78,
    179, 185
Boccacio, 20
Boethius, 104, 177
Bolt, Robert, 197
Bradford, William, 189
Bradley, A. C., 127, 131
Bride of Christ/Christ as Bridegroom
    imagery
    in *King Lear*, 169, 181
    in *Merchant of Venice*, 20, 57, 59–60,
        109
*Brideshead Revisited* (Waugh), 205
Brontë, Emily, 204
Burghley, Lord (William Cecil), 133,
    134, 141, 155

Calvin, Jean, and Calvinism, 44, 48,
    56n5, 187, 189

Campbell, Oscar James, 21n1, 196n10
Campion, Edmund, 183, 194, 195
*Canterbury Tales* (Chaucer), 204
Carlyle, Thomas, 191–92
Carpenter, Humphrey, 202n6, 205n8
Carthage, First Council of (345), 44
Cartwright, Thomas, 42–43, 44
*Catechism of the Catholic Church*, 94–95
Catholicism in Shakespeare's plays. *See* Shakespeare's plays, Catholic presence in
Cato, 44
cave, Platonic allegory of, 74
Cecil, William (Lord Burghley), 133, 134, 141, 155
Cervantes, Miguel de, 204
Chamberlain's Men, 16, 112
Chateaubriand, François René de, 191
Chaucer, Geoffrey
    as author, 204
    *Hamlet* and, 112n2
    *King Lear* and, 179, 184, 185
    *Merchant of Venice* and, 61, 82
Chesterton, G. K.
    on Catholicism of Shakespeare, 70–71, 191, 192
    Chaucer and Shakespeare compared by, 184
    on Jack and the Beanstalk, 176
    Jackson, Holbrook, response to, 199–200
    "Lepanto," 47, 69
    on lightheartedness, 110
    *Magic*, 27n1
    on relativism, 140
    Shakespeare and Milton compared by, 70–71
choice in *Merchant of Venice*
    Arragon's choice of silver casket, 55–56
    Bassanio's choice of lead casket, 58–65, 66–74
        humility of Bassanio in, 58–62
        Portia's alleged "cheating" in, 63–65
        realist argument in, 66–74
    elopement of Jessica and, 51–55

fate versus, 47–48
    Morocco's choice of gold casket, 46–51
    right choice, 46–49, 57, 58–65
    virtue of Portia and, 36–37
*Christmas Carol, A,* (Dickens), 23
*Chronicles* (Holinshed), 166
*City of God* (Augustine), 68
Clement VIII (pope), 125
Clyfton, Richard, 187–88
Coleridge, Samuel Taylor, 204
"complexion," Shakespearean meaning of, 49–51
*Confessio amantis* (Gower), 20
conscience of Lear in *King Lear*, 171–75, 182
conversions, forced, 94–95
cosmetics, *Hamlet's* reference to use of, 130, 154, 155, 157
cosmogony of *Merchant of Venice*, 102–6
Councils of the Church, 44
creative process, authority of author as to, 10, 13, 201–7
Cressida (in Gk. myth), 101
Cupid as "Lord Love" in *Merchant of Venice*, 58n1

*Daily Missal and Liturgical Manual*, 121n5
*Daemonology* (James I and VI), 124
Dante
    theological and philosophical perspective of, 204, 206
    Eliot's devotion to, 205–6
    Hamlet and, 115n7, 116
    *Merchant of Venice* and, 33, 61, 82, 104, 111
Davies, Richard, 198
Day of Antonement (Jewish holy day), 29
dead, prayers for, 120–21
death as subject of *Hamlet*, 152–53, 159–64, 165
death of Shakespeare, 198
*Decameron* (Boccacio), 20
Descartes, René, 67n2
Devil. *See* Satan

Diana (in Gk. myth), Elizabeth I
portrayed as, 105–6
Dibdale, Robert, 134, 135n3, 194, 195
Dickens, Charles, 23
Dido (in Gk. myth), 101
Diet of Worms, Hamlet's pun on, 120
Divine Comedy (Dante), 33, 35n5, 104,
111, 185, 204
divine providence in Hamlet, 157–59,
163
Don Quixote (Cervantes), 204

Eclogues (Virgil), 101
Edward I (king of England), 43n4
Edward VI (king of England), 44,
179n1
Edwardian Ordinal, 179n1
Eliot, T.S., 114, 115n7, 203–6
Elizabeth I (queen of England)
Catholics under, 169
as Diana, 105–6
Essex and, 118
López and Southwell trials, 15–17, 21,
23, 69n4, 90
music of the spheres in Merchant of
Venice and, 105
realpolitik of, 155
spymasters under, 133, 134
usury laws under, 44–45
vanity of, 155
Enos, Carol Curt, 192
Epistle unto his Father (Southwell), 17
Essex, Earl of, 118–20, 128–29, 133
Eucharist, 104

Faerie Queene (Spenser), 166
feminist theory, 37, 191
fide et operibus, 162
Fiorentino, Ser Giovanni, 20, 32n4
"fishmonger" dialogue in Hamlet,
133–35
fools and foolishness in King Lear,
171–75, 178–79
forced conversions, 94–95
Fortescue, John, 197
Four Last Things, 72, 153, 159–60

Franciscans and St. Francis in King Lear,
174–75, 181
fundamentalism, secular, 190, 192, 207

Gardiner, William, 194–95
Garrick, David, 161
Geoffrey of Monmouth, 166
Gerard, John, 195, 197
Gesta Romanorum (Anonymous), 21
Golding, William, 204
Good Friday, 29
Gooding, Thomas, 153
Gosson, Stephen, 21
Gower, John, 20
Grattan Flood, W. H., 71n9
Greenwood, John, 188
Gulliver's Travels (Swift), 204

Hamlet (Shakespeare)
advice of Polonius in, 26, 125–27
anti-Hamlet and anti-Ghost, Laertes
and Claudius as, 146–51
Cecil, William (Lord Burghley),
Polonius modeled on, 133, 134,
141, 155
climax (swordfight) in, 162–64
cosmetics, use of, 130, 154, 155, 157
death as subject of, 152–53, 159–64,
165
divine providence in, 157–59, 163
Essex, Earl of, Hamlet modeled on,
118–20, 128–29, 133
"fishmonger" dialogue, 133–35
Ghost of Hamlet's Father, appearance
of, 120–24
graveyard scene in, 152–56
honesty as theme of. See honesty in
Hamlet
justice in, 122–23
King Lear compared, 113, 125
love
Claudius's view of, 148–51
of Hamlet and Ophelia, 125–31
madness in. See under madness
Matthew 10:31–39 in, 117n9,
159–61

*Hamlet* (Shakespeare) (*continued*)
  nominalism/relativism in, 140–41,
    141n2, 144, 148–50
  play within a play in, 138–39
  poison in, 137, 148, 151, 153, 157,
    162, 163
  as problem play for critics, 113–14,
    117
  readiness in, 116–17, 158–60
  realist argument of, 67, 114–17, 132,
    140, 141, 143, 144, 155, 163, 164
  reason and will in, 143–44
  religious consciousness of, 115–17,
    129, 139, 147, 157–64, 165
  sin in, 141–45, 147, 148, 162
  "something rotten" in, 135, 165
  sources and motivations for writing,
    112–13
  spies and spying, 132–37, 140–41
  suicide in, 116, 128, 129, 143, 150,
    152, 153
  sword, swearing upon, 160–62
  vengeance in, 122–23, 141–43, 147–51
Hampton Court Conference (1604),
  188
Harrison, G. B., 155n4
Hartley, James E., 45
Harvey, Sir William, 167
Hazlitt, William, 23, 30–31, 33–34
*Henry IV, Part 2* (Shakespeare), 195
*Henry V* (Shakespeare), 118
Henry VIII (king of England), 44,
  168–69, 195
Hercules (in Gk. myth), 61, 72
Hesione (in Gk. myth), 61, 62
*hic et ubique*, 121, 161
Hitler, Adolf, 40
Hobbes, Thomas, 67n2, 141n2
Holinshed's *Chronicles*, 166
"Hollow Men, The" (Eliot), 203
homosexuality and queer theory, 27n2,
  191, 207
honesty in *Hamlet*
  cosmetics, use of, 130, 154, 155, 157
  Ghost, as honest, 124, 148, 150, 162,
    163

  lying and spying, Hamlet's disgust at,
    132–37, 140–41
  Ophelia's honesty questioned by
    Hamlet, 130
  realist argument of play, 67, 114–17,
    132, 140, 141, 143, 144, 155, 163,
    164
  tricking of Laertes by Claudius,
    148–51
Honigmann, Ernst, 206
Hopkins, Gerard Manley, 76, 204
humanism, secular, 68, 125, 141, 147
*Humble Supplication to her Maiestie*
  (Southwell), 18–19
hypocrisy in *Merchant of Venice*, 81, 82,
  91, 93, 95

insanity. *See* madness
interest, charging, 38–45, 53
Irish Catholics, 118
Irving, Henry, 23
Islam
  in *Hamlet*, 161
  in *Merchant of Venice*, 46–48

Jack and the Beanstalk, 176
Jackson, Holbrook, 199–200
James I and VI (king of England and
  Scotland), 124, 169, 188, 198
Jason (in Gk. myth), 101
Jesuits
  *Merchant of Venice* and, 15–19, 29,
    32n4, 42, 57, 59, 79. *See also*
    Southwell, Robert
  Shakespeare's association with, 183,
    194, 195, 198
*Jew, The*, 21
*Jew of Malta* (Marlowe), 15–16, 21–23
Jews and Judaism
  blood libel and, 90–91
  Day of Atonement, 29
  expelled from England, 43n4
  forced conversion of, 94–95
  *Merchant of Venice*
    anti-Semitism attributed to, 15–16,
      21–24, 39–41, 82–83, 85–86

López, Roderigo, trial of, 15–16
Puritan, Shylock as stand-in for,
    42–43, 45, 79
Johnson, Samuel, on Hamlet
    criticism of plot, 113–14, 162–64
    on Ophelia, 117, 128
    sword, practice of swearing on, 161
    vengeance, Hamlet's desire for, 142
Jonson, Ben, 138, 197
Julius Caesar, 154–55
justice
    in Hamlet, 122–23
    in Merchant of Venice, 87–96
justification by faith alone (sola fide),
    56n5, 162

Kemble, Fanny, 30
Kilroy, Gerard, 165n1
King John (Shakespeare), 112–13, 118, 167
King Lear (Shakespeare)
    blindness in, 168, 175, 177–78, 179,
        185
    Catholic metadrama of, 168–69,
        176–79, 183–85
    conscience of Lear in, 171–73,
        174–75, 182
    double plot of, 167–68
    fools and foolishness in, 171–75,
        178–79
    Franciscans and St. Francis in, 174–75,
        181
    Hamlet compared, 113, 125
    love in, 168–70, 172
    madness in, 133–34, 173–75, 180–85
    nakedness in, 173–75
    nature versus art in, 181–82
    sources and motivations for writing,
        113, 166–67
    suffering in, 172, 173, 180–81
    suicide in, 180
    as tragedy or divine comedy, 185
    treason charges in, 176–77, 183
    vice and villainy of Edmund in, 86
    wisdom in, 171–75
Klause, John, 17n4, 18, 21, 42, 108n4
Kyd, Thomas, 112–13

"Lady the Brach" in King Lear, 172, 174
Lady Windermere's Fan (Wilde), 33–34
Langley, Francis, 194
Lee, Anne and Roger, 194
Leo XIII (pope), 179n1
"Lepanto" (Chesterton), 47, 69
"Lewd Love is Losse" (Southwell), 17, 57
Lewis, C. S., 152, 201n5
light imagery in Merchant of Venice,
    107–8, 110
liturgical references
    dead, prayers for, 120–21
    Eucharist, 104
    hic et ubique, 121, 161
    Litany of Loreto, 32
    Requiem Mass, 165
López, Roderigo, 15–16, 21, 23
Lord Chamberlain's Men, 16, 112
"Lord Love" in Merchant of Venice, 58
Lord of the Flies (Golding), 204
Lord of the Rings, The, (Tolkien), 204,
    205
Loreto, Litany of, 32
love
    in Hamlet
        Claudius's view of, 148–51
        love of Hamlet and Ophelia in,
            125–31
    in King Lear, 168–70, 172
    in Merchant of Venice, 78
    sacrifice and love, relationship
        between, 78, 187
Lowenstein, Daniel H., 64, 91–93, 95n7,
    98
Lucifer. See Satan
Lucy, Sir Thomas, 193–94
Luther, Martin, 42n2, 70, 119, 120n4

Macbeth (Shakespeare), 187
Machiavelli, Niccolò, and
    Machiavellianism
    Anglican establishment in England
        and, 187–90, 195
    Hamlet and, 125, 141, 149, 150, 155,
        157, 164
    King Lear and, 173, 176, 179, 183–85

Machiavelli, Niccolò, and
    Machiavellianism (continued)
    Merchant of Venice and, 68, 69, 99,
        105, 107
    Il principe, 68n3, 125
madness
    in Hamlet
        of England, 156, 165
        of Hamlet, 129, 133–34, 137,
            139–41, 144, 157
        of Ophelia, 131, 157
        as theme of, 157, 163
    in King Lear, 133–34, 173–75, 180–85
Magi, Portia in Merchant of Venice
    identified with, 87–88
Magic (Chesterton), 27n1
Marian figure, Portia in Merchant of
    Venice as, 32–33
Marie Magdalens Funeral Teares
    (Southwell), 17n6, 18, 108n4
Marlowe, Christopher, 15–16, 21–23,
    136
Marprelate tracts, 43
marriage as metaphor for Christ the
    Bridegroom, 20, 57, 59–60, 109, 169,
    181
Mary I (queen of England), 44
Matthew, Tobias, 189
Maurras, Charles, 205
meaning. See nominalism/relativism;
    realism
Measure for Measure (Shakespeare), 187,
    188
Medea (in Gk. myth), 101
memento mori, 72, 152–56
Merchant of Venice (Shakespeare)
    anti-Semitism attributed to, 15–16,
        21–24, 39–41, 82–83, 85–86
    Belmont in. See Belmont in Merchant
        of Venice
    caskets. See under choice in Merchant of
        Venice
    choice in. See choice in Merchant of
        Venice
    elopement of Jessica and Lorenzo in,
        51–55

Essex, Earl of, possible allusions to, 118
    hypocrisy in, 81, 82, 91, 93, 95
    Jesuits and, 15–19, 29, 32n4, 42, 57,
        59, 79. See also under Southwell,
        Robert
    Jews and Judaism in. See under Jews
        and Judaism
    light imagery in, 107–8, 110
    lightheartedness in, 110–11
    literary criticism on, 21–24
    López, Roderigo, and, 15–16, 21, 23
    love and sacrifice, relationship
        between, 78
    mercy and justice in, 88–96
    music of the spheres in, 102–8
    postmodern interpretation of. See
        under postmodern literary
        criticism
    pride in. See under pride
    prodigal son parable reflected in,
        27–28, 52–53
    Protestant/Catholic theological
        divisions, reference to, 42–43, 45,
        56n5, 69–70
    queer theory applied to, 27n2
    racial discrimination attributed to,
        49–51
    racked/recked pun in, 28–29
    ring test and pragmatism versus
        principle in, 97–100, 108–11
    sources for, 20–21
    Southwell and. See under Southwell,
        Robert
    spiritual sadness and self-knowledge
        in, 25–29, 34–35
    trial of Antonio in
        multiple shipwrecks, meaning of,
            75–76
        Portia's intervention in, 87–94
        salvation history, as allegory of,
            79–81
        Southwell, as allegory of trial of,
            78–79
        testing of Shylock via, 77–78, 87–96
        vengeance, Shylock's desire for,
            81–86

vice and villainy of Shylock in, 38–45,
77–78, 81–86
virtue of Portia in, 30–37, 63–65
mercy and justice in *Merchant of Venice*,
88–96
*The Merry Wives of Windsor*
(Shakespeare), 195
Milton, John, 70–72
Milward, Peter, 42–43, 113, 167, 168,
192n4, 206
Miracle Plays and *Hamlet*, 116
More, Thomas, 125, 195–97
Morris, John, 198n13
Moser, Fernando de Mello, 33
Munday, Anthony, 196–97
music of the spheres in *Merchant of
Venice*, 102–8
Muslims
in *Hamlet*, 161
in *Merchant of Venice*, 46–48
Mutschmann, H., 191n2, 194n8,
197n11–12
Myrick, Kenneth, 38n1, 98n1

nakedness in *King Lear*, 173–75
nature versus art in *King Lear*, 181–82
Nazis and Nazism, 40, 83
Newman, John Henry, 192
"nice," Shakespearean meaning of, 50
Nietzsche, Friedrich, 147
nominalism/relativism. *See also* realism
Chaucer's rebuttals of, 204
defined, 141n2
in *Hamlet*, 140–41, 141n2, 144,
148–50, 163
literature, objective versus subjective
reading of, 199–207
in *Merchant of Venice*, 67, 105
Shakespeare claimed as relativist, 191

objective versus subjective reading of
literature, 192, 199–207
*Oliver Twist* (Dickens), 23
opening line, speeches referred to by,
83–84
*Othello* (Shakespeare), 86, 187

painting with cosmetics, *Hamlet's*
reference to use of, 130, 154, 155,
157
*Paradise Lost* (Milton), 72
Pearce, Joseph
*Flowers of Heaven*, 155n3
*Hamlet* (ed.), 112n1
*The Merchant of Venice* (ed.), 16n2,
45n5, 64n5, 91n2, 98n2
*The Quest for Shakespeare*, 9n1, 13n2,
16n3, 27n2, 135n3, 136n4, 183n1,
186n1, 193n7, 206n12
*The Tragedy of King Lear* (ed.), 134n2,
168n3
*Wisdom and Innocence: A Life of G. K.
Chesterton*, 200n1
*pecorone, Il*, (Ser Giovanni Fiorentino),
20, 32n4
Peele, George, 113, 166
Perez, Antonio, 15
Philip II (king of Spain), 15
philosophical and theological presumptions of author, 10, 13, 201–7
"Phoenix and the Turtle, The,"
(Shakespeare), 118
*Picture of Dorian Gray, The*, (Wilde), 34
Plato, 44, 67, 74, 141n2, 200
play within a play in *Hamlet*, 138–39
plays of Shakespeare, Catholicism in. *See*
Shakespeare's plays, Catholic presence
in
Plutarch, 44
poison in *Hamlet*, 137, 148, 151, 153,
157, 162, 163
postmodern literary criticism
*King Lear* viewed as tragedy by, 185
literature, objective versus subjective
reading of, 206–7
on *Merchant of Venice*
"cheating" of Portia in Bassanio's
casket scene, 63–65
Christian symbolism of, 60, 90, 102
Shylock, critical understanding of,
82n3, 83–84, 95–96
self-seriousness of, 110–11
Pounde, Thomas, 32n4

pragmatism versus principle in *Merchant of Venice*, 97–100
predestination, doctrine of, 48, 56n5
Priam, 61
pride
 in *Hamlet*, 147
 in *King Lear*, 182
 in *Merchant of Venice*
  Bassanio's lack of, 61–62, 74
  of Prince of Arragon, 55–56, 57
  of Prince of Morocco, 47, 51, 57, 62
  ring test and, 109
  of Shylock in, 38, 39
*principe, Il*, (Machiavelli), 68n3, 125
prodigal son parable reflected in *Merchant of Venice*, 27–28, 52–53
Protestantism
 Anglican establishment in England, 178–79, 187–88
 anti-Catholic bias of other plays, Shakespeare writing in response to, 112–13, 166–67
 Calvin, Jean, and Calvinism, 44, 48, 56n5, 187, 189
 Catholic/Protestant theological divisions, reference to
  in *Merchant of Venice*, 42–43, 45, 56n5, 69–72
  relative scarcity of, 187–88
 Catholicism of Shakespeare, Protestant response to, 186–90
 dead, opposition to prayers for, 120–21
 of Essex and Hamlet, 119–20
 ghosts, understanding of, 124
 in *Hamlet*, 119–21, 162
 Luther, Martin, 42n2, 70, 119, 120n4
 in *Merchant of Venice*, 42–43, 45, 56n5, 69–72
 Milton and Shakespeare compared, 70–72
 Puritans
  Anglican England, persecution in, 187–89
  *Merchant of Venice* and, 42–43, 45, 48, 79, 105, 110

*sola fide*, doctrine of, 56n5, 162
*sola scriptura*, doctrine of, 42, 70–72
providence, divine, in *Hamlet*, 157–59, 163
purgatory
 Ghost of Hamlet's Father in, 120–24, 144, 145, 162
 *Hamlet*, purgatorial spirit of, 116, 143–45, 152, 164
 in *King Lear*, 181, 185
Puritans
 Anglican England, persecution in, 187–89
 *Merchant of Venice* and, 42–43, 45, 48, 79, 105, 110

Queen's Men, 166
queer theory, 27n2, 191, 207
Quinn, Edward G., 196n10

racial discrimination attributed to *Merchant of Venice*, 49–51
readiness in *Hamlet*, 116–17, 158–59
realism. *See also* nominalism/relativism
 in Chaucer, 204
 defined, 141n2
 in *Hamlet*, 67, 114–17, 132, 140, 141, 143, 144, 155, 163, 164
 literature, applied to objective reading of, 199–207
 in *Merchant of Venice*, 66–74, 105
*realpolitik*, Machiavellian. *See* Machiavelli, Niccolo, and Machiavellianism
reason and will in *Hamlet*, 143–44
recusants and recusancy
 fines for, 119, 188, 189, 193
 *Hamlet* and, 128, 133, 156
 Shakespeare's known association with, 119, 189, 193, 194, 197, 198
relativism. *See* nominalism/relativism
*Republic* (Plato), 74
revenge
 in *Hamlet*, 122–23, 141–43, 146, 147–51
 in *Merchant of Venice*, 81–86
*Richard II* (Shakespeare), 118

Richmond, Velma Bourgeois, 42, 192n5
"Rime of the Ancient Mariner"
    (Coleridge), 204
ring test in *Merchant of Venice*, 97–100,
    108–11
Robinson, John, 198
Roman Catholicism. *See* Shakespeare's
    plays, Catholic presence in
*Romeo and Juliet* (Shakespeare), 70
Rose Theatre, London, 16
Rowe, Nicholas, 38, 51

sacrifice and love, relationship between,
    78–87
*Saint Peters Complaint* (Southwell), 19
Salmasius, 44
salvation history, trial of Antonio in
    *Merchant of Venice* as allegory of,
    79–81
Satan
    Claudius in *Hamlet* identified with, 162
    in *King Lear*, 174, 175
    self-seriousness of, 110–11
    Shylock in *Merchant of Venice*
        compared to, 38–39, 58, 83–86, 99
Scripture
    Exodus 21:23–27, 80
    Genesis, 41
    Matthew, gospel of
        5:14–16, 107n3
        6:21, 35n7
        7:1–3, 56n6
        7:1–5, 80
        10:31, 117n9, 158–59
        10:31–39, 159–61
        10:39, 60n3
        13:46, 51n3
        25:14–30, 13n1
        27:25, 90n1
    prodigal son parable reflected in
        *Merchant of Venice*, 27–28, 52–53
    *sola scriptura*, Protestant doctrine of,
        42, 70–72
secular fundamentalism, 190, 192, 207
secular humanism, 68, 125, 141, 147
seeming versus being. *See* realism

Seneca, 44
"Seven Wise Masters of Rome" *(The
    Thousand and One Nights)*, 21
Shakespeare, John (father), 119, 185,
    188, 192–93
Shakespeare, Mary Arden (mother), 193
Shakespeare, Susanna (daughter), 188,
    189, 198
Shakespeare's plays, Catholic presence in,
    9–10. *See also* specific plays, by title
    creative process, authority of author as
        to, 10, 13, 201–7
    critical reaction to, 198, 206–7
    Evidence for Catholicism of
        Shakespeare, 191–98
    Milton and Shakespeare compared,
        70–72
    objective versus subjective reading of,
        192, 199–207
    Protestant response to, 186–90
Shelley, Percy Bysshe, 202–4
Sidney, Sir Philip, 166, 167
Simpson, Richard, 191
sin in *Hamlet*, 141–45, 147, 148, 150,
    162
*Sir Thomas More* (Munday/Shakespeare),
    195–97
Socrates, 141n2, 200
Soer, Dorothy and John, 194
*sola fide* (justification by faith alone),
    56n5, 162
*sola scriptura*, 42, 70–72
*Song of Roland, The*, 47, 176
Sonnet 23 (Shakespeare), 196–97
Southampton, Earl of, 32n4, 119, 194
Southwell, Robert
    on death, 154–55
    *Merchant of Venice* and
        Antonio and Southwell, parallels
            between, 42–43, 69, 78–79
        Bassanio and Southwell, parallels
            between, 17–19, 59–60, 78
        career and martyrdom of Southwell,
            16–19
        "Lewd Love is Losse," echoes of,
            17, 57

Southwell, Robert (*continued*)
  *Merchant of Venice* and (*continued*)
    light imagery and, 107–8
    Portia on mercy and, 90
    torture and execution of Southwell,
      references to, 16, 18, 29, 79
  More, Thomas, and, 195
  Shakespeare's friendship with, 135n3,
    154, 183, 194
  Southampton, Earl of, and, 194
  torture and execution of, 16, 18, 29,
    69n4, 79, 134, 155, 188, 194
*Spanish Tragedy* (Kyd), 112
Spenser, Edmund, 166
spies and spying in *Hamlet*, 132–37,
  140–41
Stationers' Company, registration of
  plays with, 15n1, 112
subjective versus objective reading of
  literature, 192, 199–207
suffering and wisdom in *King Lear*,
  171–75
suffering in *King Lear*, 172, 173, 180–81
suicide
  in *Hamlet*, 116, 128, 129, 143, 150,
    152, 153
  in *King Lear*, 180
Süleyman the Magnificent (sultan), 47
Sutcliffe, Matthew, 43
Swift, Jonathan, 204
sword, swearing upon, in *Hamlet*, 160–62

"Tale of the Blind King of Paphlagonia,
  The," from *Arcadia* (Sidney), 167
*Taming of the Shrew* (Shakespeare), 38
Taylor, Dennis, 17n4–7, 19n9, 21n2,
  42n3, 108n4, 206
Taylor, Gary, 206
*Tempest* (Shakespeare), 27, 76, 116, 158
theological and philosophical presump-
  tions of author, 10, 13, 201–7
Third Reich, 40
Thisbe, 101
Thomas Aquinas and Thomism
  Christian Aristotelianism of, 74
  Dante, Thomism of, 204

realism of, 67, 115, 141n2, 200
  on usury, 44
*Thousand and One Nights* (Anonymous),
  21
Tillyard, E. M. W., 115–16, 201n5
Tilney, Sir Edmund, 195, 197
Tiresias, 175
*Titus Andronicus* (Shakespeare), 17
Tolkien, J. R. R., 201–5
Topcliffe, Richard, 16
torture and execution
  of Dibdale, 134, 194
  of Puritans, 188
  of Southwell, 16, 18, 29, 79, 134, 155,
    188, 194
treason charges in *King Lear*, 176–77,
  183
Trinity, doctrine of, 72, 74, 89
Troilus, 101
*Troilus and Cressida* (Shakespeare), 118
*Troilus and Criseyde* (Chaucer), 204
*Troublesome Reign of King John*
  (Anonymous), 112–13, 167
*True Chronicle History of King Leir and his*
  *three daughters* (Peele?), 113, 166–67
*Twelfth Night* (Shakespeare), 38
Tyrone (Irish rebel leader), 118

"Upon the Image of Death"
  (Southwell), 154–55
*Ur-Hamlet* (Kyd?), 112
usury of Shylock in *Merchant of Venice*,
  39–45, 53, 77–78, 86

"Venesyon Comodye" (identity unclear),
  16
vengeance
  in *Hamlet*, 122–23, 141–43, 147–51
  in *Merchant of Venice*, 77–86
Venice in *Merchant of Venice*, 31–35, 40,
  63, 68, 75, 79, 87
Virgil, 101

"Waste Land, The" (Eliot), 114, 205
Waugh, Evelyn, 205
Wayte, William, 194, 195

Weir, Alison, 118n2
Wentersdorf, K., 191n2, 194n8,
 197n11–12
Whitgift, John, 42
Wilde, Oscar, 33–34
will and reason in *Hamlet*, 143–44
will and testament
 of John Shakespeare, 192–93
 of William Shakespeare, 198
William of Ockham, 67, 141n2
Wilson, Ian, 198

Wilson, J. Dover, 118n1
wisdom and suffering in *King Lear*,
 171–75
Wittenberg, University of, 119–20
Wood, Michael, 166
"Wreck of the Deutschland" (Hopkins),
 76, 204
Wright, John, 166
Wright, T., 197n12
*Wuthering Heights* (Emily Brontë), 204

# INDEX OF FICTIONAL CHARACTERS

**Characters in Shakespeare's Plays**

Albany (*King Lear*), 178–79, 182, 185

Antonio (*Merchant of Venice*), 16, 22, 25–29, 30–31, 34, 35, 39–45, 53, 54, 59, 63n4, 74–80, 83–86, 88, 91–92, 94–96, 99, 101

Arragon, Prince of (*Merchant of Venice*), 17, 55–58, 63–64

Balthazar (Portia's alias in *Merchant of Venice*), 87, 90, 100

Bassanio (*Merchant of Venice*), 17–20, 27–29, 31, 32, 39, 53, 58–65, 66–70, 72–74, 76, 79, 83, 93, 97–102, 108–10

Bernardo (*Hamlet*), 144

Claudius (*Hamlet*), 120, 123, 125, 129, 132, 134, 135, 138, 141, 143, 146–53, 155, 157, 159–64, 187

Clown (*Hamlet*), 139, 155–57

Cordelia (*King Lear*), 167–70, 172, 182–85, 187, 191

Cornwall (*King Lear*), 177, 182–83, 185, 187

Desdemona (*Othello*), 187

Duke (*Merchant of Venice*), 78, 94–95, 98

Edgar (*King Lear*), 168, 171, 173–78, 180–82, 185

Edmund (*King Lear*), 86, 168, 173, 176–79, 182–85, 187

Fool (*King Lear*), 125, 134, 171–75, 185

Gertrude (*Hamlet*), 115, 144, 153

Ghost of Hamlet's Father (*Hamlet*), 113, 120–24, 144–45, 146–48, 150, 153, 161–64

Gloucester (*King Lear*), 167–68, 177, 180, 182, 183

Goneril (*King Lear*), 168–69, 172, 176, 178, 179, 182, 185, 187

Gratiano (*Merchant of Venice*), 16, 26–27, 31, 32, 79–82, 94, 97, 101, 109

Guildenstern (*Hamlet*), 120, 135–36, 147

Hamlet (*Hamlet*). See main entry for Hamlet in subject index

Horatio (*Hamlet*), 117, 120, 122, 144, 147, 154, 157, 160–62, 165

Iago (*Othello*), 86, 187

Isabella (*Measure for Measure*), 187

Jessica (*Merchant of Venice*), 31–32, 40–41, 47n1, 51–55, 85, 86, 101–2

Kent (*King Lear*), 168, 173, 177, 182

Laertes (*Hamlet*), 125–26, 128, 132–33, 146–51, 153, 157, 160, 162, 163

Launcelot (*Merchant of Venice*), 47n1

Lear (*King Lear*). See main entry for King Lear in subject index

Lorenzo (*Merchant of Venice*), 31, 39, 51–54, 101–2, 104–8

Macbeth and Lady Macbeth (*Macbeth*), 187

Malvolio (*Twelfth Night*), 38

Marcellus (*Hamlet*), 135, 144, 160–62

Mercutio (*Romeo and Juliet*), 70

Morocco, Prince of (*Merchant of Venice*), 46–52, 54–55, 57, 61–63

Nerissa (*Merchant of Venice*), 17, 34–36, 57, 58, 101, 106, 107, 109

Ophelia (*Hamlet*), 113–14, 117, 125–32, 135, 152, 157, 163–64

Osric (*Hamlet*), 135

Petruchio (*Taming of the Shrew*), 38

Polonius (*Hamlet*), 26, 120, 125–27, 129, 131–36, 139–41, 147–48, 155, 157, 161, 164

Poor Tom (*King Lear*), 134, 173–75

Portia (*Merchant of Venice*), 17–20, 28,
  30–38, 47, 49–51, 54–66, 66,
  73–74, 78, 83–84, 86, 87–94,
  97–100, 101–2, 105–11, 131, 187
Regan (*King Lear*), 168, 169, 172,
  176–77, 182, 183, 185, 187
Reynaldo (*Hamlet*), 132–33
Rosencrantz (*Hamlet*), 120, 135–36, 147
Salerio (*Merchant of Venice*), 26, 34,
  40–41, 51, 81, 85–86
Shallow (*Merry Wives* and *Henry IV
  Part 2*), 195
Shylock (*Merchant of Venice*), 15–17,
  22–23, 34, 38–45, 51–55, 58,
  75–86, 87–96
Slender (*Merry Wives* and *Henry IV
  Part 2*), 195

Solanio (*Merchant of Venice*), 26, 34,
  38–39, 51, 84–86
Tubal (*Merchant of Venice*), 52
Yorick (*Hamlet*), 152–55

**Non-Shakespearean Fictional
  Characters**
Darlington, Lord (*Lady Windermere's
  Fan*, Wilde), 33–34
Fagin (*Oliver Twist*, Dickens), 23
Giannetto (*Il pecorone*, Ser Giovanni
  Fiorentino), 20
Scrooge, Ebenezer (*A Christmas Carol*,
  Dickens), 23